HARRY TRUMAN AND CIVIL RIGHTS

HARRY TRUMAN
AND
CIVIL RIGHTS

MORAL COURAGE AND POLITICAL RISKS

Michael R. Gardner

With Forewords by
George M. Elsey and Kweisi Mfume

SOUTHERN ILLINOIS UNIVERSITY PRESS
CARBONDALE AND EDWARDSVILLE

Library of Congress Cataloging-in-Publication Data

Gardner, Michael R., 1942–
 Harry Truman and civil rights : moral courage and
political risks / Michael R. Gardner ; with forewords by George
M. Elsey and Kweisi Mfume.
  p. cm.
 Includes bibliographical references (p.) and index.
  1. Truman, Harry S., 1884–1972—Views on civil rights.
2. Truman, Harry S., 1884–1972—Relations with African
Americans. 3. Truman, Harry S., 1884–1972—Ethics.
4. African Americans—Civil rights—History—20th
century. 5. United States—Politics and government—
1945–1953. 6. United States—Race relations. I. Title.

E814 .G37 2002
973.9189'092—dc21

2001041154

ISBN 0-8093-2425-3 (alk. paper)

The paper used in this publication meets the minimum requirements of American
National Standard for Information Sciences—Permanence of Paper for Printed
Library Materials, ANSI Z39.48-1992. ∞

For Theresa Lennon Gardner

CONTENTS

CONTENTS

CONTENTS

Harry S. Truman's forceful statements and bold actions as president on civil rights should surprise no one who knew the man's record. In the beginning of his years in public life in the early 1920s, he denounced the Ku Klux Klan and all it stood for. It was then a potent political force in his native Missouri, but that did not deter him. He was outspoken in his conviction that all Americans should have equal rights and equal opportunities under the law.

Outraged at the mistreatment of black veterans returning from World War II service in 1946, he appointed a committee of outstanding Americans to review the civil rights situation nationwide and to bring recommendations to him for remedial action wherever rights under the Constitution were not being upheld. He said to his committee, in effect, "Tell me what we need to do to get the country's house in order."

While impatiently awaiting that report, in June 1947 he addressed a meeting of the NAACP from the steps of the Lincoln Memorial. He was the first president to accept an invitation from that body. Stirring the NAACP and the country with his words, Truman said that the time was at hand when the federal government must take the lead: "We cannot await the growth of a will to action in the slowest state or the most backward community. Our national government must show the way."

At the earliest opportunity after his Civil Rights Committee presented its recommendations, which Truman eagerly embraced, he sent a Special Message to Congress on Civil Rights. It was February 1948. An election year. He knew it was politically hazardous. Indeed, it created a firestorm of protest in many quarters. Undeterred when Congress refused to take action, Truman took the only steps open to him. By executive orders, he ended segregation in the armed forces and mandated an integrated federal civil service. He was adding to his political difficulties, but no matter. He was following the advice of Mark Twain, which he kept before him on a neatly lettered card in the Oval Office: "Always do right. This will gratify some people, and astonish the rest."

Harry Truman's convictions, commitment, and courage are admirably recounted by Michael Gardner. He describes the actions that flowed from them. He recalls long-overlooked actions taken by the Department of Justice at Truman's direction. He pointedly contrasts Truman's courage with the timidity of his two immediate successors and reminds us of the belated conversion of Lyndon Johnson to the course Truman had advocated years earlier. *Harry Truman and Civil Rights: Moral Courage and Political Risks* is an apt title. Truman had the courage. He took the risks. All of us are indebted to him.

—GEORGE M. ELSEY,
Administrative Assistant to President Truman

Harry Truman and Civil Rights: Moral Courage and Political Risks presents a riveting account of the little-known yet pivotal role President Harry Truman played in the cause for civil rights. President Truman stepped to the forefront of the fight for civil rights many times at the risk to his own political career. On July 26, 1948, he shattered the segregation laws in the federal workforce and in the U.S. armed forces with the issuance of Executive Orders 9980 and 9981 just one hundred days before the presidential election. Truman knew that his actions could end his chance to be elected president and further rupture the Democratic Party. Yet in the midst of danger and controversy, he remained undeterred in his fight for equality and justice for all citizens.

Throughout his presidential career, Truman fought side by side with the NAACP to end racism and injustice in this nation. Among his most notable achievements, Truman created the first Presidential Civil Rights Committee upon the recommendation of NAACP executive director Walter White. On June 29, 1947, he became the first president invited to speak before ten thousand NAACP members on the steps of the Lincoln Memorial during the association's thirty-eighth annual convention. In 1949, despite rigid segregation laws in Washington, D.C., Truman insisted on the complete integration of his presidential inaugural celebration.

President Truman's bravery and dogged determination opened many doors and forever changed the course of history. Michael Gardner's book is a tribute to the visionary courage displayed by this statesman who began laying the foundation to right the horrific injustices that prevailed against people of color during his time. I am certain that *Harry Truman and Civil Rights: Moral Courage and Political Risks* will serve as an important reference for the study of President Truman and his legacy and serve as an inspiration to those of us who continue in the struggle to ensure the civil rights and civil liberties of all people.

—KWEISI MFUME,
President and CEO, NAACP

PLATES

ACKNOWLEDGMENTS

When you commit to writing a book, you begin an unpredictable and engrossing journey that can be simultaneously frustrating and exhilarating. Along the way—if you're lucky—a handful of people contribute to your ultimate success . . . a book that, you hope, will inform readers for generations to come. In my case, during the seven-year-long period in which I documented Harry Truman's remarkable political courage as the United States' pioneering civil rights president, I was aided by a diverse group of people to whom I am indebted.

The initial catalyst for my book on Harry Truman's grossly underappreciated civil rights crusade was David McCullough's book *Truman*. During my first year of teaching as an adjunct professor at Georgetown University in 1992, David McCullough joined me in my classroom and shared his views about Harry Truman. McCullough's insights prompted me to do long-overdue research on the thirty-third president—a man I had cavalierly dismissed as a squeaky-voiced high school–educated presidential accident.

Because civil rights was an important element of my course at Georgetown on the modern American presidents, I determined to dig much deeper into the motivation for Harry Truman's politically high risk efforts to make racial equality a reality for the country's thirteen million African American citizens in 1946.

Following David McCullough's appearance as a colecturer before my students at Georgetown, Rex Scouten subsequently lectured with me about Harry Truman for the next six years. Rex Scouten began his remarkable White House career as a young U.S. Secret Service agent working on President Truman's personal detail; using his direct contact with the thirty-third president as a base, Rex generously shared his insights about this very special president—the first of ten presidents whom he served before retiring in 1997 as the curator of the White House. Importantly, Rex also guided me to others, such as Truman presidential aide George Elsey whose precise recollections about his extensive firsthand dealings with President Truman proved critical to my efforts to document the federal civil rights crusade that Harry Truman stubbornly launched shortly after he inherited the presidency from Franklin Roosevelt.

George Elsey, the modest Truman White House senior staffer who worked closely with President Truman and Clark Clifford during the turbulent Truman presidency, was an enormous help to me. George Elsey is unquestionably the most authoritative eyewitness to the Truman presidency alive today. It was an invaluable gift to me to be able to talk to the scholarly and thoughtful George Elsey about a president with whom he enjoyed intimate contact throughout much of Harry Truman's White House stay.

In addition to enriching my sense of Harry Truman, George Elsey confirmed my fundamental premise—that this Missouri-born president from a racist rural background acted unequivocally in the unpopular civil rights area because of his personal repugnance at the brutal and deadly racial discrimination that confronted many of the thousands of black American World War II veterans—victorious veterans of color who often returned home only to be greeted by cowardly men in white robes.

And in addition to generously sharing his insights and his unique historical perspective, George Elsey also has my gratitude for editing my evolving manuscript. No one has a sharper pencil and a keener editor's eye than George Elsey.

I am profoundly grateful for the wise counsel of my good friend Father Bob Lawton, S.J., who is now the president of Loyola Marymount University in Los Angeles. Bob Lawton is a true scholar—and his intense and rigorous commitment to the highest academic standards is still evident today at the College of Georgetown University, where Bob was dean during the 1990s. While I was teaching on the presidency at Georgetown from 1992 through 1999, and during the often frustrating times while I researched and wrote my book, Bob Lawton was unstinting with his advice—and with his keen editorial suggestions.

Truman Library archivist Dennis Bilger also deserves my thanks for his generous support. Dennis Bilger knows where every last presidential memo or draft speech is located in the endless boxes of documents at the Truman Library in Independence, Missouri. No matter how busy he might have been on myriad projects, Dennis Bilger was never too overworked to help me locate an obscure document that might shed further light on Harry Truman's civil rights crusade.

In addition to George Elsey and Dennis Bilger's key guidance in documenting Harry Truman's campaign to bring full, constitutionally protected civil rights to all African Americans, I received help in doing justice to Truman's remarkable civil rights story from a number of other people. Kathy and Jim Vance—my good friends and neighbors—were a great source of encouragement, and Kathy Vance's editorial suggestions were invaluable. Importantly, the Vances also facilitated my interview with Dr. Dorothy I. Height. As the president of the National Council of Negro Women, Dr. Height is considered by many to be the most insightful woman in America today on the civil rights movement—a movement that she helped shape and lead over the past fifty years. Dr. Height's views were a vital element of my analysis, and they helped me to better appreciate the importance of the pervasive structural changes that Harry Truman's presidential civil rights actions caused in the deeply racist America of the 1950s and 1960s.

Susan Thomases, whose passion for the academic side of the American presidency is even greater than her love for the rough and tumble of American politics, provided valuable historical insights. Without Susan's assistance, I, as have so many presidential historians, would have overlooked the ugly reality of the Wilson administration's policy of racism—a policy that led to the "whites only" restrooms and drinking fountains in the Washington, D.C., of my youth in the 1940s. Ironically, I would discover that it was high school–educated Harry Truman who moved into the White House and dismantled the shameful trappings of racism in the federal workplace—racism that was put in place by the erudite former professor and president of Princeton University, President Woodrow Wilson.

My thanks also go to Dr. Rae Alexander-Minter, the director of the Paul Robeson Cultural Center at Rutgers University and Sadie Alexander's daughter. Dr. Alexander-Minter's frank recollections of her mother's years as a pioneering civil rights activist and a black American member of President Truman's Civil Rights Committee were very helpful. That Harry Truman would empower an independent woman with the no-nonsense intellectual stamina of Sadie Alexander provides incontrovertible proof that the thirty-third president of the United States really wanted to learn the unvarnished truth about racism in America when he established his unprecedented multiracial Civil Rights Committee in 1946.

Former Congressman and Washington attorney James Symington has my gratitude for helping me to better comprehend Harry Truman's unwavering commitment to the prompt and complete integration of the vast U.S. armed services in the first years of the Cold War. Jim Symington's recollection of his father, Senator Stuart Symington's years as the first secretary of the air force under President Truman confirmed how personally determined President Truman was to expeditiously eliminating racism in the sprawling U.S. military infrastructure of the late 1940s and 1950s.

The frank and often humorous recollections of Percy Sutton were invaluable to me as I finalized my manuscript. What better person to talk to about

Harry Truman's profound impact on black Americans in the late 1940s and 1950s than a man who actually stood on the lawn of the Lincoln Memorial on June 29, 1947, when President Truman publicly articulated his explosive Magna Carta on civil rights? Who better to talk to about Truman's electrifying 1948 campaign speech before sixty-five thousand black Americans in Harlem just one hundred hours before the greatest presidential upset victory of the twentieth century than Percy Sutton—then a young civil rights activist who had papered billboards throughout Manhattan alerting African American voters about Truman's first ever presidential campaign speech in the heart of Harlem? This same Percy Sutton would one day become a successful lawyer and businessman and would buy Harlem's Apollo Theater and restore it to its old glory.

To graduates of Howard University class of 1952 Dr. Elizabeth Nelson-Ausbrooks, Major Charles J. Dashiell, Jr., and Inez R. Arrendell, I offer my sincere thanks for sharing their views about Harry Truman's positive impact on their lives. As firsthand witnesses to President Truman's civil rights address during his 1952 commencement speech at Howard University on June 13, 1952, these Howard alumni were able to confirm the more personal impact of President Truman's civil rights initiatives on the lives of young black Americans in the 1950s and 1960s. Howard University not only provided the venue for Harry Truman's final important civil rights address it also educated and empowered many of the women and men who would help advance Harry Truman's vision of racial equality in the United States.

Professor Robert Ferrell, author of numerous books on Harry Truman, also provided me with some valuable insights, including anecdotal information about Harry Truman in retirement. Professor Ferrell's suggestion that I try to document former President Truman's dealings with a black American janitor named Bob Brown proved to be an instructive exercise; it confirmed once again Harry Truman's genuine humanity toward black Americans. Truman White House aide General Donald Dawson also provided me many good insights, particularly regarding the 1948 campaign. I am also grateful to James Murray, librarian for the NAACP; Pauline Testerman, audio-visual archivist from the Truman Library; and Donna Wells and Clifford Muse of the Moorland-Spingarn Research Center at Howard University for the assistance they provided me.

Throughout this effort, I received tenacious support from my dear and witty friend, the irrepressible Jim Brady. I also received important support and valuable suggestions from Jeff Cole, director of the University of California at Los Angeles Center for Communications Policy; strategist supreme Ann Marie McSweeny Lynch; Patrick Lennon; renowned storyteller Marian Rees; Mary

Dickerson; Joe Sudbay; Steve Smith; Dr. Lori Shpunt; Rick Cannon; Florence Harrington; Rosie Forresta; Tony Scully; Bruce Johansen; Jerry Leider; Susan Grant; Stanley Sangweni; Jim Quello; Judy Hammerschmidt; Judge Ricardo Urbina; Sherrie Marshall; and Larry Fraiberg. My thanks also go to my friend Lew Wasserman, who over the past two decades has generously shared his insights about the modern American presidents—many who were his close personal friends. I am also indebted to my friend superlawyer Ken Ziffren for his wise legal advice and to Tony Vinciquerra for his strategic support of my goal to tell the Truman civil rights story to as many Americans as possible. To *Chicago Sun-Times* reporter and presidential historian Steve Neal, my profound gratitude for his proactive support in helping me get Harry Truman's civil rights story published. And to my able editors at Southern Illinois University Press, Liz Brymer, Carol Burns, Kathryn Koldehoff, and Barb Martin, my thanks for their insights and solid professionalism.

Sincere thanks also go to a whole chorus of Washington, D.C.–based college and graduate students who worked with me as tenacious researchers during my seven years of researching and writing this book. Whether it was tracking down obscure news articles and books at the Library of Congress or exhuming long-forgotten amicus briefs at the U.S. Supreme Court, my researchers were splendid, and many of them grew to share my passion about making certain that Truman received appropriate historical credit for his courageous pioneering civil rights crusade. Special thanks go to Corinne Cannon and Molly Clancy of Trinity College, Mike Gerdes of Georgetown Law School, Mike McIntosh of the University of Virginia Law School, and Katrelle Jones of Howard University; and, last but not least, my thanks to an extremely efficient and dedicated young Truman scholar, Molly Cannon of Trinity College, who never gave up in her pursuit of the most hard to find fact that would add to this book's integrity.

In writing this book, I had to balance my competing day-to-day professional responsibilities. I could not have managed this task without the unfailing professionalism of my steadfast assistant, Esther Gabriel, who never dropped the ball and never lost her sense of humor.

In today's fiercely competitive publishing world, every would-be author should have compelling prayers on his or her behalf. In my case, Mother Margaret Mary and her joyful Poor Clare Sisters in Washington, D.C., were a constant source of encouragement and support; and even though Harry Truman was not a Catholic, Mother Margaret was as determined as I was that this God-fearing Baptist president from Missouri get full credit for his efforts to bring about civil rights reform.

Finally, as any member of an author's family knows, it is a real challenge to remain supportive when the family's author becomes obsessed with his or her "book." In my case, my family was particularly challenged because weekends and evenings presented my primary windows to write. So, I say with total humility, thank you to my two daughters, Courtney and Christine, for their support and sometimes feigned interest in my frequent and often redundant stories about Harry Truman.

To my bride and best friend, Theresa Lennon Gardner, my complete gratitude for her unfailing encouragement, her substantive comments and edits, and her consistent good humor during the seven-year period when I was working on "the book." In my case, writing this book was truly a joint venture that was realized in large part because of my spouse's determined belief that Harry Truman's remarkable civil rights story ultimately would be told.

HARRY TRUMAN AND CIVIL RIGHTS

Introduction

When Harry Truman suddenly became president on April 12, 1945, the United States was at war against one of the world's most notorious racists, Adolf Hitler. The country was also engaged in a much more subtle war at home—a simmering racial war waged by a reenergized Ku Klux Klan (KKK) that was threatened by the return of nearly nine hundred thousand black American veterans to the United States.[1] The KKK's fears were based on the fact that many of these returning African American veterans had been "liberated" during their World War II service—service in a segregated military that often took these black Americans to areas of the world where one's skin color was largely irrelevant.

Long before he became president, Harry Truman knew firsthand about the KKK and their cowardly but intimidating form of racism. The Klan had a real presence in young Truman's rural life in Jackson County, Missouri, during the early 1920s. With more than twenty thousand active Klan supporters in Jackson County in the early 1920s, Harry Truman got a direct taste of the Klan's tenacious racism when the Klan refused to support Baptist Truman for Jackson County judge because of his work with Catholic politicians.[2]

In addition to having direct knowledge of the Klan, Harry Truman also knew about slavery. Both sets of his grandparents, the Anderson Trumans and the Solomon Youngs, had owned slaves.[3] His beloved mother, Martha Ellen Young Truman, who died at the age of ninety-four, nurtured throughout her long life a fierce hatred for the Great Emancipator, Abraham Lincoln—the president whose actions altered the slave-dependent Missouri farm life of Martha Young's childhood.[4]

By April 12, 1945, not much had changed for black Americans since Lincoln freed the slaves throughout much of the rebellious South with his Emancipation Proclamation of January 1, 1863. The South and border states, such as Missouri, were segregated; the vast U.S. armed services were segregated; much of corporate America was segregated; and even the nation's capital—the sacred seat of America's constitutional democracy—was segregated.[5] In fact, many of the obvious trappings of the apartheid lifestyle of Cape Town, South Africa, circa 1985 existed in Washington, D.C., in 1945. "Whites only" rest rooms, theaters,

I

hotels, cafeterias, and drinking fountains were the commonplace signs of the rigidly segregated lifestyle of the nation's capital when Harry and Bess Truman and their daughter, Margaret, moved into the White House after Franklin Roosevelt's death.

Even though America's slaves had technically been freed eight decades before Truman became president, black Americans were nonetheless largely trapped in second-class—or worse—segregated lifestyles. On April 12, 1945, few Americans—except for some "liberal" politicians from the North or Midwest, seemed to notice or care about the rampant racism in America. Why should they?

There was no Black Caucus in the Congress.[6] There were no black federal judges in the continental United States. Blacks could not vote throughout most of the South, where poll taxes and other discriminatory hurdles kept "the Negroes" out of the voting booths.[7] And even though the National Council of Negro Women (NCNW) and the National Association for the Advancement of Colored People (NAACP) had large memberships, there was no pervasive, nationwide political pressure for civil rights reform.

Importantly, during Truman's presidency, scores of cities across America were not burning as they would during the violent race riots of the 1960s. In the 1940s, if black Americans misbehaved or "acted uppity," laws that took care of any alleged lawlessness by Negroes were enforced by all-white juries in much of the country. And when the laws were inadequate, there were always those white-sheeted citizens who could handle "Negro problems"—in fact, they hanged at least six of those "problems" in the twelve months after Harry Truman became the first Cold War president of the United States.[8]

In this environment, how was it possible that the nation's foremost black American female civil rights advocate, Mary McLeod Bethune, would write the following letter to Harry Truman on February 13, 1948?

Dear Mr. President:

The National Council of Negro Women rejoices in the thought that in this day when courage, real understanding and a forthright stand are needed, we find in you the embodiment of that need. We congratulate you with all our hearts on your stimulating, humane, democratic message to Congress.

Your insistence upon the passing of the ten points of the Bill of Rights, in our judgment, is the greatest possible sword and ammunition that can be used to bring about lasting world peace, and to give to America its rightful leadership on the affairs of world unity and brotherhood.

God bless you, Mr. President. We will stand by your philosophy and may you know that men like you can never die. Like Lincoln and Gandhi, your work will ever be alive in the hearts of the people of the world.

Sincerely yours,
Mary McLeod Bethune
Founder-President[9]

What happened to make Harry Truman rise above the racism of his background and take actions that would prompt Bethune to put this president in the lofty company of "Lincoln and Gandhi"?

Did Truman deserve this high praise and the praise of the NAACP's executive director, Walter White, who characterized Truman's first ever presidential speech to the NAACP in 1947 as "more courageous" than Lincoln's Gettysburg Address?[10]

In the following chapters, I provide the factual basis for understanding why these African American architects of the early civil rights movement place Harry Truman in the special company of Abraham Lincoln and Mahatma Gandhi. The record of Harry Truman's efforts on behalf of black Americans is a remarkable presidential story of moral courage and political recklessness. It is a story that should inspire similar moral courage, vision, and political boldness in future presidents, who must successfully complete the American civil rights journey begun by Lincoln and Truman.

CHAPTER ONE

The Historical Background for Truman's Civil Rights Crusade

In August 1863, a [Union] General [Thomas] Ewing issued Order Number 11
. . . by which everybody in these parts [of Missouri] moved into what they
called posts. There was one in Kansas City where all my family had to go.
They called them posts, but what they were, they were concentration camps.
—HST, reflecting on his family's Southern heritage in Miller, *Plain Speaking*

When Harry Truman was born in Lamar, Missouri, on May 8, 1884, the Civil War had concluded less than two decades earlier. His parents personally experienced the hard lessons of that brutal war—a war in which Union soldiers "evacuated" Truman's mother, Martha Young, at age eleven, and her five siblings from their rural Missouri farm in August 1863. Truman's grandparents, as did so many working-class farm families in the border state of Missouri, depended on slave labor prior to the Civil War and utilized this form of economic servitude to make ends meet on the rugged frontier of America in the mid 1800s.[1]

Because of the harsh treatment of "occupying" Union soldiers toward Martha Young and countless citizens of Missouri, and because of the pervasive attitude of a master-slave way of life in Missouri even after the Civil War, Harry Truman was conditioned to be a racist. His mother's deep hatred of President Abraham Lincoln stayed with her even to the days almost a century later when this aged vestige of Civil War America visited her son in the White House. Martha Young Truman's disdain for Lincoln, fueled by bitter memories of her forced internment as a youngster in a Kansas City Union army "post," prompted the president to label his mother an "unreconstructed rebel."[2] Knowing his mother's still virulent Southerner's hatred for Lincoln even after her ninetieth birthday, President Truman took delight in teasing his mother by suggesting that she sleep in the Lincoln

4

Bedroom when visiting the Truman White House—a suggestion that Martha Young Truman soundly rejected.[3] According to Clark Clifford, who was a trusted aide to Harry Truman, the president welcomed his mother to the White House early in his presidency by saying, "Tonight, Mother, we are going to give you a special treat, a chance to sleep in the most famous room in the White House, the Lincoln Room, and in the very bed in which Abraham Lincoln slept."

Clifford, who witnessed this incident, went on to note, "There was quiet in the group for a minute, and [the senior] Mrs. Truman—brought up on the myths of the Old Confederacy by parents who had owned slaves—looked at her daughter-in-law and said, 'Bess, if you'll get my bags packed, I'll be going home this evening.'"[4] As humorous as this incident was to the president, it illustrates the degree of unyielding anti-Union anger that permeated the Truman family eight decades after Harry Truman's grandparents were forced to alter their slave-dependent farm life.

Another revealing insight into Martha Young Truman's strong Confederate feelings is offered by Alonzo Fields in his memoirs of his twenty-one years as chief White House butler.

> For her age, she was most charming and refreshing. She would not have anything to do with the Lincoln Room. . . . To me the funniest thing she said was one night at dinner with Mr. Joseph Davies, the former ambassador to Russia. During the conversation between the President and the former ambassador a name was mentioned which attracted Mother Truman's interest. She remarked, "Isn't he a Yankee?"
>
> Miss Mary Jane Truman, the President's sister, said, "Now, Mother—"
>
> "Well, isn't he?" she insisted.
>
> The President spoke up and said, "Yes, Mother, but you know there are good Yankees as well as bad and good Rebels."
>
> Mother Truman retorted, "Well, if there are any good Yankees, I haven't seen one yet."[5]

While there were no Yankee soldiers lingering in the Missouri of Harry Truman's youth, the racism that had been a core element of the Civil War remained. Segregated schools and neighborhoods were commonplace in post–Civil War Missouri. Truman also heard about lynchings that were rarely publicized but were well known to Missourians—particularly Missourians who were former slaves and their children, who lived as freedmen in the ever-present fear of a KKK party arriving at their front yard. Young Harry Truman saw firsthand the potency of the KKK, and years later, in the Senate and the White House, he spoke with certainty about the racial intimidation and discrimination that was an accepted way of life in the Missouri of his youth.

Predictably, within his immediate family, racism was a reality. Not only had the Youngs owned slaves, Grandfather Anderson Truman also was a slave owner who apparently inherited his slaves from his wife's family.[6] For families like the Trumans who relied on this form of human chattel, the use of the term *nigger* was acceptable, and while the Young and Truman families seem to have been committed Christians, racial equality was not part of their Judeo-Christian ethic.

Despite the racist culture that permeated Missouri in the post–Civil War environment of his youth, Truman evolved into a man who was not put off by a person's lesser economic status or skin color. During his early, life-defining experiences as a frail student devouring Roman classics, then as a young farmer stoically laboring a dozen hours a day on the family's farm, and later as an army captain leading the rowdy Battery D during the final months of World War I, Truman grew to understand and enjoy his fellow man.[7] He was as comfortable with farmhands and brawling Irish American laborers as he was with the reserved no-nonsense teetotalers of Independence's best churches. He simply liked people, and as a veteran of World War I, he appreciated the enormity of the sacrifice that each soldier and sailor was prepared to make to preserve the democratic way of life guaranteed by the U.S. Constitution. That same Constitution became Truman's solid anchor when he entered politics in the early 1920s. And from that point forward—throughout Truman's life, both private and public—it was his Constitution-grounded belief in the equality of opportunity and civil rights for all Americans that shaped Truman's words and actions.

When thirty-eight-year-old Harry Truman first sought elective office as a Jackson County judge in 1922, he was schooled not only in the Constitution but in the dogged ways of the KKK—a revitalized Klan that had a formidable presence in Independence and throughout Jackson County, Missouri. As Truman campaigned in the summer of 1922 for the position of county judge—a largely non-legal job that included the management of Jackson County's road construction program—the Klan in Missouri was flexing its political muscle. The *Jackson Examiner* of July 14, 1922, focused on the newfound potency of the Klan, reporting in a front-page story that

> within three miles of Independence just off one of the main roads toward the south was held Thursday night a Ku Klux Klan meeting. It is said that a class of 200 mostly from Independence was initiated.

The meeting was on a country lawn. Cars, most of them from Kansas City, lined the roads leading to the farm. Guards in white caps and white wraps stopped every machine seeking entrance. Only those properly identi- fied were permitted to pass. The guards remained on duty during the pro- ceedings. A number present by invitation got their first ideas of the order and many familiar faces from Independence were in the crowd.

An address was made to the entire audience by "Mr. Jones." The speaker stated that this was the first open air meeting held in Jackson County. He told of the purposes of the order and explained the objects of the Klan. Then all those who did not care to join were asked to retire and the class was initiated.

The crowd present was estimated at 2,000 and until late at night the roads leading to the place of meeting were lined with cars. It is said that with the 200 initiated last night there are approximately 600 members in and near Independence.[8]

The Klan's opposition to Truman's candidacy for the county judgeship was later confirmed by the *Independence Examiner* of November 6, 1922, which reported that

men stood Sunday morning at the doors of several protestant Churches in Independence as the people were leaving after the service and passed out pink "Sample Ballots." When asked what it meant the answer was "100 Per Cent" American: It sounded like Andy Gump's great slogan, "I wear no man's collar." It was the Ku Klux Klan ballot.

On the county ticket on this ballot only one Democratic nominee is endorsed. Judge O. A. Lucas for circuit judge. Opposite each name on the ticket is a paragraph which purports to give the religious affiliation of the candidate. Opposite the name of Judge Lucas is printed "Church affili- ation, protestant, Record Good." . . .

Opposite the name of Harry Truman the Democratic nominee for County Judge appears "Church affiliation, protestant, endorsed by Tom and Joe." . . .

"The Tom and Joe referred to are two Roman Catholic Political- Bosses who dominate and control political affairs and Government of Kansas City and Jackson County."

This would indicate that no candidate is endorsed who has the sup- port of "Tom and Joe." . . . Harry Truman is the one man on the ticket who was not endorsed by the fifty-fifty agreement, was bitterly opposed at the primary by the Shannon faction and only supported by the Pendergast faction after he had been out campaigning for some months. . . .

An advertisement appears on the front page of this paper . . . which announces, "Klansmen, special meeting tonight. Independence Klan."[9]

While the Klan failed to defeat Truman in his first campaign in 1922, their power to intimidate blacks in Jackson County was a reality that Truman experienced firsthand in his first campaign for elective office, and it was a lesson in racism that stayed with Truman as he progressed from county judge to U.S. senator to vice president serving under the frail President Franklin Delano Roosevelt. Pervasive racism remained largely unchallenged in America as Truman evolved into a major political force in the United States; through the Great Depression that dominated the 1930s, and during the first half of the 1940s when winning World War II was the nation's top priority, there was little focus on the Klan or on the racism that the KKK sympathizers fomented throughout the South and border states. During that challenging time when he was elected four times, President Roosevelt was a skilled and inspirational president who had more pressing priorities than taking controversial actions on behalf of one minority segment of the American family. Nonetheless, FDR became the nation's beloved father figure—a man who was revered by all types of Americans who had survived the horrendous depression and were close to victory against Hitler in April 1945.

On April 12, 1945, Vice President Harry Truman's life changed dramatically with President Roosevelt's death. Not only was Truman stunned, but the nation, still at war in Europe and the Pacific, was traumatized with grief. With FDR's death, the nation lost far more than a president who had led the nation for thirteen years. For many Americans, including African Americans, the nation lost a comforting and articulate father.[10] In his place was a little-noticed politician from Missouri—a border state automatically viewed with suspicion by many black Americans who, like Truman, knew of the Klan's longtime presence in Missouri.

To many Americans, high school–educated Truman was a pathetic successor to the unflappable, erudite Roosevelt. By contrast to FDR, Harry Truman was barely known to American voters—except those living in Missouri or in the nation's capital—in 1945. Based on the contrasting public images of the legendary Roosevelt and the unimpressive Truman, it was not surprising that, in the traumatic days immediately following President Roosevelt's death, many in the press and troubled citizens throughout the United States wondered, How could this little man from Missouri provide the intellectual and moral leadership for a nation that was still at war in April 1945?

The public's concerns were addressed quickly as the nation watched their new president take bold, yet measured actions—actions that confirmed how quietly resolute Truman was. Ending the war in Europe on May 8, 1945; launching the United Nations on June 26, 1945; confronting the legendary Joseph Stalin and Winston Churchill at Potsdam just ninety-four days after he became president; dropping the atomic bomb on Japan on August 6, 1945, to expedite the end of World War II in the Pacific theater—these were among the more important and well-known actions taken by President Truman in the first months of his presidency—a profound presidency that was soon confronted at home with the unprecedented challenge of absorbing twelve million returning veterans into a fractured post–World War II domestic economy.[11]

As the new president faced the complex challenges attendant to the tidal wave of victorious veterans returning to both coasts of the United States, Truman simultaneously confronted, with increasing clarity, the reality of an aggressive Stalin tenaciously committed to expanding the Soviets' global footprint. The Soviet menace gained momentum in the months following the war's end, requiring prompt and creative presidential responses as Stalin's Communism was forced on millions of war-weary survivors throughout Eastern and Central Europe. In this chaotic environment, Truman—with virtually no preparation for the presidency—became the necessary architect of a global strategy that included the Truman Doctrine, the Marshall Plan, and the creation of the North Atlantic Treaty Organization (NATO)—programs that would successfully shape the foreign policy of the United States for the next four and one-half decades, until the Soviet threat finally dissipated.

While addressing these complex and interrelated domestic and international postwar challenges facing the United States, Truman's presidency remained largely free of the overwhelming civil rights pressures that began to burden the presidency after the Supreme Court's 1954 *Brown v. Board of Education* decision—a decision that finally ended the judicially protected separate-but-equal doctrine established by the Supreme Court in its notorious *Plessy v. Ferguson* holding of 1896. *Plessy v. Ferguson*, decided on May 18, 1896, by a divided Supreme Court, effectively neutralized the equal protection clause of the Fourteenth Amendment by ruling in favor of a Louisiana statute that mandated separate, segregated public carriers for blacks and whites: "The object of the [Fourteenth] Amendment was undoubtedly to enforce the absolute equality of the two races before the law, but, in the nature of things, it could not have been intended to abolish distinctions based upon color, or to enforce social, as distinguished from political, equality, or a commingling of the two races upon terms unsatisfactory to either."[12]

In sharp opposition to the majority in *Plessy*, Justice John Marshall Harlan entered a vigorous dissent that argued, "Our constitution is color-blind, and neither knows nor tolerates classes among citizens." Notwithstanding Harlan's dissent, the Court's majority view that separate but equal was constitutionally sound became the solid legal foundation for segregation throughout the United States for much of the next half century.[13] Simply put, after the Court's *Plessy* ruling in 1896, state-enforced segregation was generally a Court-protected right— a right that Truman's four appointees to the Supreme Court, including Chief Justice Fred Vinson, would challenge and ultimately alter through a series of controversial rulings handed down by the Vinson Court in the years before *Brown* became law.

After 1954, with *Plessy* gone and *Brown v. Board of Education* in its place, racial ferment gripped the nation first in the 1950s with riots in Little Rock, Arkansas, and then in the 1960s with race riots in the Watts neighborhood of Los Angeles; in Detroit, Michigan; in Washington, D.C., and in scores of other American cities. While pervasive race riots and violent inner-city turmoil would become a decade-long reality in the 1960s, that era's racial turmoil was largely unthinkable for U.S. citizens when Truman became president in 1945.

In 1945, there was a vacuum of nationwide political pressure for civil rights reform in the United States. For a nation still at war, the priority was peace—and that overwhelming national obsession blurred the reality of increasing racism throughout much of the United States.

Increased racism and the economic and social discrimination that resulted from that racism in the United States in the mid 1940s was confirmed by evidence presented in a University of Chicago round-table discussion during a February 6, 1949, radio broadcast. In a live radio debate, which pitted Truman's civil rights supporter Senator Hubert Humphrey (D-Minn.) against racist Senator Allen J. Ellender (D-La.), the University of Chicago provided compelling data of the abysmal state of segregated life for Negroes in America during the mid and late 1940s. Besides a disturbing increase in lynchings, the evidence compiled by the University of Chicago confirmed the vast economic and educational canyon dividing black and white Americans during this period, a period when median annual income of Negro high school graduates was at $775, just over half the $1,454 annual average income for white high school graduates; there was a staggering shortage of Negro doctors—one for every 3,400 Negroes, compared to one doctor for every 750 white Americans; per pupil expenditure ratios throughout the South ranged from South Carolina's $57 per year for each white student compared to a mere $15 a year for each black student, with Texas's $73 to $28 white-to-black student ratio only slightly better.

In the nation's capital, where Harry, Bess, and Margaret Truman had resided since Truman's senate victory in 1934, pervasive racism was a commonplace reality for black Americans when the Trumans moved into the White House in the spring of 1945. Although Abraham Lincoln signed legislation in March 1862 that freed the three thousand slaves living in the District of Columbia, a 1948 report by the National Committee on Segregation in the Nation's Capital confirmed that the city's two hundred fifty thousand black citizens were still denied their basic constitutional rights to equality because of segregationist policies put in place by President Woodrow Wilson.[14] The report confirmed that Washington, D.C., "hotels in the downtown area will not rent rooms to Negroes [and] . . . downtown area restaurants will not serve Negroes. At lunch counters Negroes must stand to be served. . . . Negroes will not be admitted to downtown theaters."[15] In every aspect of life—professional and personal—black Americans living in and visiting the nation's capital in the 1940s were second-class citizens, repeatedly humiliated and discriminated against as a result of active racism, which directly conflicted with Washington's symbols of its democratic government, symbols that included the Lincoln Memorial.

Despite these grim realities of the apartheid-like environment that existed throughout much of the South and Washington, D.C., when Truman became president, there simply was no groundswell of support for federal civil rights reform. Truman historians Donald R. McCoy and Richard T. Ruetten, in their detailed civil rights treatise *Quest and Response: Minority Rights and the Truman Administration,* confirmed the pervasive nationwide antipathy toward civil rights reform in the 1940s. While they acknowledge some progress for black Americans during the 1940s, particularly for upper- and middle-class blacks, McCoy and Ruetten concluded, "True, a small and increasing number of whites agreed that change should come, and still others were willing to yield under moderate pressure. The struggle would continue bitterly, however, because most whites would seldom grant even minor concessions graciously—and sometimes not at all."[16]

In this environment of pervasive racial inequality, President Truman's energies in 1945 were necessarily focused primarily on global challenges, including hastening the end of World War II and preventing Soviet expansionism in the wake of the war's end. Notwithstanding these awesome and pressing tasks, Truman also determined that the time had come for the president of the United States to address civil rights reform—reform that was long overdue for black American veterans returning home, often to communities where they were greeted by angry white citizens.

Less than a month after becoming president, Truman met with the NAACP's executive director, Walter White. Truman's meeting with the articulate spokesman for the NAACP was symbolically important to African Americans who had felt a kinship with President Roosevelt. By virtue of White's May 5 visit to the Oval Office less than a month after FDR's death, black Americans knew they retained ready access to the new president—even if he was a former senator from the border state of Missouri. By June 5, 1945, Truman also won applause from black leaders for his public commitment to a permanent Fair Employment Practices Committee (FEPC)—a commitment that Roosevelt would not make while he was president. By contrast, Truman supported a permanent FEPC, and that support was another early indication that Truman was genuinely committed to civil rights reform.

Truman also used his presidential appointment powers during his first months in the White House to signal to black Americans that he would be proactive on their behalf. In October 1945, the president nominated a black American attorney from Chicago, Irvin C. Mollison, to the United States Customs Court, an appointment that was unprecedented in 1945 for a black in the continental United States.[17]

While many African Americans were gratified by these early indications that the new president was sensitive to their concerns, Truman knew that, for the vast majority of the American population in late 1945, civil rights reform was a non-issue. But Truman also knew from his own life experiences that racism was a deadly disease that had to be addressed before the United States could be a credible beacon of democracy for a war-ravaged world. He knew, even without the violent race riots of the 1960s that would haunt his successors in the White House, that the federal government had to act promptly and aggressively to address the country's rampant racism.

In this regard, Truman was different from his predecessor, Roosevelt, and from later presidents—Dwight David Eisenhower, John F. Kennedy, and Lyndon B. Johnson; Truman did not need political pressure to do what he felt was morally right and constitutionally mandated for black Americans. Even though he confronted monumental domestic and global challenges, the thirty-third president could not ignore a racist trend in this country, a country that had just defeated one of mankind's grossest racists, Adolf Hitler.

Importantly, as a veteran of an earlier and brutal war, where one hundred twenty-six thousand Americans lost their lives, Truman also knew what it meant to serve one's country in potentially mortal combat. Thus, when this president learned of the chilling stories of racial abuse directed at returning black American veterans of World War II, he could not and would not look the other way.[18]

Ironically, as the record of his presidency confirms, Martha Young Truman's son Harry would become Abraham Lincoln's direct heir on the often sad and still unresolved civil rights journey of the United States. Eighty-four years after Lincoln issued the Emancipation Proclamation, President Truman would begin the next leg of the country's journey for federal civil rights reform. That journey formally commenced early in Truman's presidency—on December 5, 1946—with his issuance of Executive Order 9808, creating the first Presidential Civil Rights Committee.

CHAPTER TWO

Truman's Committee on Civil Rights: December 5, 1946

The Federal Government is hampered by inadequate civil rights statutes.
The protection of our democratic institutions and the enjoyment by the
people of their rights under the Constitution require that these weak
and inadequate statutes should be expanded and improved.
—HST, December 5, 1946

In the fall of 1946, President Harry Truman's popularity had sunk to the low thirties, making him a serious liability for Democratic congressional candidates who steadfastly avoided campaign contact with the Democratic incumbent in the White House. Not surprising to most political pundits of the day, the Democrats were soundly trounced during the midterm elections in November 1946, when the Republicans gained overwhelming control of both houses of Congress.[1] In the House, the GOP enjoyed a staggering fifty-seven-vote advantage, and a six-vote margin of Republicans dominated the Senate. As a former senator, Truman knew all too well that the GOP majority in the Senate would be bolstered by Southern Democratic senators any time the contentious civil rights issue was raised in the Congress.[2] Despite his party's overwhelming rejection by American voters—tired of meat shortages, labor strikes, and inadequate housing—Truman determined just weeks after the political humiliation of the 1946 election to pick up where Lincoln left off and embark on a predictably unpopular moral crusade—civil rights reform in a racist America.

THE COMMITTEE'S PRESIDENTIAL MANDATE

On December 5, 1946, in a chaotic postwar environment, while the Truman administration was addressing a growing Soviet menace abroad and significant union unrest at home, President Truman issued Executive Order 9808, which established a multiracial Civil Rights Committee of fifteen distinguished U.S. citizens. Truman instructed his committee to prepare a written report containing "recommendations with respect to the adoption or establishment, by legislation or otherwise of more adequate and effective means and procedures for the protection of the civil rights of the people of the United States."[3] Truman's creation of the Presidential Committee on Civil Rights was unprecedented, but even the use of the term *civil rights* represented a new semantic approach to the old problem of racial discrimination in America. Truman White House aide Philleo Nash, in an extensive oral history for the Truman Library, explained that, prior to the president's creating the committee, racial discrimination was commonly referred to as "violations of civil liberties" or "violations of human rights," not as violations of civil rights. Nash, who worked extensively with members of the President's Civil Rights Committee, confirmed that the "use of the word 'civil rights' . . . came about in the course of our staff studies. We thought it advisable to find a term that was slightly fresh, and the word civil rights was not used for this function at that time, but it was as soon as we created a President's Committee on Civil Rights, it acquired its own meaning."[4]

Truman was politically fearless as he took this controversial unilateral action in the area of civil rights when, according to Gallup polls, 47 percent of the American public already disapproved of his leadership and another 18 percent were undecided.[5] Despite the negative poll numbers, Truman pushed forward on a program of civil rights reform for the country. As a politician, Truman felt that polls and public opinion should not control his decisions; instead, Truman felt that his presidential decisions should be based on what was right or wrong for all Americans. Truman's disdain for polls—now an essential element of contemporary presidential politics—was captured by Truman historian Robert H. Ferrell in *Off the Record,* where he details a memo that Truman wrote: "I wonder how far Moses would have gone if he'd taken a poll in Egypt? What would Jesus Christ have preached if he'd taken a poll in Israel? Where would the Reformation have gone if Martin Luther had taken a poll? It isn't polls or public opinion of the moment that counts. It is right and wrong and leadership—men with fortitude, honesty and a belief in the right that makes epochs in the history of the world."[6]

Truman's contempt for polls was also confirmed by his trusted White House aide General Donald Dawson, who reflected on his years of service with President Truman: "When people on the staff would caution the president about this or that issue—claiming that public opinion was against some action that the president was planning to take, Harry Truman would interrupt by asking his advisers to tell him what they thought was the best thing—the right thing for the country. It was just that simple—polls didn't matter; the good of the country did."[7]

Regardless of what the polls might say, down deep, Harry Truman knew something was wrong and getting worse in terms of race relations in the post-war society of the United States. While the mainstream white media of the mid 1940s were primarily focused on war-related developments and not on reports of civil rights abuses, the president heard reliable nonpublic reports in 1946 about increasing KKK-inspired violence against African Americans, particularly black veterans who had served in a segregated U.S. armed services and were now returning home to the segregated South.

Truman's concerns about the newly potent KKK were confirmed in a September 19, 1946, meeting with a delegation of civil rights leaders led by the NAACP's executive director, Walter White. In that meeting, the president heard horrendous stories about racially motivated violence directed at black veterans—stories that further convinced Truman how inflamed the racial situation had become in the postwar South. White, in his autobiography, *A Man Called White,* portrays a troubled Truman who "exclaimed in his flat, Midwestern accent, 'My God, I had no idea it was as terrible as that! We've got to do something.'"[8]

Truman's shock about increased racial violence against black American veterans triggered a presidential directive just one day after Walter White and the NAACP delegation visited the president in the Oval Office. On September 20, the president wrote to Attorney General Tom Clark,

Dear Tom:

I had as callers yesterday some members of the National Association for the Advancement of Colored People and they told me about an incident which happened in South Carolina where a negro [*sic*] Sergeant, who had been discharged from the Army just three hours, was taken off the bus and not only seriously beaten but his eyes deliberately put out, and that the Mayor of the town had bragged about committing this outrage.

I have been very much alarmed at the increased racial feeling all over the country and I am wondering if it wouldn't be well to appoint a commission to analyze the situation and have a remedy to present to the next Congress—something similar to the Wickersham Commission on Prohibition.

I know you have been looking into the Tennessee and Georgia lynchings, and also been investigating the one in Louisiana, but I think it is going to take something more than the handling of each individual case after it happens—it is going to require the inauguration of some sort of policy to prevent such happenings.

I'll appreciate very much having your views on the subject.

Sincerely yours,
Harry S. Truman[9]

Attorney General Clark knew how troubled the president was by the increased racial violence—particularly the repulsive form of physical abuse suffered by Sergeant Isaac Woodard, who was blinded by the racist Batesburg, South Carolina, police chief Lynwood Lanier Shull just hours after his discharge from the army.[10] The attorney general, whose father had been a slave owner, was a liberal, University of Texas–educated lawyer who had been named attorney general only after the president had confirmed Clark's commitment to an aggressive civil rights approach by Truman's Justice Department.[11] Based on Clark's own strong views on civil rights and this latest directive from the president, the attorney general reacted promptly to President Truman's letter about Woodard, issuing on September 26, 1946, a Department of Justice press release that confirmed that the Truman administration viewed racial violence as a criminal offense.[12]

For Immediate Release:

THURSDAY, SEPTEMBER 26, 1946

DEPARTMENT OF JUSTICE

Attorney General Tom C. Clark . . . announced that criminal charges have been filed against Lynwood Lanier Shull, Batesburg, South Carolina[,] Chief of Police. Shull is accused of having "beaten and tortured" Isaac Woodard, Jr., Negro veteran residing at 1100 Franklin Avenue, Bronx, New York, last February 12, in violation of a Federal Civil Rights Statute, which prohibits police and other public officials from depriving anyone of rights "secured by the Constitution and the laws of the United States." Woodard is permanently blind as a result of the alleged beating. The mistreatment is said to have occurred after Shull had arrested Woodard in the South Carolina town for allegedly creating a disturbance on a bus on which the latter was returning home after his discharge from the Army earlier that day. Shull is charged with the violation of Woodard's "right to be secure in his person and immune from legal assault and battery" and

"the right and privilege not to be beaten and tortured by persons exercis-
ing the authority to arrest". The Information containing the charges was
filed by United States Attorney Claud N. Sapp, Columbia, South
Carolina, in the Federal Court in that city.[13]

While Attorney General Clark's announcement may be viewed today as an
understated reaction by the Justice Department, in 1946, it was highly significant, if not unprecedented, for the attorney general of the United States to file
criminal charges against a prominent Southern police chief. Truman himself
encouraged this uncompromising response by the federal government in the
Woodard case despite the predictable political backlash throughout the South,
where white racists often dominated state and local law enforcement bureau-
cracies.

When the Woodard case came to trial on November 5, 1946, in a federal
courtroom in Columbia, South Carolina, the 215-pound Sheriff Shull admitted
using force to restrain the uniformed, decorated black veteran who had boarded
a Greyhound bus just five hours earlier on February 12, 1946, after his honorable
discharge from the army.[14] Sheriff Shull acknowledged on the witness stand that
the physical force he used on Sergeant Woodard resulted in one of Woodard's
eyes being gouged out and in the other eye being so badly damaged that the
young sergeant was blinded for life. Notwithstanding the horror of this civil
rights violation, the *New York Times* on November 6, 1946, reported, "After
deliberating thirty minutes, an all-white federal court jury tonight cleared
Lynwood L. Shull, chief of police of Batesburg, S.C., of a charge of violating the
civil rights of Isaac Woodard, of Bronx, N.Y., a Negro veteran."[15]

While the Truman administration's efforts to convict Police Chief Shull
failed, the president's meeting with the NAACP's Walter White and other civil
rights leaders on September 19, 1946, convinced Truman that a full-blown investigation of civil rights abuses in the United States was urgently needed. However,
as a politician familiar with the leadership of the Congress, Truman also recognized that the White House would not be able to secure even modest congressional support for a comprehensive review of the largely toothless civil rights
protections available to African Americans in 1946.[16]

According to White's account of their September 19 meeting, the president
confirmed the dismal prospects for congressional cooperation, giving as his reason the Southern Democrats' filibuster prowess; notwithstanding Truman's
obvious appreciation of that prowess, White reported in his autobiography that
"the President nodded his head in agreement as he said, 'I'll create [the Civil

Rights Committee] by Executive Order and pay for it out of the President's Contingent Fund.'"[17]

White's firsthand account of the president's reaction to the stories of racial abuse was reiterated by former Truman aide George Elsey, who worked closely with the president and other members of his White House staff on a variety of civil rights initiatives. Elsey recalled Truman's repulsion at the gruesome racial attacks on returning black American veterans and confirmed that these events were pivotal to Truman's decision to create the Presidential Civil Rights Committee—a committee that the president could only launch through an executive order, which did not require congressional approval.[18]

To effectively address the country's racial problems about which White and others spoke, Truman had to quantify this problem—fully assessing its causes, as well as its possible remedies. Accordingly, the president on December 5, 1946, asked the members of his Civil Rights Committee to document civil rights abuses in the country as nearly nine hundred thousand black veterans were returning home victorious from World War II. Truman also instructed and empowered his Committee on Civil Rights to propose federal legislation and other means by which the White House and the Congress could correct civil rights abuses.[19]

Creating a Presidential Committee on Civil Rights today would not be viewed as a particularly important or courageous development by students of the modern U.S. presidency. In today's presidential environment, a difficult political problem, ranging from campaign reform to financing Medicaid, often gets detoured to an ad hoc presidential commission, which takes the heat until the political storm passes. More often than not, these presidential committees have a brief public life, then fade away with little meaningful impact. By contrast, in 1946, Truman's creation of the Presidential Committee on Civil Rights was significant because of the general absence of political heat to act on civil rights.

In reality, Truman was subjected to little, if any, serious nationwide political pressure in 1946 to act on civil rights reform for black Americans. When Truman established this Civil Rights Committee, there was no Congressional Black Caucus to galvanize support for black Americans in Congress; despite a national population of thirteen million black Americans, there were only two African Americans in Congress throughout Truman's presidency, Congressman William Dawson, a Democrat from Chicago, and Adam Clayton Powell, a Democrat from New York City.[20] If anything, Truman had widespread pressure not to focus on the civil rights needs of a distinct minority of the population while the country was struggling to employ and house twelve million returning veterans from both the European and Pacific theaters. Basic problems, including holding down labor costs while increasing U.S. food production and housing construction, dominated the domestic agenda in 1946, not racial reform.

In this environment, committing political capital to addressing the relatively narrow issue of civil rights for black Americans seemed illogical to many Democrats, particularly states' rights advocates in the South—a South whose elected leaders effectively used the filibuster to control the domestic legislative agenda of the House and Senate during the 1940s. And while the NAACP, the NCNW, the Urban League, and other civil rights groups were agitating for civil rights reform in the mid 1940s, these groups were not collectively able to generate the nationwide outcry that was evident in the editorial comments and protests of the 1960s.

From a national standpoint, the civil rights movement in 1946 was at an embryonic stage and certainly nowhere near the political boiling point that it reached in the early and mid 1960s when a reluctant President Kennedy and his successor, President Johnson, were literally forced to respond to urban riots, massive civil disobedience, and the acute political pressures that these events generated. Ironically, while John Kennedy significantly advanced his chances to capture the White House in 1960 with spirited campaign rhetoric directed at African American voters, those same voters had to wait almost thirty months, near the end of Kennedy's presidency, for the president finally to commit to introducing civil rights legislation in an impassioned speech on June 11, 1963.[21]

Why then did Truman make the civil rights and human freedoms of the country's thirteen million black Americans a top priority—a priority that was added to a long list already crowded with compelling national and global goals? Why, when confronted with so many pressing national and foreign priorities in 1946, did President Truman formally launch a full-blown federal investigation to document civil rights abuses in the United States?

The best insight into Truman's motivation comes from his own words in his statement issuing Executive Order 9808 on December 5, 1946.

> Today, Freedom From Fear, and the democratic institutions which sustain it, are again under attack. In some places, from time to time, the local enforcement of law and order has broken down, and individuals—sometimes ex-servicemen, even women—have been killed, maimed, or intimidated.
>
> The preservation of civil liberties is a duty of every Government—state, Federal and local. Wherever the law enforcement measures and the authority of Federal, state, and local governments are inadequate to dis-

charge this primary function of government, these measures and this authority should be strengthened and improved.

The Constitutional guarantees of individual liberties and of equal protection under the laws clearly place on the Federal Government the duty to act when state or local authorities abridge or fail to protect these Constitutional rights.[22]

When officially announcing the creation of his Civil Rights Committee, he clearly stated that his overarching concern was that "ex-servicemen, even women—have been killed, maimed, or intimidated"[23] Truman was presiding over a challenging postwar economy in 1946, and while the nation had vigorously celebrated its hard-fought victories in Europe and the Pacific a year earlier, the country now had to move forward, providing hope and the rewards of victory to all of its successful veterans, both white and black.

Based on his brief, yet life-altering military service during the last months of World War I, Truman knew firsthand about the enormity of the sacrifices that so many returning World War II veterans had made. Truman's World War I service was profoundly important to his development on several levels, including gaining his first real global experience when the thirty-three-year-old Truman sailed for France in early April 1918 aboard the USS *George Washington*. In France, Truman commanded the rowdy group of 194 men of Battery D—a group largely made up of Irish Americans from Kansas City. To his surprise, Captain Truman learned that he was a natural leader of men, in this case a challenging but rewarding group of enlisted men from ethnic and religious backgrounds entirely different from Truman's own Anglo-Saxon, Protestant heritage.

In letters to his fiancée, Bess Wallace, postmarked "Somewhere in France," July 14 and 22, 1918, Truman talked about the men of Battery D, many of whom would remain his lifelong friends.

> They made me captain of Battery D. . . . I have the Irish Catholic Battery but they seem to like me pretty well and I am satisfied that, if I don't blow up with too many worries, I'll have a good Battery. I hope the best in the brigade.[24]

> They gave me a Battery that was always in trouble and bad, but we carried off all the credits this week. . . . It is the Irish Battery. . . . The men are as fine a bunch as were ever gotten together but they have been lax in discipline. Can you imagine me being a hard-boiled captain of a tough Irish

Battery? I started things in a rough-cookie fashion. The very first man that was up before me for a lack of discipline got everything I was capable of giving.[25]

By September 1918, Captain Truman's leadership skills were confirmed and his deep affection and empathy for his men in Battery D were evident in another "Dear Bess" letter postmarked "Somewhere in France" on September 15, 1918: "My Battery was examined by the chief ordnance officer the other day and he said it was in the best condition of *any in France,* and he has seen them all. . . . I am plumb crazy about my Battery. They sure step when I ask them to."[26]

Besides discovering that he enjoyed having strong leadership skills—skills that had not been tested during the prior decade when young Harry Truman was primarily working on the family farm, taking orders from his tireless father—Captain Harry Truman's World War I experience proved to be an invaluable lesson in the brutal price that many Americans paid as part of their military service. Truman saw firsthand a degree of human waste in the French battlefields in the last months of 1918 that showed war and carnage at its worst. The profound and lasting impression of his World War I experience provided the basis for President Truman's empathy and deep respect for the twelve million U.S. servicemen returning home in 1945 and 1946.

Because of the president's special empathy for the returning servicemen, who literally flooded the U.S. marketplace in 1946, Truman was repulsed at horrific stories involving black American veterans, such as Isaac Woodard, who returned to the United States—often to their Southern homes—only to suffer some great indignity or, worse, death. And because of his repulsion at the stories that Walter White and others shared with him, it was politically unwise for, yet predictable that former Captain Harry Truman would take his unprecedented civil rights action by issuing Executive Order 9808.

As a veteran himself who had returned home with other World War I veterans to a grateful nation in 1918, President Truman also had to be troubled by the inhospitable and humiliating treatment that victorious black veterans of World War II received in his own adopted hometown of Washington, D.C. One incident that received considerable notoriety involved black veterans who were refused seats in the fall of 1946 to see actress Ingrid Bergman in the play *Joan of Lorraine* at George Washington University's Lisner Auditorium. When Bergman learned that black American veterans had been denied admission to a university-owned theater in the capital city of the United States, the actress issued a public statement that captured her horror at America's racism. "If I had known of discrimination before I signed I wouldn't have come. I heard in the midst of rehearsal a few days ago that no Negro can come into the theater. And in the capital city, too. Before I came to America, I didn't know there was any place where colored people could not come in."[27]

Based on the escalating racism in America in 1946—whether deadly racism directed at returning black veterans like Isaac Woodard or the humiliating racism inherent in denying blacks seats in theaters and restaurants in the nation's capital, Truman knew he had to take presidential action to address America's pervasive racism. Truman's action of December 5, 1946, in issuing Executive Order 9808 set in motion the far-flung efforts of the Presidential Civil Rights Committee—efforts that would result ten months later in the release of a comprehensive and politically explosive presidential civil rights report that would chart the course of federal civil rights reform for the next two decades.

THE "NOAH'S ARK" MAKEUP OF TRUMAN'S CIVIL RIGHTS COMMITTEE

To conduct its comprehensive survey of the civil rights landscape in the United States in 1946, President Truman and his White House staff recruited a high-powered and diverse group of fifteen citizens to serve as committee members. According to White House aide Philleo Nash, who helped the president in identifying his fifteen multiracial appointees, "We were so meticulous to get balance that we wound up with two of everything: two women, two southerners, two business [leaders], two labor [leaders], and many people were there in more than one role, but it was a very carefully balanced commission." Nash also noted in his oral history that the White House staff "finally came up with what has since been called the 'Noah's Ark Committee.'"[28]

Truman's goal of nationwide balance in the committee's membership was evident when the committee members' names were announced on December 5, 1946. The committee's chairman, Charles E. Wilson, president of the General Electric Corporation, was one of the country's leading industrialists. President Roosevelt's son Franklin D. Roosevelt Jr. was also named to the committee, bringing with him the active civil rights legacy of his outspoken mother; Rabbi Roland Gittelsohn, Catholic Bishop Francis Haas, and Bishop Henry Sherrill of the Episcopal Church provided serious ecumenical voices. The remaining members were industrialist Charles Luckman, president of Lever Brothers; James B. Carey of the Congress of Industrial Organizations (CIO); Boris Shishkin of the American Federation of Labor (AFL); Frank P. Graham, president of the

University of North Carolina; John S. Dickey, president of Dartmouth College; Dr. Channing H. Tobias, director of the Phelps-Stokes Fund; Mrs. M. E. Tilley of the Methodist Church; Morris L. Ernst, a civil rights advocate; Francis P. Matthews, former head of the Knights of Columbus; and Sadie Tanner Alexander, a black female lawyer from Philadelphia.[29]

According to the NAACP's Walter White, the makeup of the committee was intentionally broad based so that the committee's findings would enjoy maximum credibility outside of the more narrow and largely regionally based civil rights movement in 1946. In recalling his discussions with President Truman about the composition of the Civil Rights Committee, White took credit for alerting President Truman to the fact that General Electric Corporation's president, Charles E. Wilson, was troubled by the growing potential for increased racial discord in the post–World War II environment. Both White and President Truman felt that Charles Wilson was an ideal figure to head the committee because of his passion about race relations and also because of his prominence in the U.S. marketplace. While the committee included academic, corporate, religious, and labor leaders, it also included several respected black Americans whose appointment clearly signaled that this first ever Presidential Civil Rights Committee would in no way soft-pedal the hard issues of race relations and discrimination.[30]

In this regard, Truman's appointment of Sadie Tanner Alexander, who was well known amongst the legal and academic black American leadership of 1946 as an uncompromising civil rights advocate, confirmed how genuinely committed he was about documenting the brutal realities of civil rights in a post–World War II America. "Sadie Alexander minced no words and she did not suffer fools easily," said her daughter, Dr. Rae Alexander-Minter, fifty years later when recalling her mother's vigorous involvement in the then-nascent civil rights movement in the United States.[31] When her mother was appointed to the president's committee, Alexander was the assistant city solicitor of Philadelphia. She prepared herself for this and other important professional assignments by being the first Negro woman in America to earn a Ph.D. in economics. She had also been an assistant to Dr. Dorothy I. Height, who was working with the legendary Mary McLeod Bethune, founder and first president of the NCNW. White House staffer Philleo Nash, who worked on the final list of possible appointees to the Civil Rights Committee recalled that Sadie Alexander was "a very distinguished woman lawyer from Philadelphia. . . . She is one of the people I had in mind when I said it was a 'Noah's Ark Committee' because she was a Negro, a woman and a northerner. So, there you've got three roles taken care of with one appointment."[32]

Throughout her life, Sadie Alexander had been a forceful advocate of civil rights in a country that was a checkered mosaic of communities where basic civil rights for blacks were often nonexistent. For Alexander and her family, the road to marginal economic security and professional achievement from their ancestors' days as slaves had been a long and determined journey. By 1946, the Alexander and Tanner families had reached an educational and professional level that equipped them to be role models for other blacks who valued Sadie Alexander's articulate advocacy and leadership. Accordingly, President Truman's appointment of Sadie Alexander to his committee was more than symbolic; it guaranteed that the committee's work would be shaped and directly influenced by people who knew firsthand how arduous the civil rights journey had been, and continued to be, for the vast majority of African Americans in 1946. Insight, passion, real-world pain and the wisdom it produced were fully rooted in Sadie Alexander's own experiences—experiences that the Truman White House officials wanted to learn from when naming her to the committee.

In her acceptance letter of December 9, 1946, to President Truman, Sadie Tanner Alexander wrote,

> I accept this appointment, realizing the intricacies of the problem involved in carrying out your directive to prepare a report containing concrete recommendations, which millions of people of every race and faith await with hope.
>
> May I say, Sir, that your creation of this Committee is, in my opinion, the greatest venture in the protection of civil liberty officially undertaken by the government since reconstruction. I shall endeavor to give to its successful conclusion all the ability at my command.[33]

By including Sadie Alexander on his Civil Rights Committee, President Truman empowered a black woman who would not compromise or shade the truth when telling the president, and through him the country, what really was wrong with the country's civil rights infrastructure—and what needed to be done to remedy it. In a curious yet appropriate turn in civil rights history, Sadie Alexander's daughter would ensure in 1996 that the Alexander and Tanner families were once again at the center of another civil rights first. At a special White House ceremony in 1996, Alexander-Minter presented her great-uncle Henry Ossawa Tanner's painting *Sand Dunes at Sunset—Atlantic City* to the president and the American people.[34] In accepting the Tanner masterpiece as the first painting by an African American to be hung in the White House, President Bill

Clinton spoke of the leadership role played by the Alexander and Tanner families in this country's civil rights struggle—a struggle that was energized when President Truman launched his Civil Rights Committee.

THE NEW "FEDERAL" ROLE IN CIVIL RIGHTS

President Truman's own words in creating his committee illuminate his emerging yet highly controversial philosophy about civil rights reform: that the federal government was the only possible vehicle for correcting the significant yet only partially documented civil rights deficiencies in the United States in 1946. Setting the tone for the committee's deliberations, President Truman told his newly appointed committee members that the federal government had the duty to act when state or local authorities abridge or fail to protect the constitutional rights of all of its citizens.[35]

While speaking to the committee members at an early organizational meeting on January 15, 1947, President Truman made it clear that he wanted immediate federal civil rights reform for two basic reasons. First, the Bill of Rights guaranteed the civil rights of all Americans; second, there was a noticeable increase in the kinds of KKK activities that he had observed firsthand in 1922 in Missouri.

> I want our Bill of Rights implemented in fact. We have been trying to
> do this for 150 years. We are making progress, but we are not making
> progress fast enough. This country could very easily be faced with a situation similar to the one with which it was faced in 1922. That date was
> impressed on my mind because in 1922 I was running for my first elective
> office—county judge of Jackson County—and there was an organization
> in that county that met on hills and burned crosses and worked behind
> sheets. There is a tendency in this country for that situation to develop
> again, unless we do something tangible to prevent it.
> I don't want to see any race discrimination. I don't want to see any
> religious bigotry break out in this country as it did then.[36]

In 1946, Truman's vision of the federal government as the primary vehicle for curing the country's civil rights problems was revolutionary. Ultimately, Truman's stubborn insistence on a comprehensive federal vehicle for civil rights reform in the United States provided the public policy framework almost two decades later for enactment of the 1964 Civil Rights Act and the 1965 Voting Rights Act by the Eighty-eighth and Eighty-ninth Congresses—Congresses in which racist Southern Democrats and reluctant Republicans collapsed under relentless pressure from President Lyndon Johnson.

It is remarkable—yet often historically overlooked—that President Truman, when empowering his Civil Rights Committee in 1946, publicly articulated his view that there was a fundamental flaw in American society that prior presidents, since Lincoln, had largely ignored: "The Federal Government is hampered by inadequate civil rights statutes. The protection of our democratic institutions and the enjoyment by the people of their rights under the Constitution require that these weak and inadequate statutes should be expanded and improved."[37] With these words, President Truman for the first time put down an explicit public policy marker, serving notice on the country's entire governmental structure—federal, state, and local—that it was the constitutional responsibility of the federal government to do more, much more, to protect and expand the civil rights of black Americans.

In establishing his Civil Rights Committee, Truman acted without the public pressure caused by inner-city race riots, without daily denunciations by black leaders, without a groundswell of public opinion or editorial comment clamoring for presidential action on civil rights. Nonetheless, in an environment relatively free of serious nationwide public pressure to act, Truman decided in 1946 to force a very reluctant and largely segregated federal government to assume its rightful leadership role on civil rights. And even though the president faced a Congress dominated by states' rights Southern Democrats and Republicans who wanted to minimize the role of the federal government, Truman unilaterally empowered his Civil Rights Committee with the mandate and the legal tools necessary to recommend federal legislation and other federal actions whereby he could ensure that civil rights equality for all African Americans would become a priority.

For the ten months following the December 5, 1946, issuance of Truman's Executive Order 9808, the fifteen members of the Committee on Civil Rights labored to shape the long-overdue federal blueprint for massive civil rights reform in the United States. Yet even before President Truman received the final report of his Civil Rights Committee, this president knew where he was taking the country on its civil rights journey. Truman would make his intentions perfectly clear to black Americans and the country at large on June 29, 1947, when he addressed the NAACP.

CHAPTER THREE

Truman's Speech to the NAACP at the Lincoln Memorial: June 29, 1947

We must make the Federal Government a friendly, vigilant defender of the rights and equalities of all Americans. And again I mean all Americans.
—HST, June 29, 1947

On Sunday, June 29, 1947, a humid summer day in Washington, D.C., Harry Truman jauntily marched up the steps of the Lincoln Memorial to address the closing session of the thirty-eighth annual conference of the NAACP. Though Truman was the thirty-third president of the United States, he was the first president to address the NAACP since its founding in 1909.[1] Truman also set another precedent in his NAACP speech when he became the first president unequivocally to commit himself and the federal government to "civil rights and human freedom of black Americans."

Appropriately, Truman's public declaration of support for the civil rights of African Americans was made on the steps of a federal monument dedicated to Abraham Lincoln, the Great Emancipator, who eighty-four years earlier had freed slaves throughout the South in a bitterly divided United States fighting a civil war over the enslavement of black Americans. It was the Civil War that had embittered many Missourians, including the president's ninety-four-year-old mother, who still disdained Abraham Lincoln even as her beloved Harry walked up the steps of Lincoln's memorial to deliver his landmark civil rights address.

Truman's audience on this Sunday afternoon consisted of ten thousand people gathered around the reflecting pool and the steps of the Lincoln Memorial for the closing session of the NAACP's annual conference. The weekly *Baltimore Afro-American* newspaper, in its July 5 front-page coverage of Truman's speech, claimed that "white and colored persons sat next to each other all through the audience," an audience that included 612 official NAACP delegates from 45 states of the union.[2]

While Truman's NAACP audience had been drenched with afternoon showers, the *Baltimore Afro-American* reported "Skies Smile on Crowd at Truman Talk" as "the rains came—and went—an hour before the President was scheduled to address the closing session." With the sun shining brightly, the sixty-three-year-old Truman spoke with a passion about civil rights that future Americans would often associate with the young and vigorous John F. Kennedy.[3] Ironically, sixteen years later, on August 28, 1963, President Kennedy would refuse to go to these same Lincoln Memorial steps to address black Americans participating in the march on Washington. Equally ironic, the broad federal goals for African Americans that were voiced during the 1963 march on Washington were articulated publicly for the first time not by Harvard-educated JFK but on June 29, 1947, by President Truman—a high school graduate who grew up in a rural, agrarian border state, where slavery had been a way of life when President Lincoln issued the Emancipation Proclamation. In fact, just 24 years before Truman's birth, Missouri boasted a slave population of 114,931, 9.7 percent of the state's total pre–Civil War population of 1,182,012.

President Truman's NAACP address—an address lasting only twelve minutes—is historically important for several reasons. Broadcast live nationwide on four major radio networks at 4:30 P.M.—prime time in 1947 for many Americans who gathered around their radios—Truman's NAACP speech was the first public address by a U.S. president wherein the full weight of the federal government was committed to the fledgling civil rights movement. Truman's no-nonsense speech was also significant because it conveyed a new sense of urgency about the critical need for the United States to put its civil rights house in order through federal action.

> It is my deep conviction that we have reached a turning point in our
> country's efforts to guarantee freedom and equality to all our citizens.
> Recent events in the United States and abroad have made us realize that it
> is more important today than ever before to insure that all Americans
> enjoy these rights.
> When I say all Americans, I mean all Americans.[4]

For one young black American veteran in Truman's audience, twenty-seven-year-old Percy Sutton, the president's unequivocal public call for equality for "all Americans" was a noble and courageous thing. Sutton, who was then attending both Columbia's graduate school and the Brooklyn Law School in New York, traveled to Washington on roads where African Americans were routinely arrested for merely seeking food and water from restaurants along the busy New York to Washington corridor. Notwithstanding his rigorous academic schedule and the vagaries of interstate travel for a black man in 1947, young Percy Sutton knew that Truman's first ever presidential address to the NAACP was an important event—an event worth enduring the various and predictable humiliations of segregation that governed life. Sutton recalled, "Washington was a totally segregated city in the 1940s—and those policies would remain in place well into the sixties." In 1961, Sutton and a group of NAACP protesters would be arrested for attempting to buy food at a restaurant outside of Baltimore—a city that was in many respects as rigidly segregated as Washington was when President Truman issued his civil rights Magna Carta on June 29, 1947.

Expressing his "delight" at Truman's call for full civil rights for all Americans, Sutton also spoke of the surprise that was evident from many in the predominately black audience as they heard the thirty-third president repeatedly and publicly commit to full equality for African Americans. Sutton recalled, "All around me, blacks in the audience were reacting with *uh huh*s and *God bless you*s as President Truman repeated his words pledging civil rights equality for all Americans."[5]

When the president delivered his unprecedented call to action for federal civil rights reform, his mother was still an alert and outspoken senior citizen living in Missouri. Martha Truman's strongly held Confederate views were well known to her son Harry, who remained devoted to his feisty mother until her long life ended on July 26, 1947, less than a month after Truman delivered his civil rights speech at the Lincoln Memorial.[6]

Truman's affection for his mother and his family and his full appreciation of their racist views were reflected in a letter that he wrote to his sister, Mary Jane, on June 28, 1947, the day before he spoke to the NAACP. In a typically frank letter that covered a variety of subjects, ranging from criticism of the Taft-Hartley Law to his upcoming speech to the NAACP, Harry Truman wrote:

> I've got to make a speech to the Society for the Advancement of Colored People and I wish I didn't have to make it. . . . Mamma won't like what I say because I wind up by quoting old Abe. But I believe what I say and I'm hopeful we may implement it. . . .
>
> Love to you & Mamma
> Harry[7]

His letter of June 28, 1947, confirms that, despite his deep loyalty to his family and obvious sensitivity to his mother's views, Truman had determined to say what he felt had to be said in the most explicit public words about the need for full civil rights equality for all Americans. In addition, when he wrote, "I'm hopeful we may implement it," Truman was optimistic about his ability to make civil rights equality a reality. Based on his decision to make civil rights equality a top priority for his administration, President Truman stood before his audience made up largely of African Americans and reiterated the fundamental point of his 1,227-word speech—that the time had finally come when "all Americans" were entitled to full civil rights and human freedoms.[8] Truman's genuine passion about full civil rights equality for black Americans was evident as he repeatedly assured his largely disenfranchised audience that this president of the United States was committing the full resources of the federal government to guaranteeing their civil rights.

Many of the black Americans in Truman's NAACP audience in 1947—people who enjoyed only a modicum of the political clout that blossomed more than a decade later under Martin Luther King Jr.'s leadership—were incredulous as they heard President Truman unequivocally, explicitly, and publicly commit the federal government to their cause. Even optimists in the civil rights movement of 1947 knew that their movement was, at best, regional in terms of political muscle. In the industrial North, Northeast, and Midwest, the NAACP enjoyed limited political support, often aligning itself with the Americans for Democratic Action and other largely urban, liberal organizations. While NAACP executive director Walter White claimed that the NAACP had six hundred thousand American members that June, the NAACP's political power in 1947 paled in comparison to the NAACP's power today and to the political influence held in 1947 by such major, nationwide organizations as the United Steel Workers, the Brotherhood of Railroad Trainmen, or the AFL.[9] The relatively weak political position of African Americans in terms of national clout in 1947 is further evidenced by the fact that only two black Americans served in the House of Representatives in 1947—and the politically potent Congressional Black Caucus would not be created until 1970.[10]

For African Americans in 1947 who were aware of the president's racially unenlightened Missouri family background, it was an extraordinary experience to see him stand before them on the steps of the Lincoln Memorial to publicly embrace their radical movement for full racial equality in a widely segregated United States. Walter White knew that a speech like the one Truman delivered on June 29, 1947, would, as White stated in his autobiography, make "the Southern Democrats . . . want to run him out of the country."[11] White and other black American leaders also knew, as did the president, that the NAACP of 1947 had not yet evolved into the high-powered, nationwide political force that could provide political cover for the president; in 1947, the NAACP simply could not energize widespread editorial support around the country for Truman's revolutionary vision.

Despite Truman's appreciation of the predictable adverse reaction that his speech would provoke, President Truman decided to use the live nationwide radio forum to tell his African American audience, as well as the country at large, that the time had come for this country to move forward with a bold new federal civil rights program to safeguard America's democratic heritage. "The extension of civil rights today means not protection of the people against the Government, but protection of the people by the Government. We must make the Federal Government a friendly, vigilant defender of the rights and equalities of all Americans. And again I mean all Americans."[12]

In his autobiography, White concluded that Truman literally launched the federal civil rights program on June 29, 1947, by making the first major civil rights address by a U.S. president over the national airwaves.[13] White, who sat with Truman on the steps of the Lincoln Memorial, claimed that "several hundred million listeners in all parts of the globe heard the speeches" on June 29, 1947, of President Truman and other NAACP Speakers. "It was by far the largest single audience in history to hear the story of the fight for freedom for the Negro in the United States."[14]

While several respected Truman historians, including Robert Ferrell, David McCullough, and Alonzo Hamby, have noted the civil rights efforts of Harry Truman, historians and journalists often overlook the moral imperative for civil rights reform articulated in Truman's NAACP speech—a speech that marked an end to the eight-decade-long period of presidential silence on civil rights.[15] An example of the pervasive ignorance of Truman's early leadership role in civil rights was evident in a December 4, 1997, ABC Television feature about President John F. Kennedy, in which anchorman Peter Jennings used footage of President Kennedy's brilliant, but long-overdue civil rights address to the nation on June 11, 1963, and referred to Kennedy as the first president to view civil rights reform as a "moral" issue. Jennings and his ABC researchers, like so many contemporary journalists, failed to take appropriate notice of Truman's June 29, 1947, speech to the NAACP—a public address that was delivered sixteen years before John Kennedy finally acted decisively on civil rights.[16]

One historically important civil rights figure who directly observed Truman and appreciated his morally anchored view on civil rights was William H. Hastie. Hastie, one of the foremost black lawyers in America during the mid 1900s, felt strongly that Truman's leadership in civil rights was solidly grounded in Truman's no-nonsense ability to know right from wrong. Hastie was the former dean of the Howard University Law School and a frequent legal advocate in early civil rights cases before the Supreme Court, where he often collaborated on behalf of the NAACP with attorney Thurgood Marshall. Years after President Truman appointed Hastie to the Third Circuit Court of Appeals—an unprecedented appointment of an African American to a federal bench—Chief Judge Hastie, in a 1972 oral history for the Truman Library, explained why Truman would make the unpopular issue of civil rights equality a top priority in the early years of his presidency. Judge Hastie recalled,

> I think one of the many remarkable things about him was that though he had been brought up and his public career back in Missouri had developed in machine politics, he was a person who had very firm convictions, and when he reduced an issue in his own mind to a position that, 'This is right; and that is wrong,' he would not allow political considerations to cause him to disavow the position that he regarded as morally wrong. And I think in his mind the positions taken in the report of his [Civil Rights] Commission and in his message to Congress, represented something that he had become convinced was right and that the contrary position was wrong, and political considerations were not going to budge in front of him.[17]

Walter White shared Hastie's view that Truman's convictions about the need for civil rights reform were deeply and genuinely felt. For Truman, the need for civil rights reform was being documented by the President's Civil Rights Committee, which had been hard at work for over six months by the time Truman climbed the steps of the Lincoln Memorial. In White's view, Truman's remarks before the NAACP on that June day were made in anticipation of the expected political reaction to the committee's report, which was released four months later, on October 29, 1947. White and other NAACP leaders had urged President Truman to make a forthright civil rights statement "to let the people of the world know that while Americans frequently failed to live up to their declarations of democracy, we were constantly at work to narrow the margin between our protestations of freedom and our practice of them."[18] In his autobiography, White confirmed that he and his NAACP colleagues heard far more than anyone expected from the president on June 29, 1947. In fact, Truman's call for a comprehensive federal civil rights program was directly at odds with states' rights leaders in the Congress, many of whom were ranking Southern members of Truman's Democratic Party. Notwithstanding the angry political reaction that the president expected following his NAACP speech, Truman ignored the predictable political eruption; he did so because he already knew the direction that the federal government must take: it must be "a friendly, vigilant defender of the rights and equalities of *all* Americans" (emphasis added).[19]

In President Truman's view, the federal government must not only assume the lead role in civil rights reform but must do so promptly—not next month or next year. "We can no longer afford the luxury of a leisurely attack upon prejudice and discrimination. . . . We cannot, any longer, await the growth of a will to action in the slowest State or the most backward community. Our National Government must show the way."[20]

Truman's sense of urgency about the need for civil rights reform was based on a number of compelling national, as well as global, considerations. In the global arena, the United States was playing a new, almost unilateral leadership role amongst the noncommunist, "free" governments of the world. This new leadership role was accelerated due in part to the fact that our most important ally, the United Kingdom, was financially crippled, while many other "free" governments were wasted and unstable. These realities obviously placed considerable pressure on Truman, who had helped launch the United Nations just twenty-four months earlier on June 26, 1945.[21] Mindful of the potential diplomatic benefits that could accrue to the Truman administration as it attempted to nurture democratic governments throughout the globe, the State Department transmitted Truman's NAACP speech by shortwave radio to audiences around the world.[22]

In its front-page story of June 30 on Truman's landmark civil rights address, the *Washington Times-Herald* focused primarily on the foreign policy implications of the president's NAACP speech. With the headline "U.S. Must End Racial Bias, Says Truman—Calls Action Vital to Foreign Policy," the *Times-Herald* referenced the president's belief that a vital nexus existed between domestic civil rights reform and the country's ability to be a credible global advocate for democracy.

> President Truman . . . called for a swift and vigorous campaign to wipe out race prejudice and discrimination in the U.S. so desperate people abroad will have faith in democracy and not fall for the false security being peddled by totalitarian regimes.
>
> The nation can no longer afford the luxury of a leisurely attack on

these problems, he declared, because we must prove that democracy really works. The Federal Government must lead the way, and not wait for the slowest State or most backward community to protect the civil rights of all citizens, he added.[23]

When Truman delivered his NAACP speech, the new global leadership role of the United States within the context of the recently launched United Nations was very much on the president's mind as his administration confronted repeated international crises being addressed by the United Nations. That the United Nations was a pressing concern for the president is confirmed by the June 30, 1947, *New York Times*'s positioning its front-page report on Truman's NAACP speech between two articles dealing with other important United Nations–related developments, including increased "Zionist dissident" attacks on British soldiers in Palestine.[24]

By June 29, 1947, the president had not only learned of increasing racial violence directed at returning black veterans in the United States but had been fully informed about the horrors of the Holocaust, where racism was the driving force. Accordingly, Truman knew how important it was promptly to harmonize the interests of the fractured, war-torn global community that had only two years earlier defeated Hitler. Yet how could Truman's goals for global harmony be realized when the African diplomats stationed at the United Nations in New York were routinely denied access to food, housing, and rest room facilities when traveling on the roads between Washington and New York? How could a nation seeking to inspire new democracies in the decimated countries of Western Europe and the Pacific Rim hold itself out as a model of human liberties when its own African American citizens lived in real fear of being lynched? And how could the United States build a new global order if Truman's "democratic" federal government tolerated a discriminatory system of laws in the United States that perpetuated a permanent group of second-class citizens—citizens who were economically and legally discriminated against simply because of the color of their skin?

In view of these troubling realities of American life in 1947, President Truman spoke frankly in his NAACP speech about the international importance of putting our own house in order from a civil rights and human freedoms standpoint.

The support of desperate populations of battle-ravaged countries must be won for the free way of life. We must have them as allies in our continuing struggle for the peaceful solution of the world's problems. Freedom is not an easy lesson to teach, nor an easy cause to sell, to people beset by every

kind of privation. They may surrender to the false security offered so tempt-
ingly by totalitarian regimes unless we can prove the superiority of democracy.
Our case for democracy should be as strong as we can make it.[25]

For Harry Truman, the United States in 1947 immediately had to correct
the civil rights abuses and neglects of the past if it were to succeed as the leader
of the free world in the highly unstable period following World War II. Just four
months earlier, on March 12, 1947, President Truman announced the Truman
Doctrine, wherein he articulated a new global policy, later augmented by the
Marshall Plan; the Truman Doctrine would effectively contain communism and
totalitarian governments around the globe. In this challenging global environment,
Truman appreciated the unavoidable linkage between the federal government's
ability to provide for the civil rights of all United States citizens and the nation's
ability to promote democratic, nontotalitarian governments in a war-ravaged
world where the United States emerged relatively unscathed—and clearly the
preeminent democratic power.[26]

Truman was a practical man whose brief World War I service in Europe and
his crash course in diplomacy prior to meeting Stalin and Churchill at Potsdam
in the summer of 1945 had provided him with valuable insights into the new
world order. And while Truman never had the opportunity to earn even an
undergraduate degree, he nonetheless had become an insightful globalist by the
time he stood before the ten thousand NAACP members and supporters on June
29, 1947.[27] As a globalist, President Truman understood the critical nexus between
having our own house in order, from a civil rights perspective, and the United
States' ability to persuade tentative new governments to embrace democratic
forms of government that would free the world of the next generation of Benito
Mussolinis and Adolf Hitlers.

Putting our civil rights house in order was becoming a pressing issue for
President Truman as his administration was increasingly confronted with embarrassing diplomatic incidents caused by the racism that permeated America's segregated capital city. Since the United States had become the national host for the
recently created United Nations in New York, the East Coast—and especially
Washington, D.C.—were popular attractions for visiting African diplomats.
Unfortunately, because of their skin color alone, these diplomats and their families were often subjected to nightmarish hospitality in the segregated federal city
and on the roadways and railroads that these diplomats used when visiting
Washington, D.C. The 1948 report of the National Committee on Segregation in
the Nation's Capital recounted numerous cases where black ambassadors and mini-

sters from developing countries were refused hotel accommodations or even the privilege of being seated at lunch counters in Washington, D.C., unless they could produce documentation that they were "alien Negroes." The report confirmed,

> Often an alien Negro will be allowed to eat sitting down at a lunch counter if he has a diplomatic pass, or some other means of proving that he is not an American Negro.
>
> Four Negro students from the British West Indies sat at a downtown lunch counter. The waitress informed them that they would have to stand to be served. But when they produced their British diplomatic passes she apologized, remarking that she didn't realize they were "not niggers."[28]

In addition to Washington's segregated hotels and restaurants, theaters and meeting facilities in the nation's capital also proved to be venues for embarrassing international incidents involving foreign diplomats of color. One incident, which took place in September 1948, threatened diplomatic relations between Ethiopia and the United States. Typical of the shabby treatment received by countless African diplomats in Washington in the late 1940s, Ethiopia's minister to the United States was asked to vacate his seat while attending a meeting of the American Association for the Advancement of Science at Washington's Constitution Hall. Following the diplomat's humiliating public ordeal, Truman's State Department received a blistering protest from the Imperial Ethiopian Legation, stating, "The Ethiopian government considers the offense of its accredited representative as grave and prone to create serious implications, especially so because the offense occurred in a public place and in the presence of the President of the United States."[29]

Whether it was "accredited" African diplomats or leaders of color from much of the post–World War II globe where new governments were taking root, President Truman knew that the United States must end all forms of segregation if America's democratic form of government were to be a credible option to the Soviet's socialist form of government—an option being aggressively advanced around the world by Joseph Stalin.

Although international considerations were no doubt important to Truman as he addressed the NAACP audience, the president's overriding sense of urgency for civil rights reform was based on repugnant reports reaching Truman about the treatment of many black veterans returning to their families in the South. Accordingly, it was no surprise to his White House staff when, in his address on the steps of the Lincoln Memorial, Truman repeatedly spoke of the immediate need for major civil rights reform. "Our immediate task is to remove the last remnants of the barriers which stand between millions of our citizens and their birthright. There is no justifiable reason for discrimination because of ancestry, or religion, or race, or color."[30]

In publicly addressing America's rampant racism in his NAACP speech, Truman was not merely condemning discrimination—discrimination that he saw firsthand in his youth in Missouri.[31] He was going much further when he explicitly outlined a set of basic rights to which he believed all Americans were entitled. "Every man should have the right to a decent home, the right to an education, the right to adequate medical care, the right to a worthwhile job, the right to an equal share in making the public decisions through the ballot, and the right to a fair trial in a fair court."[32] To young Percy Sutton and the thousands of African Americans gathered at the Lincoln Memorial on June 29, 1947, Truman's words— never spoken publicly by any U.S. president—represented a bold and gratifying new course of federal action in civil rights. Importantly, President Truman was not merely sharing his private views on civil rights with a roomful of presidential advisers; instead, he was publicly stating his expansive vision of civil rights in a nationwide radio address heard by millions of Americans who were now fully informed about what this president demanded for all citizens of the United States.

With Truman on this hot Sunday afternoon in June were two men who would play pivotal roles in helping Truman achieve his goal of federally prompted civil rights reform in America. As reported by the *Washington Post*, "Among those who listened to President Truman's words against intolerance were Chief Justice Fred Vinson [and] Attorney General Tom Clark," men who together would subsequently vote as members of the Vinson Court for sweeping, structural changes in the civil rights landscape. On this hot, sunny afternoon in late June, both Fred Vinson and Tom Clark once again heard publicly what they had heard privately from Truman, that the United States must put its civil rights house in order.[33]

In addressing the thirty-eighth annual NAACP conference, President Truman also used this valuable media forum to serve notice on politicians in Washington and around the country that, despite potential congressional opposition, he was personally committed to a comprehensive and immediate federal civil rights effort. For ranking Southern Democrats, including Congressman Sam Rayburn (D-Tex.), Senator Harry Byrd (D-Va.), and Senator Richard Russell (D-Ga.), who wanted to regain control of the Congress in 1948, the last thing they wanted the Democrat in the White House to do was launch a liberal, anti–states' rights civil rights program.[34] For states' rights leaders around the country, such as the racist governor of South Carolina, Strom Thurmond, Harry Truman's nationwide radio address on June 29, 1947, was political dynamite because the president articulated such an expansive view of absolute civil rights for all Americans. "We must insure that these rights—on equal terms—are enjoyed by every citizen. To these principles I pledge my full and continued support."[35]

While these words were applauded by young activists like Percy Sutton, as well as Walter White and other NAACP leaders gathered at the Lincoln Memorial, Truman's no-nonsense pledge for full-fledged federal civil rights reform constituted political fighting words throughout the South. For Southern Democrats who retained their political powers through forced segregation, it was appalling that Truman would publicly commit to eliminating the poll tax and other states' rights devices that traditionally denied full voting rights to black citizens. Truman also called for "fair trials in fair courts"—a repugnant concept throughout much of the South, where selecting a black American to serve on a jury was largely unthinkable.[36]

Semantically, Truman's NAACP speech contained a directness about civil rights that emboldened his audience. In Truman's typically blunt style, his speech was not hobbled by the rhetorical generalities that modern U.S. presidents often rely on to avoid political controversy. In Walter White's view, Truman's specificity and urgent call to action were unprecedented as "President Truman called for federal, state and individual action against lynching, disenfranchisement, the poll tax, educational and employment inequality, and the whole caste system based upon race or color."[37]

In his NAACP speech, Truman the populist was at his best. While Truman privately still occasionally used the pejorative word *nigger*—a demeaning word that was commonly used throughout the segregated federal city in 1947—Truman on June 29, 1947, publicly articulated a provocative and positive vision in which African Americans would live in dignity with full equality throughout the United States.[38] As president of the United States, Truman had come a long way—and the racism that had been a part of his family's heritage was long gone on that day in June when this son of Missouri used simple, unequivocal words to make it clear that he was committing the full weight of the federal government to a bold new effort to make comprehensive civil rights a reality for all black Americans.

In its front-page story about Truman's NAACP speech, the *New York Times* reported that the president articulated "new concepts of civil rights."

President Truman declared . . . that the nation has reached the turning point in the long history of its efforts to guarantee freedom and equality to all Americans.

"And when I say all Americans, I mean all Americans," he said. . . .

President Truman . . . said that civil rights laws enacted in the early years of our Republic were precious to us and were written "to protect the citizen against any possible tyrannical act by the new government in this country."

The nation must go beyond this point, since there is a need for new concepts of civil rights to safeguard our heritage, the Chief Executive asserted. . . .

The President agreed that many of our citizens still suffered the indignity of insult, the harrowing fear of intimidation and the threat of physical injury and mob violence since the prejudice and intolerance in which these things are rooted still exist. He said that the nation could not wait, "another decade or another generation to remedy these evils."[39]

For Truman, standing on the steps of Abraham Lincoln's memorial, the nation had "reached the turning point," in its long and often disgraceful history regarding the civil rights of African Americans. While Truman had a strong sense of urgency about the need for civil rights reform, the vast majority of the American people disagreed with Truman's vision as articulated before the NAACP. A Gallup poll released in early 1948—just six months after Truman's call for civil rights reform before the NAACP—confirmed that 82 percent of the fifteen hundred adults surveyed nationally opposed Truman's civil rights program.[40]

Notwithstanding the obvious widespread public antipathy to the civil rights vision that Truman articulated to the NAACP, the president knew from some unmistakable inner compass what direction he would take on civil rights. In retrospect, it is clear from Truman's public and private words that his compass on civil rights was morally, not politically, anchored. In fact, if Truman was thinking primarily about enhancing his 1948 presidential election prospects when deciding whether to speak to ten thousand black Americans assembled at the Lincoln Memorial on June 29, 1947, the president would have stayed home in the White House, just as President Kennedy would do sixteen years later.

Truman clearly demonstrated his indifference to public opinion polls, yet the president no doubt would have been pleased with the editorial that appeared in the *Baltimore Afro-American* of July 5, 1947. Titled "Civil Rights, Human Freedom," this leading African American paper concluded,

President Truman, by his assurance of a "sensible and vigorous" program of action regarding civil rights and human freedom in the United States, put himself squarely on record, Sunday afternoon. . . .

The President made it plain that he is strongly in favor of federal anti-lynching legislation and the unrestricted use of the ballot. . . .

America's claim to world leadership is at stake each time a right is abridged or a privilege denied. Mr. Truman stated it plainly when he said: "Our case for democracy . . . should rest on practical evidence that we have been able to put our own house in order."

We were glad to hear him admit it officially.[41]

For Truman, the time had come to put our house in order, and with his often shrill voice and simple words on June 29, 1947, the president publicly articulated in the most explicit of terms his commitment to the fullest and promptest realization of sweeping civil rights reforms for black Americans. Always the realist, the plainspoken but optimistic Truman concluded his remarks:

The way ahead is not easy. We shall need all the wisdom, imagination and courage we can muster. We must and shall guarantee the civil rights of all our citizens. Never before has the need been so urgent for skillful and vigorous action to bring us closer to our ideal.

We can reach the goal.[42]

When the president sat down after delivering his address, he asked his host, Walter White, what White thought of his remarks. In his autobiography, White reported, "When I told him how excellent I believed it to be, [the president] assured me, 'I said what I did because I mean every word of it—and I am going to prove that I do mean it.'" In White's view, "If he had any premonition of the savage assaults which were destined to be made upon him by Southern governors, senators, and congressmen when he asked the Congress to act upon the issues he had discussed in his speech, or if he had any fear of the consequences, he showed no signs of it."[43]

To White, Truman's NAACP speech was profoundly important—in some ways more important to the civil rights movement than Lincoln's Gettysburg Address. "I did not believe that Truman's speech possessed the literary quality of Lincoln's speech but in some respects it had been a more courageous one in its specific condemnation of evils based upon race prejudice which had too long disgraced America, and its call for immediate action against them."[44]

For Truman, it was indeed high praise to have his NAACP speech described as more important than the Gettysburg Address by Walter White, one of the early architects of the civil rights movement in America. However, for Truman, who knew he would be vilified by Southern Democrats for his stubborn and public commitment to black Americans, praise or condemnation appear to have been of little importance. As is evident in the letter he wrote to his sister, Mary Jane, just twenty-four hours before he would address the NAACP, Truman knew he would publicly commit on June 29, 1947, to massive federal civil rights reform because, in the president's own words, "I believe what I say and I'm hopeful we may implement it."[45]

CHAPTER FOUR

The Report of Truman's Committee on Civil Rights: October 29, 1947

[This report] will be a declaration of our renewed faith in the American goal—the integrity of the individual human being, sustained by the moral consensus of the whole Nation, protected by a [federal] Government based on equal freedom under just laws.
—HST, October 29, 1947

Four months after his speech to the NAACP at the Lincoln Memorial, President Truman on October 29, 1947, was presented with the 178-page report of his Civil Rights Committee—a committee that had been hard at work since December 5, 1946.[1] Walter White characterized this "explosive Report" as bringing "down upon [Truman's] head vilification and denunciation from the South as great as that heaped upon Abraham Lincoln."[2]

In publicly accepting the report formally submitted to him by the Committee on Civil Rights, President Truman praised the fifteen members for "their unselfish, devoted service." He once again conveyed his sense of urgency to see major federally inspired civil rights reform in the United States. "I created this Committee with a feeling of urgency. No sooner were we finished with the war than racial and religious intolerance began to appear and threaten the very things we had just fought for."[3] Truman's words confirm his continued alarm about increasingly overt signs of racism in a country that had just a year earlier won a global victory against racism and massive human rights violations. In view of the president's growing sense of urgency about the need to address the ugly racism that he first encountered in Missouri, the president, on October 29, 1947, was now armed with a comprehensive document that had been developed over the past ten months by a group of distinguished Americans who were determined to give Harry Truman the unvarnished truth about racism in America.

THE COMMITTEE AT WORK

While the President's Committee on Civil Rights was legally established on December 5, 1946, with the explicit "Assignment from the President" to tell him what the federal government must do to ensure the civil rights of all Americans, the committee's first formal meeting did not take place until January 15, 1947. At that meeting, Truman personally addressed his fifteen appointees.

> You have a vitally important job. . . . You people can, I think, make a real contribution here, with the assistance of the Attorney General and the Office of the President, that will get us tangible results. . . . You may get more brickbats than bouquets. Your willingness to undertake the job shows that your hearts are in the right place.
>
> I know you will go to work in earnest and I hope that you will bring me something tangible by which we can accomplish the purposes which we have been trying to accomplish for 150 years, ever since the adoption of the Constitution. . . . It's a big job. Go to it![4]

The attorney general then addressed the committee members and informed them of the significant legal tools available to them as a result of the president's issuance of Executive Order 9808. The Texas-born attorney general, Thomas Clark, was already building a reputation as a civil rights activist based on his aggressive prosecution of white supremacists charged with civil rights violations earlier in 1946. Truman historians McCoy and Ruetten, in *Quest and Response: Minority Rights and the Truman Administration,* focused on the racial violence that occurred in the summer of 1946—a summer when returning black veterans were confronted by violent Klansmen throughout the South. "As summer came there was also news of a lynching in Georgia, which had just nominated a leading racist, Eugene Talmadge, for governor. Macio Snipes, the only Negro to vote in his district, was killed in his front yard by four white men. More shocking was the lynching on July 25 outside Monroe, Georgia, of Roger Malcolm, who had just been released from jail on bond for stabbing his employer. Two Negro women and another black man, who happened to be with Malcolm, were also shot and killed. That set off a tidal wave of protest which was not soon to subside."[5]

In a proactive response to the lynching and gross civil rights violations in

Monroe, Georgia, Clark, with support from the president, immediately ordered a federal investigation.[6] Clark announced that the Truman Justice Department was investigating the activities of the reenergized KKK in seven states.[7] Thus when Attorney General Clark briefed the fifteen members of the Truman Civil Rights Committee on January 15, 1947, he spoke with a credibility that was based on the record of civil rights activism he had built since being named attorney general by President Truman on June 15, 1945. As the country's ranking legal authority, Clark explained that the committee members' assignment was made easier by virtue of the explicit language of President Truman's Executive Order 9808, which required the full cooperation of "all executive departments and agencies of the Federal Government."[8]

By authorizing the committee's access to all things federal, Truman empowered his committee to probe the federal bureaucracy at all levels to determine exactly what was and was not happening with regard to civil rights in the United States. He also empowered the committee to tell him what he and the federal government should do to ensure an environment of "freedom from fear" for all U.S. citizens, regardless of skin color. "The Committee shall make a report of its studies to the President in writing, and shall in particular make recommendations with respect to the adoption or establishment, by legislation or otherwise, of more adequate and effective means and procedures for the protection of the civil rights of the people of the United States."[9]

While grade school students in the United States typically learn at an early age that all Americans are protected under the Constitution and that access to those constitutional rights is generally enforced by the federal government, in 1946 it was an unprecedented presidential action for Truman to have mandated a full-blown, federally supported civil rights investigation. It was even more provocative for voters in the South and throughout much of the country that this thorough civil rights investigation was premised on Truman's stubborn belief that the federal government had the ultimate obligation to protect and ensure the civil rights of all Americans, regardless of their race.

To make certain that this federal civil rights investigation would be in-depth and comprehensive, Executive Order 9808 mandated that federal employees produce "any and all materials" and testify, "even under oath," before the Civil Rights Committee.[10] These legal tools given to the committee were formidable; they equipped it with the unfettered ability to probe the federal bureaucracy to determine where soft spots and opportunities existed in regard to civil rights reform. This legal authority was particularly relevant in regard to the committee's investigation of the Federal Bureau of Investigation (FBI) and the Department of Justice—a department that had jurisdiction over federal prosecutors and district attorneys throughout the South.

For many African Americans in the 1940s, including navy veteran Carl T. Rowan, the FBI was a grossly inadequate federal force for preventing criminal acts of racial violence. As a young, pioneering black journalist in postwar America, Rowan explained in his autobiography, *Breaking Barriers,* he was "outraged to read, again and again, that crimes of race were not the business of the FBI or any other part of the federal government because states' rights under the constitution precluded any federal jurisdiction."[11] Under the broad charter of Executive Order 9808, the FBI's activities—or lack thereof—would be scrutinized by the fifteen members appointed by President Truman.

Equipped with the legal authority to examine every aspect of racism in America—both within and outside of the federal government—the president's committee set out on its uncharted journey, and as the committee chairman, Charles Wilson, explained, "almost exclusively focused our attention on the bad side of our record—on what might be called the civil rights frontier."[12] The committee members—for the most part public, or quasi-public, figures in their own rights—decided to define their committee's collective task and "to go beyond the specific flagrant outrages" mentioned by President Truman in his statement launching his Civil Rights Committee.

At the committee's second formal meeting on February 6, 1947, Chairman Wilson announced that Franklin D. Roosevelt Jr., the late president's son, would serve as cochair of the committee. Dartmouth College's president, John S. Dickey, was named as the committee's other cochair. Dartmouth College would play a vital role in the work of the committee with the appointment of Dartmouth's professor of government, Robert K. Carr, as executive director of the Civil Rights Committee. Carr had worked during the prior two years on a study of the Civil Rights Division of the Justice Department; thus Carr's selection as executive director gave the committee an informed head start as it began its formidable task. To attack the broad areas of review, the committee also agreed to divide itself into three subcommittees that would facilitate the completion of the comprehensive report requested by the president when he had met with the committee a month earlier. One subcommittee would determine the adequacy of existing federal legislation, as well as possible new legislation that was needed to effectuate racial equality; another subcommittee would focus on the broader social, economic, and educational aspects of promoting full civil rights for all Americans; the final subcommittee would evaluate the effectiveness of private organizations that impacted civil rights in the United States in 1947.[13]

With their internal subcommittee structure in place, and with a deep sense of history about their unique undertaking, the fifteen presidential appointees agreed that, because individual cases of civil rights abuses were only a superficial reflection of a much deeper civil rights disease in the United States, their focus must be broader. "We believe we must cure the disease as well as treat its symptoms. Moreover, we are convinced that the term 'Civil Rights' itself has with great wisdom been used flexibly in American history."[14]

The committee's use of the word *disease* in reference to its challenge to attack the pervasive racism that existed in America circa 1946 is significant because it echoed Truman's earlier characterization of racial discrimination as a nationwide disease that "must be attacked wherever it appears." In an August 28, 1946, letter from the president to Charles G. Bolte, the chairman of the American Veterans Committee, Truman wrote of the "disturbing evidence of intolerance and prejudice" that plagued a United States that had just months earlier won a war rooted in part in racism. In his letter to the chairman of the American Veterans Committee, Truman reiterated his view that discrimination was a national disease that must be eliminated. "Discrimination, like a disease, must be attacked wherever it appears. This applies to the opportunity to vote, to hold and retain a job, and to secure adequate shelter and medical care no less than to gain an education compatible with the needs and ability of the individual."[15] Truman's view that the country needed a civil rights program that addressed more than the symptoms of racism was fundamental, and the members of the Civil Rights Committee clearly agreed. Based on the president's expansive view of their role and with broad legal tools to function, President Truman's Civil Rights Committee began to search out the core viruses of civil rights inequality in the United States, and importantly, they looked for remedies that were primarily federal in nature. The remedies sought were not temporary Band-Aid approaches merely to address the symptoms but long-term cures to the underlying racial disease that afflicted the United States, both North and South.

THE POSTWAR LEGAL LANDSCAPE FOR CIVIL RIGHTS

In creating his federal Civil Rights Committee, Truman moved aggressively away from the dominant states' rights philosophy of the 1940s; this philosophy provided a governmental safe harbor for racism throughout much of the country—a country in which twenty states still compelled segregation in all public accommodations and only eighteen states, primarily in the North and Northeast, prohibited discrimination in public accommodations.[16]

Truman's home state of Missouri was one of ten states that had no public accommodations law on the books in 1946 when the committee commenced its work.[17] While Missouri was silent on public accommodations laws, this border state's constitution of 1875, adopted more than a decade after Lincoln's issuance of the Emancipation Proclamation and just seventy years before Truman took office, explicitly mandated that "separate schools shall be provided for white and colored children, except in cases otherwise prescribed for by law."[18] In reality, the Missouri Constitution rendered the state as segregated as most Southern states until Missouri, like the rest of the South, was forced by federal statute in 1965 to enact nondiscriminatory public accommodations laws.[19]

Segregationist public accommodations laws like Missouri's were only a subset of the state laws and local ordinances that the committee critically surveyed from December 1946 through October 1947.[20] The committee's examination was comprehensive, ranging from a review of the adverse cultural impact of the odious poll taxes, which discriminated against blacks, as well as low-income whites, to an examination of the de facto exclusion of blacks from leadership positions in the U.S. military, where black Americans were generally relegated to "Stewards' Services."[21]

Throughout its ten-month deliberations, the committee met ten times in full committee and more frequently in subcommittee meetings that focused on what needed to be done to advance the goal of "freedom from fear"—a concept articulated by President Truman in his opening statement to the committee on December 5, 1946.[22] "Freedom from fear" was an important and fundamental goal for the committee because most of the thirteen million African Americans in the United States in 1946 lived with a very real and legitimate fear not just of being deprived of their rights to vote, to serve in the armed services, or to equal justice or fair employment but of lynching. Sadly, in 1946 and 1947, lynching by out-of-control white mobs was still a reality for African Americans throughout the South where this grossest violation of a person's civil rights often occurred with the acquiescence or even the active cooperation of elected and local law enforcement officials.[23] As an enterprising young journalist in the late 1940s, Carl Rowan noted that he "was especially troubled to find that white political demagogues were encouraging lynching and other racial atrocities. In Georgia, Eugene Talmadge said that when elected Governor he would assign to every sheriff an assistant 'to take care of the nigger trouble.'"[24] Taking care of "nigger trouble" was shorthand for an increasing level of white supremacist vigilante justice, which meant lynching for black Americans, including decorated returning veterans. The committee confirmed that the threat of lynching was a fear that affected all blacks who lived in the South or contemplated travel throughout the southern states, where quick and brutal mob violence remained a real possibility.[25]

Committee members living in the nation's capital had independent confirmation, through the *Washington Times-Herald* of February 21, 1947, that lynching and other deadly acts of racial violence remained a very real and growing problem throughout the postwar South. The *Washington Times-Herald* carried a United Press story from Greenville, South Carolina: "Authorities disclosed . . . that 23 men had signed confessions in the lynching of Willie Earle, [a] 24-year-old Negro who was removed from his jail cell at dawn Monday by a mob armed with shot-guns. . . . Earle's body, slashed and blasted with shotgun shells, was found inside Greenville county less than an hour after a mob estimated at 30 raided the Pickens county jail."[26]

While the committee noted the decline in documented lynchings from fifty-nine in 1921 to six or fewer per year in the early 1940s, it also confirmed that at least six black Americans were lynched by mobs in 1946.[27] It obviously was impossible for the committee to document all of the lynchings, as well as the attempted but failed lynchings that still occurred in the mid 1940s; nonetheless, the committee documented the sad reality of six certain lynchings in 1946—lynchings that traumatized black Americans who often were the targets of KKK-inspired vigilante justice. Thus while the number of documented lynchings in 1946 had dropped to six, the horror of a still viable and widespread lynching mentality throughout the South was very much a factor in the committee's deliberations.[28]

In addition to documenting that lynching remained an ugly reality, primarily in the South, the committee also focused on the real potential for increasing racial violence beyond the South owing to the new mobility of the post–World War II U.S. population, particularly minority populations, which "were carrying certain of our civil rights problems to all parts of the country. In the near future it is likely that the movement of Negroes from rural to urban areas, and from the South to the rest of the country, will continue. . . . Unless we take appropriate action on a national scale, their civil rights problems will follow them."[29] In the committee's view, the continued significant migration of black Americans out of the South to urban centers of the North, Northeast, and Midwest made it all the more imperative that a national program be mounted to fight racism in other regions of the country where the African American population was increasing.

THE COMMITTEE'S FEDERAL SOLUTION

Emboldened by President Truman's urging that the committee recommend a comprehensive federal solution that would protect the rights of black Americans, regardless of where they lived, the committee's final report looked to a bold national solution to civil rights abuses, such as lynching.[30] By proposing a national civil rights solution, with the federal government at the helm of that reform program, the committee was offering a radical proposal. The explosive nature of the report was confirmed in a front-page article in the *Washington Post* on October 30, 1947, that heralded the committee's report as "social dynamite." The *Post* reported that the committee "called on the Nation to take immediate and bold action to wipe out segregation and discrimination from the American way of life. . . . The report, 176 pages of social dynamite entitled 'To Secure These Rights,' demanded 'action now' on 35 recommendations, including some of the most controversial domestic issues of our time."[31]

The report was necessarily controversial because it articulated the fundamental goal that every citizen—regardless of skin color or ethnic background—must be able to enjoy "freedom from fear." This fundamental concept was particularly offensive to states' rights politicians since the committee concluded that this goal could only be realized through a multifaceted federal plan implemented on a national scale.[32] Based on its determination that only a national solution would achieve civil rights equality, the committee necessarily gave secondary status to state and local authorities—authorities that often were unable, or unwilling, without an overriding federal mandate, to ensure the constitutionally guaranteed civil rights of black Americans. In urging a national solution, the committee recommended simultaneous federal action on numerous levels, including federal court rulings, congressional legislation, and presidential executive orders.[33]

Rather than focus only on specific quantifiable remedial actions, the committee also determined that its sweeping recommendations should create that important, yet missing, element in the cultural and social environment of life for black Americans in the 1940s: "life without fear." The report concluded that fear was as debilitating as any of the more tangible incidents of civil rights abuse that the committee documented; fear, in the committee's view, constantly demeaned the black population while reinforcing a false but potent sense of superiority amongst bigoted members of the white population.[34]

In the committee's view, as horrendous as any of the six documented lynchings were in 1946, the fear of lynching—the mere possibility of this horrific event—cast a far greater psychological shadow than the actual event. This kind of fear worked to inhibit and often mentally cripple minority residents of Southern towns. Black Americans knew that if accused of some unpardonable social sin in a segregationist society, an accused Negro had no protection under the law no matter how upstanding a citizen that individual might have been throughout his or her lifetime.[35]

The committee also documented the often dysfunctional nature of the local judiciary and the Southern "whites only" jury system. The committee focused on the insidious antiblack conspiracy that was occasionally forged between local police who joined with some misguided federal prosecutors and federal district attorneys scattered throughout the South to abrogate the civil rights of blacks. The report also highlighted the sad irony that occasionally existed when some federal officials in the South, who were the intended guardians of the constitutional promise of equality, were active conspirators against the civil rights of African Americans.[36]

FOUR BASIC—USUALLY ABSENT—CIVIL RIGHTS IN 1946

After focusing in some detail on the various documented civil rights deficiencies of American life in the 1940s, the committee's 178-page report detailed four sets of constitutionally guaranteed basic rights. The pervasive absence of these rights in 1946 was confirmed by the committee members's need to enumerate and propose these basic rights, which Americans today take for granted. The four fundamental rights enumerated by the committee were

1. The Right to Safety and Security of the Person
2. The Right to Citizenship and its Privileges
3. The Right to Freedom of Conscience and Expression
4. The Right to Equality of Opportunity[37]

The Right to Safety and Security of the Person

When the committee's report focused on a person's right to safety and security, it necessarily addressed the lingering problem of lynching in America. Describing lynching as the ultimate "terrorist device," this section of the report documented countless situations in which local police, sometimes working with federally appointed prosecutors and district attorneys, failed to provide black citizens even minimal protections under the law.[38] The report also highlighted official police misconduct, including widespread police brutality toward black Americans. FBI director J. Edgar Hoover's testimony before the committee confirmed the prevalence of this problem, as evident by Hoover's assertion that, at a particular prison, "It was seldom that a Negro man or women [*sic*] was incarcerated who was not given a severe beating, which started off with a pistol whipping and ended with a rubber hose."[39] In addition to Director Hoover's testimony, volumes of similarly disturbing and often repulsive evidence were made available to the committee by the Department of Justice, which in 1946 maintained only a small, seven-attorney staff within the Criminal Division to handle civil rights complaints.[40] This limited staff would be enlarged under Attorney General Tom C. Clark who, together with the president, used the committee's report to lobby for expanded funds and personnel to address the serious increase in racial violence documented as black American soldiers returned home after World War II.[41]

While Hoover's testimony before the Truman Civil Rights Committee implies that Hoover was publicly supportive of civil rights reform in the mid and late 1940s, his private attitude, according to Attorney General Clark, was much different. In a 1972 oral history, Justice Clark, who retired in 1967 from the Supreme Court to which Truman had appointed him in 1949, confirmed that J. Edgar Hoover was anything but a civil rights activist when Clark was the attorney general trying to implement recommendations in the committee's report. "We enlarged the Civil Rights Section; it is now a Division. . . . Hoover was against it. He inserted in his investigative directives that he sent to agents that all civil rights complaints be referred back to him, in the Department in Washington, without taking any action. Then he would refer them to me, and when I'd approve the investigation Hoover would say, 'Well, the Attorney General ordered me to come in.'"[42]

An equally harsh view of J. Edgar Hoover was provided by Truman White House aide Clark Clifford in his autobiography, *Counsel to the President.* Clifford, in reflecting on Hoover's dealings with the Truman administration, discussed Hoover's long-term grip on the reins of the FBI. "J. Edgar Hoover was fifty-two years old in 1947. He had served in the FBI and its predecessor, the Bureau of Investigation, since 1917, and had been the nation's chief domestic intelligence officer since 1936. . . . He felt that everyone else in the Truman Administration was a novice compared to him."[43]

Harry Truman's own dim view of Director Hoover can be deduced from the 1983 oral history of President Truman's only child, author Margaret Truman Daniel. In her oral history for the Truman Library, focusing on life in her family's home at 219 N. Delaware Street in Independence, she reacted spontaneously in a revealing comment when asked about J. Edgar Hoover instead of President Truman's friend former President Herbert Hoover. "Oh, not J. Edgar! We never discuss that. Don't ever mention that name in this house!"[44] Margaret Truman Daniel's comments and the characterizations of J. Edgar Hoover's attitude toward the Truman White House by Clark Clifford and Justice Clark strongly suggest that President Truman had a negative view of the egotistical director of the FBI.

While Hoover's testimony before Truman's Civil Rights Committee helped to document the obvious racial biases and deficiencies inherent in many local police operations throughout the South, the committee also addressed the more fundamental flaws inherent in the jury system—a system that frequently provided a safe haven for whites, often at the expense of blacks. The committee documented the commonplace inability of black men to be judged by a jury of their peers throughout the South, where the traditional all-white jury rarely had difficulty convicting a black defendant, especially when it was the defendant's word against a white's.[45] That commonplace flaw in the South's judicial system of the mid 1940s was compellingly demonstrated by Harper Lee in her book *To Kill a Mockingbird*.

The Right to Citizenship and Its Privileges

In addressing the right to citizenship and its privileges, the committee's report discussed the "many backwaters in our political life where the right to vote is not assured to every qualified citizen. The franchise is barred to some citizens because of race; to others by institutions or procedures which impede free access to the polls."[46]

The discriminatory procedures referred to by the committee included several practices that were prevalent in 1946 yet simply defy credulity today. A vivid example of the procedural tactics employed to block black American voting was Alabama's Boswell amendment, adopted in November 1946. By requiring black voters to explain various provisions of the state's constitution as a prerequisite to voting, the Boswell amendment empowered white voting officials in Alabama to determine both who would be tested to vote and who would fail the subjective test.[47] In addition, throughout much of the South in 1946, the committee documented other well-established and often inventive schemes for denying African Americans the basic right to vote—a right that, in the committee's view, was tantamount to the right of citizenship.

The report also included a compelling graph that demonstrated the adverse impact of poll taxes—taxes that remained in effect in 1946 in Alabama, Arkansas, Mississippi, South Carolina, Tennessee, Texas, and Virginia. For example, the committee's graph dramatically illustrated how the voter turnout in the presidential elections of 1944 averaged 68.74 percent of U.S. citizens in forty non–poll tax states, compared to 18.31 percent of the voting population in the eight Southern States that retained the poll tax.[48] While poll taxes had an adverse impact on lower-income whites, as well as black Americans, the committee concluded that the most pervasive effect of the poll tax was to inhibit the voting rights of black

Americans.[49] The report also focused attention on the voting potential of the disenfranchised black Americans, primarily in the South, who were not able to vote in 1946 because of the poll tax and other onerous forms of discrimination designed to keep blacks out of the polling booths in the 1940s.

For decorated World War II veteran Percy Sutton, who served his country in Italy and North Africa, the harsh reality of life in 1946 was that poll taxes remained in place in his home state of Texas. Black veterans like Sutton, who later provided tenacious leadership in the civil rights movement of the 1950s and 1960s, had earned the right to vote—a vote that Texas-born Sutton would necessarily cast for Truman in 1948 in New York, where his right to vote was ensured.[50]

Another significant yet missing element in the right of citizenship for African Americans was the right to serve their country in wartime with dignity, free from discrimination. Notwithstanding the fact that nearly nine hundred thousand black American veterans were returning home in 1946, the committee confirmed that blacks continued to suffer widespread and deep-rooted racial discrimination in the service of their country, "even as they fell in battle."[51] The committee further confirmed that "Negroes, for example, are faced by an absolute bar against enlistment in any branch of the Marine Corps other than the steward's branch, and the Army cleaves to a ceiling for Negro personnel of about ten percent of the total strength of the service."[52] And while the committee found no official policy of discrimination against blacks in the navy and Coast Guard, the report nonetheless concluded that de facto discrimination existed because only 4.4 percent of navy personnel were Negroes in 1946, and only 4.2 percent of the Coast Guard's ranks were minorities. The report also focused on the revealing fact that, in the U.S. Army of 1946, only one black in seventy was a commissioned officer compared to a ratio in the white ranks of one officer for every seven white enlisted men.[53]

While some progress had been made in integrating the armed forces during the war years, the committee concluded, "There is much that remains to be done, much that can be done at once. Morally, the failure to act is indefensible."[54] The committee's outrage at the pervasive segregation in the armed services was heightened by the fact that, just over a year earlier, the United States had celebrated V-E Day and V-J Day—victories that were achieved with the collective efforts and sacrifices of white and black Americans.

In regard to continued de facto segregation within the vast United States armed forces in 1946, the report concluded, "The war experience brought to our attention a laboratory in which we may prove that the majority and minorities of our population can train and work and fight side by side in cooperation and harmony. We should not hesitate to take full advantage of this opportunity."[55]

The Right to Freedom of Conscience and Expression

The third basic right articulated by President Truman's Civil Rights Committee was the right to freedom of conscience and expression. In addressing this right, the committee's concern reflected a reaction to civil rights violations resulting from postwar concerns about a growing communist menace at home. Even before Senator Joseph McCarthy's tirades made national headlines, the committee was concerned that "red hunting" amongst civil servants and the growing public alarm about possible communists in government and in the arts would ultimately undercut the civil rights of minorities, just as Japanese Americans had suffered severe civil rights abuses after Pearl Harbor.[56]

A related committee concern involved widely circulated, anonymous hate literature, which played an important and racially divisive role in the campaign of 1940—a campaign in which one-third of the campaign propaganda distributed was circulated without author or sponsor identification. The committee expressed its serious collective concern about this trend in American politics in 1946, as some well-financed proponents of racial and religious discrimination had gone underground and could continue anonymously to propagandize against blacks with well-financed hate literature. While the committee argued for the continued protection of the right to express one's views, no matter how controversial, the report advocated a concomitant responsibility to identify the campaign literature's author so voters would know what groups were attempting to influence them.[57]

The Right to Equality of Opportunity

The fourth and final basic civil right that the committee addressed was the right to equality of opportunity. The report characterized this basic principle as follows: "A man's right to an equal chance to utilize fully his skills and knowledge is essential. The meaning of a job goes far beyond the paycheck."[58] Citing the compelling testimony of witnesses who appeared before them, the committee's report concluded that "discrimination in employment damages lives, both the bodies and the minds, of those discriminated against and those who discriminate. It blights and perverts that healthy ambition to improve one's standard of living which we like to say is peculiarly American. It generates insecurity, fear, resentment, division and tension in our society."[59] Ironically, these words from the committee's report in 1946 were echoed almost fifty years later, on May 10, 1994, by white and black South Africans, the oppressors and the oppressed, as they jointly celebrated their common sense of liberation when President Nelson Mandela was inaugurated as the first president of an integrated Republic of South Africa.

In addressing the right to equality of opportunity, the president's committee argued that the black population of the United States deserved the opportunity to be full participants in America's somewhat chaotic and explosive postwar economy. The committee recognized that anything less than full equality of opportunity would destroy a black person's spirit as surely as the hunger and homelessness that often resulted from discrimination-based unemployment.[60]

While acknowledging that some progress had been made in the early 1940s in eliminating discriminatory employment practices as a result of Roosevelt's 1941 issuance of an executive order creating the temporary FEPC, the Truman committee's report was equally critical of corporate America, the unions, and even the federal government. Example after example of racial discrimination in hiring and on-the-job practices were cited by the committee as the basis for its sweeping recommendations. And even when the committee praised the federal government's improved employment practice of hiring black Americans during World War II—a period when black Americans' employment in the federal government increased from forty thousand before 1941 to three hundred thousand in 1944—the committee nonetheless warned of the recent noticeable slippage in minority hiring in 1946 when the economy was no longer frenetically fueled by a wartime industrial engine.[61]

To achieve equality of opportunity, the committee stressed the critical need of equal education for all citizens of the United States, black and white, in every part of the country. While it noted modest progress in some areas, the committee stated, "We have not finally eliminated prejudice and discrimination from the operation of either our public or our private schools and colleges. Two inadequacies are extremely serious. We have failed to provide Negroes and, to a lesser extent, other minority group members, with equality of educational opportunities in our public institutions, particularly at the elementary and secondary school levels. We have allowed discrimination in the operation of many of our private institutions of higher education, particularly in the North with respect to Jewish students."[62] In this regard, the Truman Civil Rights Committee was essentially restating the obvious regarding the seriously inadequate but allegedly separate but equal public schools in the South and elsewhere.

The committee also pointed a damning finger at the North's institutions of higher education that were not only indifferent to black students but were pointedly discriminatory in not providing educational opportunities for Jewish students—often highly qualified students who applied to elite institutions but who were frequently rejected without explanation.[63] The committee reached beyond its more limited racial focus and confirmed that discrimination in education was both a Southern and a Northern problem; discrimination injured blacks who struggled to get even a modest grade school education in the South, and discrimination also injured young Jewish Americans who, no matter how gifted or academically prepared they might be, were kept from attending the country's leading colleges and universities in the more integrated liberal states of the North.

Beyond the need for equality of education, the committee also addressed the issue of fair housing for African Americans. For blacks, as well as for many white Americans in 1946, there simply was not adequate housing available, and the shortage was exacerbated by the return of twelve million veterans. But for black Americans, widespread racial discrimination in housing created an often insurmountable hurdle. Restrictive covenants, which today provoke disbelief in law school property classes around the country, were just fifty years ago often ironclad legal impediments to black Americans seeking housing throughout the country. As documented by the committee, restrictive covenants were relied on equally in aristocratic Yankee neighborhoods of the North and in magnolia tree–lined neighborhoods of the South. For the members of the Truman Civil Rights Committee, these restrictive covenants had "become the most effective modern method of accomplishing such segregation." The committee documented its conclusion that segregation in housing was not an exclusively Southern phenomenon by showing that, in 1946, 80 percent of Chicago's land was subject to racial restrictions.[64]

Beyond the dismal state of education and housing opportunities for minorities in the United States in 1946, the committee's report also focused on the gross inequalities in the availability of basic health care for African Americans, whether in the hands of federal, state, or local providers.[65] A black American's right to public services and equal accommodations in 1946 often was only a paper right—and not even marginally available to many black Americans across the country. That twenty states in 1946 legally compelled some form of segregation while another ten were silent on the subject of legal equality, was, in the committee's view, ample evidence of the fictional right blacks had to housing, education, medical care, and public services.[66] In this regard, the committee noted the cruel inconsistency under which black American veterans were welcome on the battlefields of World War II, but these same black veterans returned home in 1945 and 1946 to many communities across America where they were unwelcome because of their skin color.

In discussing the fiction of separate but equal, the committee's report detailed the shortcomings for African Americans in education, housing, and public services that resulted from the separate-but-equal doctrine throughout much of the country. While condemning the policy of separate-but-equal services in the United States in 1946, the committee nonetheless reiterated its collective belief that, "in a democracy, each individual must have freedom to choose his friends and to control the pattern of his personal and family life. But we see nothing inconsistent between this freedom and a recognition of the truth that democracy also means that in going to school, working, participating in the political process, serving in the armed forces, enjoying government services in such fields as health and recreation . . . distinctions of race, color, and creed have no place."[67] Here, the committee balanced its call for massive federal civil rights reform with its respect for the constitutionally protected right of association; and while the report's explicit language stressed the right of free association, its overwhelming rejection of *Plessy*'s separate-but-equal doctrine was the dominant theme of this section of the report—a theme that would prove to be politically incendiary.

THE COMMITTEE'S THIRTY-FIVE RECOMMENDATIONS

During the ten-month drafting process for their report to the president, the committee's fifteen members and twelve full-time professional staff were thorough in documenting the prevalence of gross civil rights abuses in the post–World War II United States. But the president had asked them on December 5, 1946, to do more than merely document racism and its impact in America; Truman also told his appointees that he wanted their recommendations about what needed to be done to remedy the pervasive racism and its ugly by-product, discrimination, throughout the United States. In response to the presidential mandate, the committee's final report provided President Truman a detailed set of thirty-five recommendations—recommendations that the *Washington Post* on October 30, 1947, called "some of the most controversial domestic issues of our time."[68]

In the committee's view, adoption of all thirty-five recommendations was essential if the country were to begin effectively and promptly to address the underlying causes of the civil rights disease. The cornerstone of the committee's report was the basic, albeit controversial, belief that "the National Government of the United States must take the lead in safeguarding the civil rights of all Americans."[69] While this belief and the recommendations that flowed from it may seem logical today, the Truman committee's insistence on the federal government's assumption of the leadership role in the civil rights area was a radical proposal in 1946.

The belief that the national government must take the lead in civil rights also represented a sharp departure from the views of President Truman's predecessor in the White House, Franklin Roosevelt. FDR was much beloved by African Americans who benefited, as did much of the impoverished U.S. population, from many of his New Deal policies. While Roosevelt was a hero to African Americans, he had in fact been very reluctant to risk alienating Southern members of Congress by advancing even a limited federal civil rights program during his twelve years in the White House. As noted by many historians, including Ted Morgan in *FDR: A Biography,* Roosevelt never proposed comprehensive federal civil rights legislation and only issued a single executive order designed to address the rights of black Americans.[70] While Roosevelt's Executive Order 8802 created a temporary federal FEPC as part of the wartime effort, it was issued on June 25, 1941, only after President Roosevelt was confronted with a threatened march on Washington that was organized by A. Philip Randolph, founder of the Brotherhood of Sleeping Car Porters.[71]

Although Roosevelt's issuance of Executive Order 8802 aborted the 1941 march on Washington, in the words of Supreme Court Justice Tom C. Clark, it nonetheless, "caused a hullabaloo down in the South." Even though Texan Tom Clark was an admirer of President Roosevelt, Clark acknowledged in a 1972 oral history, "Although Mr. Roosevelt, whom I loved, had talked much about the plight of the Negro and things of that kind, why, he never got around to integrating the armed services"—an armed services that swelled significantly during Roosevelt's final years in the White House and included more than eight hundred eighty thousand African Americans by the end of World War II.[72]

In contrast to Truman's civil rights legacy, which triggered structural and permanent changes in the country's segregated landscape, Roosevelt's federal FEPC established only a temporary program to free up jobs for blacks in the wartime defense industry. Accordingly, its long-term impact was marginal. In regard to broader civil rights reform during his twelve years in office, Roosevelt remained timid. Even when Roosevelt's feisty secretary of the interior, Harold Ickes, eliminated the demeaning trappings of the segregated federal workforce at the Department of the Interior—a workforce that had become rigidly segregated under President Woodrow Wilson, President Roosevelt did not follow Ickes's courageous lead and failed to issue an executive order that would make Ickes's integration policy at the Department of the Interior universally applied throughout the vast federal bureaucracy.[73]

Unlike Truman, President Roosevelt generally dodged the civil rights issue—an issue that was of persistent concern to his wife, Eleanor, who repeatedly sought to break down the segregationist traditions of the federal city. This view of a politically cautious and rhetoric-only President Roosevelt on civil rights matters was shared by Walter White, who enjoyed frequent contact with President Roosevelt and his wife during the Roosevelt presidency.

White's criticism of FDR's civil rights record was publicly articulated in a February 1948 article for White's *Graphic Syndicate,* where the NAACP leader acknowledged that FDR was opposed to lynching and other civil rights evils, "But [FDR] repeatedly told me that the time was not yet ripe for a head-on collision with the Southern Senators and Congressmen who, under the seniority rule of the Senate . . . chaired important Senate and House committees."[74] In White's opinion, "Roosevelt issued his famous Executive Order 8802 establishing a Fair Employment Practices Committee only when he was convinced that a threatened March on Washington was not a bluff."

In sharp contrast to FDR's reluctance to offend racist members of Congress by using the powers of the executive branch to advance civil rights reforms, the members of Truman's Civil Rights Committee recommended presidential action that would directly attack the status quo politics of states' rights politicians. These politicians dominated many congressional committees, state assemblies, and local governments throughout much of the United States in 1946. In this regard, the committee's recommendation for "the national government" to assume the leadership role in civil rights reform was tantamount to a political declaration of war against the Southern Democrats—a wing of the party that traditional political pundits viewed as essential to President Truman's ability to effectively govern, as well as his ability to win the presidential election for the first time in 1948.

For the federal government to fulfill its constitutional responsibility to all Americans, the report devoted twenty-two pages to a detailed discussion of its thirty-five recommendations.[75] The recommendations included

- creation of a full-fledged civil rights division in the Department of Justice to replace the understaffed and largely ineffective Civil Rights Section in the Justice Department's Criminal Division that was started in 1939;[76]
- establishment of a permanent commission on civil rights in the Executive Office of the president, with the simultaneous creation of a joint standing committee on civil rights in Congress;[77]
- enactment of a federal antilynching law, as well as a federal statute to criminalize police brutality;[78]
- action by states and Congress to end poll taxes as a voting prerequisite;[79]
- enactment of comprehensive federal voting rights legislation;[80]

- enactment by Congress of legislation prohibiting any and all forms of discrimination against a member of the United States armed forces;[81]
- adoption of federal and state laws requiring the full identification of groups seeking to influence public opinion;[82]
- elimination, by federal and state governments, of segregation in America based on race, color, creed, or national origin;[83]
- enactment of a federal fair employment practices act;[84]
- enactment by state legislatures of fair education laws;[85]
- outlawing of "restrictive covenants."[86]

In view of the scope and radical nature of its thirty-five recommendations, it was not surprising that the release of the committee's final report on October 29, 1947, proved to be "explosive" throughout the South. According to the *Washington Post* of October 30, 1947, when the president accepted his committee's comprehensive report, "President Truman said he hoped the Committee had given the Nation a document as broad as the Declaration of Independence— 'An American Charter of Human Freedom in our time.'"[87] By publicly comparing his Civil Rights Committee's report to one of the most important documents in the nation's history, Truman further infuriated states' rights advocates throughout the country. Journalist Carl Rowan concluded that, when the president publicly embraced the committee's report, "Mr. Truman became the nation's first president to say unequivocally that the federal government has the primary responsibility to secure the basic civil rights of minority group citizens."[88]

While Carl Rowan and other black journalists praised Truman, press reaction in the South was instant and harsh, putting Truman on public notice that any efforts to effectuate civil rights reform would be politically costly. On October 30, 1947, the *Washington Post* reported that the Civil Rights Committee's report was vilified by the Nashville, Tennessee, *Banner*, which editorialized that the report "originated in the left wing of imported politics." In North Carolina, the *Charlotte News* editorially described the report as "a bombastic demand for upheaval," while the Alabama's *Mobile Register* characterized the report as "unwarranted and impractical."[89] Even the normally more reasoned *Atlanta Constitution* editorialized on October 31, 1947, "You Can't Legislate Tolerance":

We believe the Committee's insistence upon immediate action is especially unwise at this particular time and that, instead of assisting in solving a serious problem, it serves only to confuse the issue.

For racial segregation is merely an outward manifestation of an inner state of mind. Whether this state of mind is proper or improper is immaterial. It is there, and it can be eradicated not by laws but only by the evolutionary process and the acquirement by the human race of the spiritual qualities which effectively eliminate it.[90]

Although the *Atlanta Constitution* was only mildly critical of the committee's report, other leading publishers and editors throughout the South were outraged, and they sent Truman an unmistakable signal that his political chances for election to the White House in 1948 would be compromised if he gave the committee's report more than lip service.

In addition to often vitriolic Southern press reaction to his committee's report, President Truman received an outpouring of letters and telegrams of protest from voters throughout the South, many of whom characterized his civil rights program as a political dead end. This point was succinctly made in a November 4, 1947, letter to the president from a resident of Virginia named Mrs. M. R. Baker. Her letter was forwarded to Truman by his former senate colleague, the formidable Harry F. Byrd—the legendary Virginia senator whose "Byrd machine" dominated Virginia politics for decades. To Byrd's letter was attached a press clipping that included a photo of the president's multiracial committee. Mrs. Baker had obviously been prompted to write the president after seeing the photo, which showed the black and white Americans who were members of the President's Civil Rights Committee as they formally presented their report to the president.

Dear Mr. Truman:

Do you expect the South to vote for you after seeing this picture and reading what is under it? If you do away with segregation, allow negro [*sic*] children in white schools, churches, etc. you might as well drop a few bombs on us and not prolong the agony. Just come down here (southern Va.) and live awhile, and you'll see why we are right.

Very truly,
M. R. Baker[91]

Notwithstanding harsh public reaction like Baker's and the widespread editorial threats of Southern publishers, Truman publicly embraced the report of his Civil Rights Committee. For the first time in his presidency, Truman was equipped with a comprehensive civil rights policy game plan. Unlike FDR, who privately knew from his well-traveled wife that there were serious unaddressed civil rights problems throughout the country, President Harry Truman now was formally empowered by his multiracial committee with public documentation about exactly what was wrong with civil rights in America.[92]

For Walter White, the report of the Committee on Civil Rights became the seminal document in the unprecedented federal civil rights campaign that was launched by Truman. Looking back on the committee's efforts, White concluded,

> The report which these representatives of business, labor, education, the law and the public generally presented to the President and the American public in the autumn of 1947 under the title *To Secure These Rights* is without doubt the most courageous and specific document of its kind in American history. There are of course some omissions and deficiencies. But these are so minute in importance and number as to be insignificant when compared to the explicit recommendations of things to be done by the Congress, administrative bureaus of the federal and state governments, by state legislatures and by private organizations and individuals. An almost perfect yardstick was thus established by which can be measured the gap between what Americans say they believe and what they do.[93]

White was one of the nation's most respected black leaders in the 1940s, and in his opinion, President Truman had successfully inspired the diverse group of citizens on his committee to do exactly what he had asked them to do: they established the public "yardstick" by which federal civil rights reform would be measured in the future. In White's view, with the report's formal submission to the president, the nation for the first time had a definitive record and public policy road map for the massive action that the federal government must take.

For Supreme Court Justice Tom Clark, who served as Truman's attorney general from June 1945 to April 1949, the Truman committee report *To Secure These Rights* was profoundly important in shaping the modern American civil rights movement. In Justice Clark's 1972 oral history, given more than twenty-five years after the public release of the committee's civil rights report, he stated, "If you will study [the report,] . . . you will find it is a blueprint of most everything that's been done in the area of civil rights since that time."[94] Clark's views are particularly relevant because he had frequent and direct contact during this period both with President Truman and with Truman's good friend and appointee Chief Justice Fred Vinson. Clark's professional contact with Vinson was initially as

Truman's proactive attorney general and subsequently as Vinson's fellow justice on the U.S. Supreme Court—a court that handed down a number of landmark civil rights rulings that effectively dismantled much of America's segregationist policy under *Plessy v. Ferguson*'s separate-but-equal doctrine. Justice Clark was also one of the nine justices on the Warren Court when it unanimously overturned *Plessy v. Ferguson* in 1954 with *Brown v. Board of Education*.

According to Dr. Dorothy I. Height, the renowned civil rights leader and former president of the NCNW, the Truman committee report was vitally important because "it laid it all out." "The Report told Americans what a lot of them did not want to hear" about the terrible inequality and racism that permeated life in America in the 1940s.[95]

For Carl Rowan, the respected journalist who chronicled the civil rights movement for almost five decades following his service in a segregated U.S. Army in World War II, the committee's report "shocked the nation with its documentation of lynchings, of the denial of voting rights, of inequality of educational opportunities, of discrimination in our armed services."[96] In a 1959 *Ebony* article following his interview with Truman, Rowan concluded that the report "perhaps, as much as any other single thing in recent decades, . . . drew the people's attention to the special problems of the Negro in America and to the need for government to do something about them."[97]

In evaluating the final report that the committee submitted to the president on October 29, 1947, Chairman Charles Wilson described the report as deliberately focused "on the bad side of our record—on what might be called the civil rights frontier."[98] Wilson realized, as did Walter White, Dorothy Height, Tom Clark, and Carl Rowan, that the committee's report was revolutionary primarily because it explicitly called on this American president, who was the product of a slave-owning heritage, to take comprehensive federal actions on behalf of African Americans—actions that, if taken, would impact every phase of American life. Wilson also knew that, equipped with the committee's thirty-five recommendations, it was now up to Truman to demonstrate that he had the moral courage to lead the country on a journey into the uncharted civil rights frontier, a journey that had been stalled since Lincoln liberated America's slaves eight decades earlier.

Grandview farmhouse. For young Harry Truman, shown here with his beloved mother, Martha Young Truman *(left)*, and his grandmother, Harriet Gregg Young, their Grandview, Missouri, farmhouse was a palace. While the Trumans were respected farmers, Harry's hope of attending college ended with his father's business failures, making Truman the only modern American president to govern with merely a high school degree. *Courtesy of the Harry S. Truman Library.*

HST on plow. Rural Missouri farm life was rugged and demanding for young Harry Truman at the turn of the century, when Missouri farmers, including Harry's slave-owning grandparents, could no longer count on slave labor to help with the rigors of farm life. *Courtesy of the Harry S. Truman Library.*

HST and Battery D boys. In April 1919, then Captain Harry Truman *(first row, second from left)* returned home from France, where he had taken charge of "his boys" in the rowdy Irish American Battery D, shown here at Camp Mills, New York. On inauguration day, January 20, 1949, the veterans of Truman's Battery D marched down Pennsylvania Avenue beside the car carrying Commander-in-Chief Harry Truman. *Courtesy of the Harry S. Truman Library.*

Segregated public health service facilities. For federal workers, shown above at Public Health Dispensary no. 32 (circa 1920) in Washington, D.C., segregated restrooms, cafeterias, and even "whites only" waiting rooms became the norm after Woodrow Wilson became president in 1913. *Courtesy of the Library of Congress.*

HST's Sedalia speech. Long before the White House became a political option for the former Missouri farm boy, Senator Truman bluntly told his fellow Missourians in a 1940 senate campaign speech in Sedalia, Missouri *(shown above)*, that he was committed to equality of opportunity for all Americans, including African Americans. *Courtesy of the Harry S. Truman Library.*

HST's swearing in. At 7:09 P.M., April 12, 1945, a stunned Vice President Harry Truman assumed the office of president, surrounded by President Roosevelt's cabinet appointees, as well as Truman's dear friends House Speaker Sam Rayburn (D-Tex., *fifth from right*) and Kentucky native Fred Vinson *(fourth from right)*. Ironically, Truman was sworn in under the portrait of President Woodrow Wilson, whose segregationist policy for federal employees would be eliminated by Truman. *Courtesy of the National Park Service and the Harry S. Truman Library.*

Segregated privies at the Manhattan Project. When Truman became president, the humiliating policy of segregation reached every aspect of a black federal employee's life—including even the use of outhouses at the federal government's top-secret Manhattan Project in Oakland, Tennessee. As president, Harry Truman dropped not only the first atomic bomb, to expedite the end of World War II; he also dropped a civil rights bomb in 1948 when, by executive order, he eliminated all forms of racial discrimination in the federal workplace. *Courtesy of the National Archives, Still Pictures.*

HST and Walter White. Walter White, the tenacious executive secretary of the NAACP *(on Truman's left)*, used the NAACP's September 19, 1946, visit to the Oval Office to "educate" Truman about racial abuse and Ku Klux Klan–inspired lynching parties directed at African American veterans returning home after service in World War II. *Reprinted by permission of Corbis Images.*

HST's Civil Rights Committee. Sadie Tanner Alexander *(on Truman's right)* was an articulate African American civil rights pioneer who was one of the fifteen members of the first Presidential Civil Rights Committee established by Truman on December 5, 1946—just weeks after his humiliation in the fall elections. *Reprinted by permission of Corbis Images.*

State of the union address, 1947. As unhappy Republicans looked on, a pugnacious Truman delivered an uncompromising speech to the GOP-controlled Eightieth Congress in which he told GOP leaders and Southern Democrats that civil rights equality for all Americans was a top priority of his administration. *Reprinted by permission of Corbis Images.*

HST and Fred Vinson on train. President Truman and his appointee, U.S. Supreme Court Chief Justice Fred Vinson (shown departing Washington, D.C., for the 1946 Army-Navy football game) were trusted friends who shared a love of cards, as well as a deep concern about racial inequality in America. As chief justice from 1946 to 1953, Vinson would author several landmark civil rights opinions that laid the legal foundation for the Warren Court's 1954 decision in *Brown v. Board of Education. Reprinted by permission of Corbis Images.*

Purple Heart awardees. A grateful President Truman and First Lady Bess Truman were never too busy to greet returning World War II veterans—here shown at a May 25, 1946, ceremony on the White House lawn that honored twelve hundred Purple Heart veterans. *Reprinted by permission of Corbis Images.*

NAACP speech, June 29, 1947. With Eleanor Roosevelt in attendance, President Truman delivered his provocative civil rights address to the thirty-eighth annual NAACP convention on the steps of the Lincoln Memorial. Truman was the first U.S. president formally to address the NAACP. *Courtesy of the National Park Service and the Harry S. Truman Library.*

Protest at Washington's National Theater. The National Theater, then Washington's premier theater, was the scene of a peaceful demonstration in 1948 by black citizens who could not attend theatrical performances throughout the nation's capital. *Courtesy of the Moorland-Spingarn Research Center–Howard University Archives.*

CHAPTER FIVE

Truman's State of the Union Address: January 7, 1948

Our first goal is to secure fully the essential human rights of our citizens.
—HST, January 7, 1948

On Tuesday, January 6, 1948, just seventy days after Harry Truman formally accepted the report of his Civil Rights Committee, the president prepared to deliver his third state of the union address to members of a Congress already focused on their own reelection and on the election of a president later that year. As a former member of the U.S. Senate, the president knew exactly what he was up against with the GOP-led Eightieth Congress, where Southern Democrat leaders were still a formidable force even though they were temporarily relegated to minority-party status.[1] Truman also knew how deeply his Southern Democratic colleagues treasured their states' rights philosophy, which had provided the legal foundation for the racist, segregated traditions that dominated life throughout the South—and the South would be critical to his election hopes ten months later.

As he prepared his address to the Congress, the ever blunt Harry Truman made the following entry in his diary on January 6, 1948:

Congress meets—Too bad too.
They'll do nothing but wrangle, pull phony investigations and generally upset the affairs of the Nation.
I'm to address them soon. They won't like the address either.[2]

Truman knew that this Congress would definitely not like his state of the union address, primarily because the president would tell them that a federal civil rights program was his top priority.

For young White House aide and trusted Truman speech writer George Elsey, the 1948 state of the union address was particularly important.

> It was clearly apparent to all of us in the White House staff, certainly to the President himself, that the 1948 State of the Union message would be the opening gun—might well be the opening gun in the '48 presidential campaign. . . . The '48 message very consciously was an effort to epitomize, to wrap up, to summarize, the Truman program, and by now we felt there was a Truman platform, a Truman program, a coherent, consistent, cohesive body of ideas that President Truman was advocating, was fighting for and stood for. . . . By the time the '48 State of the Union message was ready for delivery, it was thoroughly Trumanesque.[3]

Beginning his state of the union address promptly at 1:30 P.M. on Wednesday, January 7, 1948, a determined President Truman addressed the Republican-controlled Congress with neither a hint of compromise nor a shift to the center as seen so frequently in contemporary presidential politics. Initially invoking a spiritual tone in his remarks, Truman reminded both his states' rights Democratic colleagues from the South and the conservative GOP chieftains, "The basic source of our strength is spiritual, for we are a people with a faith. We believe in the dignity of man. We believe that he was created in the image of the Father of us all."[4]

The president also spoke about the moral basis for each person's dignity in the United States. Reflecting the moral posture of Baptist ministers from his Missouri past, a stern but confident Truman reminded the members of the Congress that, in his view, the federal government had a responsibility to serve all people: "We do not believe that men exist merely to strengthen the state or to be cogs in the economic machine. We do believe that governments are created to serve the people and that economic systems exist to minister to their wants."[5] Once again, as he had stated in previous speeches, Truman envisioned the federal government in an important, supportive, yet subordinate role to each citizen. Citizens' basic dignity must be maintained and protected by the federal government.

Like his speech to the NAACP six months earlier, the president's 1948 state of the union address stressed the urgent need for a vigorous federal government in the civil rights arena; while not excluding state and local governments, Truman articulated an important and implicitly dominant role for the federal government in the realm of civil rights—a role that needed prompt and comprehensive attention from Congress.[6]

The consummate optimist, Truman addressed Congress with a positive attitude about the civil rights challenges facing the nation less than three years after
the end of World War II.

On all sides there is heartening evidence of great energy—of capacity for
economic development—and even more important, capacity for spiritual
growth. But accompanying this great activity there are equally great questions, great anxieties, and great aspirations. They represent the concern of
an enlightened people that conditions should be so arranged as to make
life more worthwhile.

We must devote ourselves to finding answers to these anxieties and
aspirations. We seek answers which will embody the moral and spiritual
elements of tolerance, unselfishness, and brotherhood upon which true
freedom and opportunity must rest.[7]

While not actually preaching to the members of Congress, Truman nonetheless unabashedly spoke of the country's morality in the context of the civil rights
of all Americans. Moreover, despite the fact that his state of the union message
was delivered to a hostile Eightieth Congress dominated by states' righters from
both parties, Truman ignored this political reality and directly confronted these
congressional leaders, telling them firmly that the country must do more—much
more—in the area of tolerance and brotherhood.

To Southern members of Congress who were stubbornly fighting to preserve
segregation in much of the United States in 1948, Truman's use of such words
as *tolerance* and *brotherhood,* uttered in reference to relations between black and
white Americans was anathema. By choosing these provocative words for his state
of the union address, the president conjured up the vision of a color-blind United
States, a vision that Truman knew all too well was far from a reality on January
7, 1948.

Urged on by the troubling findings of his Civil Rights Committee, Truman
told Congress that they must work together to enact the remedial public policy
initiatives that would lead to a United States in which brotherhood amongst the
races could be a reality. In Truman's view, this was the collective moral imperative
for both the executive and the legislative branches of the government in a postwar
America in which the economy must be harnessed by the federal government to
provide meaningful opportunities for all Americans.

Truman also used his 1948 state of the union address to articulate his vision
for a ten-year plan that would focus on five top priorities. Using his highly publi-

cized speech to put human rights, which is to say civil rights, at the top of his congressional to-do list, Truman said,

> Our first goal is to secure fully the essential human rights of our citizens.
> The United States has always had a deep concern for human rights. Religious freedom, free speech, and freedom of thought are cherished realities in our land. Any denial of human rights is a denial of the basic beliefs of democracy and of our regard for the worth of each individual.
> Today, however, some of our citizens are still denied equal opportunity for education, for jobs and economic advancement, and for the expression of their views at the polls. Most serious of all, some are denied equal protection under laws. Whether discrimination is based on race, or creed, or color, or land of origin, it is utterly contrary to American ideals of democracy.[8]

With these words, Truman confirmed that he had no illusions about the serious civil rights malaise in the United States; he also publicly confirmed that he fully recognized the comprehensive societal ills that his Committee on Civil Rights had recently documented. With that documentation in hand, the president promised the GOP leadership and Southern Democrats, "I shall send a special message to the Congress on this important subject."[9]

Once he established civil rights reform as his top priority, the president went on to enumerate four additional priorities that must be addressed by Congress and the White House:

- Protect and develop America's human resources.
- Conserve and utilize the country's natural resources.
- Lift the standard of living for all Americans by strengthening the country's economic system.
- Achieve world peace based on principles of freedom and justice and the equality of all nations.[10]

After detailing the priority actions that the Eightieth Congress must take to achieve these goals, President Truman returned to his fundamental theme of human rights and equality for all Americans—black and white. He concluded his state of the union address as he had begun it—with another unequivocal public statement confirming that he and his administration would continue to work to ensure equality for every citizen.

We are determined that the productive resources of this Nation shall be used wisely and fully for the benefit of all.

We are determined that the democratic faith of our people and the strength of our resources shall contribute their full share to the attainment of enduring peace in the world.

It is our faith in human dignity that underlies these purposes. It is this faith that keeps us a strong and vital people.

This is a time to remind ourselves of these fundamentals. For today the whole world looks to us for leadership.

This is the hour to rededicate ourselves to the faith in mankind that makes us strong.

This is the hour to rededicate ourselves to the faith in God that gives us confidence as we face the challenge of the years ahead.[11]

Concluding his address on this spiritual note, President Truman publicly put the members of Congress on notice that he would remain fully committed to his civil rights program during the presidential election year that lay ahead. No matter how distasteful Truman's federal civil rights program was to Southern Democrats, and no matter how important those Democrats were to his nomination in July and his election in November, the president remained stubbornly and unalterably committed to civil rights.

As Truman expected, his state of the union address received a "chilly reception" from GOP leaders and Southern Democrats in the Congress. As *New York Times* journalist C. P. Trussell put it in a front-page headline on January 8, 1948, "Congress Is Cool to Truman Pleas." He noted that the "silences indicate displeasure even among Democrats."[12] While Truman's words to Congress would result in "long periods of silence," Truman once again made it clear to the Congress and to the American people that massive federal civil rights reform was the number one priority of his presidency.[13] It was a bold and politically unpopular assertion to make at the beginning of a presidential election year when he needed the robust support of every Southern Democrat in the Congress if he were to be elected president on November 2, 1948.

In Tom Clark's view, it was no surprise that President Harry Truman would ignore public opinion by making such a controversial and well-covered statement about the need for massive civil rights reform in an election year. Clark recalled that Truman "had a faculty that no one else had—any of the Presidents that I know of, and that was of forgetting the decision as far as the effects of it on his political life or on his image, you might say, in the public mind. He didn't particularly care how people felt about it. It was his decision and that was it, period! It was over with. He went on to another problem of which there were always plenty."[14] When he had prepared his 1948 state of the union address, Truman had known that his remarks on civil rights would prove offensive to many members of Congress. But obviously, as Clark noted, Truman, "didn't particularly care how people felt," if what he was proposing was morally right. And notwithstanding the predictable "chilly reception" that his election year state of the union address provoked, Truman was morally certain of his constitutional responsibility to ensure civil rights equality for all Americans. And as his actions throughout his days in the White House would show, it was a moral position from which Truman would not retreat, no matter what the political risks were to his presidential election aspirations.

As the Eightieth Congress would soon find out, when President Truman promised them a full-blown civil rights proposal, he would deliver.

CHAPTER SIX

Truman's Special Message to Congress on Civil Rights: February 2, 1948

We cannot be satisfied until all our people have equal opportunities for jobs,
for homes, for education, for health, and for political expression, and until
all our people have equal protection under the law.
—HST, February 2, 1948

On Monday, February 2, 1948, less than a month after he delivered his state of
the union address, Harry Truman kept his promise and sent the Republican-
controlled Congress a detailed message outlining his revolutionary vision for civil
rights reform in a racist America. In uncompromising words, the president's special civil rights message told this postwar Congress that he was putting his ten-
point civil rights legislative proposals before them to achieve his top priority: "to
secure fully the essential human rights [—the civil rights—] of our citizens."[1]
The president referenced the five "great goals" that he had outlined to Congress
just twenty-six days earlier and reiterated his belief that the comprehensive civil
rights proposal that he placed before them was the most important challenge for
the Eightieth Congress.

In preparing to send this first ever presidential civil rights message to the
Congress of the United States, Harry Truman knew from his own years in the
Senate that his message would be bitterly opposed by some of his closest friends
in Congress. Truman's political acumen is reflected in his diary entry of February
2, 1948: "I send the Congress a Civil Rights message. They no doubt will receive
it as coldly as they did my State of the Union message. But it needs to be said."[2]
That Truman would insist on making his unpopular civil rights program a top priority in 1948 is particularly noteworthy since the president and Congress were
simultaneously facing a panoply of troublesome unrelated issues that were far

more important to most citizens in the postwar United States than the issue of civil rights.

By early 1948, the Cold War had grown more grim as Stalin's determination to expand communism's influence around the globe had become increasingly evident. Western Europe remained largely wasted and while Truman and his secretary of state had proposed the Marshall Plan in June 1947, by early 1948 the multibillion-dollar Marshall Plan had not yet been enacted by the GOP-led Congress.[3] With legislation like the Marshall Plan pending before the Congress, Truman's antagonism of the Southern Democrats and states' rights GOP leaders in the Congress by insisting on the enactment of a comprehensive federal civil rights bill was a high-risk move. Journalist Carl Rowan reported,

> Angry Southern congressmen threatened to sabotage the European Recovery Program (the Marshall Plan) and desert the president in his fight against a six and one-half billion dollar tax cut being pushed by the Republicans. Truman now was faced with the traditional Southern threat: "If you persist in your civil rights efforts, we will wreck the rest of your program. You cannot afford to have us do that." According to Mrs. Roosevelt, similar threats often had forced FDR to back away from strong civil rights proposals, primarily because Roosevelt was convinced that some Southerners actually would sabotage his legislative program and risk the country's losing World War II before they would permit the Negro to emerge from peonage. Roosevelt felt that he could not afford to gamble.
>
> These threats also came at a crucial period for President Truman. Europe was in economic chaos and there was fear that Communism would overrun the continent unless Congress voted the aid necessary to produce economic recovery. Still, Truman refused to back down. He gambled that he could defy Deep South congressmen and still get the laws and funds that he needed to save Europe. Truman won that gamble.[4]

In addition to securing congressional support for the all-important Marshall Plan, Truman, in early 1948, was also wrestling with the increasingly vexing Palestine issue, the outcome of which remained uncertain when Truman sent his special civil rights message to the Congress on February 2.

Truman subsequently took bold action on the Palestine issue when on May 14, 1948, he formally recognized the State of Israel—action bitterly opposed by Truman's secretary of state, General George Marshall. In this challenging public policy environment, Harry Truman's expansive view of essential civil rights for all Americans was politically audacious. With explicit and unequivocal language, the president's Special Message to the Congress on Civil Rights called for unprecedented equality for African Americans: equality under the law, equality of opportunity in the workplace and the armed services, equality in access to "good" housing and medical care, and equality in the voting polls. "We believe that all men are created equal and that they have the right to equal justice under [the] law. We believe that all men have the right to freedom of thought and of expression and the right to worship as they please. We believe that all men are entitled to equal opportunities for jobs, for homes, for good health and for education. We believe that all men should have a voice in their government and that government should protect, not usurp, the rights of the people."[5] In the president's view, these broad rights were "the basic civil rights which are the source and the support for our democracy."

In 1948, Truman's expansive vision of civil rights and equality of opportunity for all Americans as outlined in his special message had never been publicly annunciated by an American president. Significantly, Truman articulated his broad view of constitutionally guaranteed civil rights during a period in this country's history when the violent civil rights protests of the late 1950s and 1960s were largely unthinkable. Those violent civil rights riots ripened into major explosions in the 1960s—a period that one of this country's most tenacious civil rights activists, Congressman John Lewis, described in *Walking with the Wind* as a time "when America itself felt as if it might burst at the seams—so much tension, so many storms."[6]

In contrast to the 1960s, during Harry Truman's presidency the country simply was not energized over civil rights, nor was it "burst[ing] at the seams" with the kind of widespread civil disobedience and race riots that Congressman Lewis detailed in his book. Ironically, while President Truman aggressively attempted to push civil rights reform in an environment largely devoid of racial unrest, Truman's two immediate successors at 1600 Pennsylvania Avenue—Presidents Eisenhower and Kennedy—steadfastly dodged the civil rights issue until major civil rights upheavals forced them to act.

While Dwight Eisenhower was clearly not proactive on the civil rights front during his early presidency, ugly race riots in 1957 prompted him to sign the substantially watered down Civil Rights Act of 1957 on September 9, 1957—a compromise bill that renowned Eisenhower historian Stephen E. Ambrose described as "emasculated" in his biography entitled *Eisenhower: Soldier and President.*[7] This limited civil rights legislation focused primarily on voting rights reform and was ushered through the Senate by Majority Leader Lyndon Johnson after violent civil rights protests erupted in Little Rock. Leading white citizens in Little Rock and other Southern segregationist strongholds refused to adhere to the Supreme Court's 1954 *Brown v. Board of Education* decision rejecting *Plessy*'s separate-but-equal doctrine—a doctrine that had been condemned seven years earlier by Truman's Civil Rights Committee and had been attacked in numerous amicus curiae briefs filed by Truman's Department of Justice before the Supreme Court.[8]

By the late 1950s, the relatively peaceful civil rights movement of Truman's presidency had been replaced by a much more confrontational form of protest, and President Eisenhower, together with the Senate, firmly under the control of Majority Leader Johnson, was forced to react. In evaluating President Eisenhower's impact on the emerging civil rights upheaval in the United States in the late 1950s, Ambrose, who generally holds President Eisenhower in high regard, concluded, "Essentially, Eisenhower passed on to his successors the problem of guaranteeing constitutional rights to Negro citizens."[9] Ambrose's reference to President Eisenhower's lack of commitment to civil rights reform was echoed by Carl Rowan, who wrote in 1959,

> Eisenhower who entered the White House with the reputation of a great leader, is inclined not to get ahead of the public. He urges patience, and in effect asks Negroes to place their ultimate faith in time. . . . Truman declared civil rights to be a basic federal responsibility; Eisenhower is in many respects a "states righter," and he has made this clear even when bold federal action has been forced upon his administration.
>
> Nothing highlights the difference between these two presidents more than their stands on the 1954 Supreme Court decision outlawing school segregation. Mr. Eisenhower has urged that the rulings of the federal court should be obeyed "even if they are unpalatable"—leading many to believe that Ike himself finds the 1954 decision unpalatable. He has refused to state publicly his approval or disapproval of the ruling.
>
> In New York last October Truman told a Democratic party rally that the 1954 decision not only is the law of the land but "it is morally right."[10]

Eisenhower's successor in the White House, John Kennedy, while a visionary in promoting global sharing through the Peace Corps, the Space Program, and the Alliance for Progress, nonetheless avoided the thorny issue of civil rights reform until well into his presidency. According to Martin Luther King Jr. historian Taylor Branch, by late 1962 King was deeply disappointed with Kennedy's performance in the civil rights area, particularly his actions in responding to the deadly violence that gripped the University of Mississippi campus after a young black American named James Meredith enrolled at Ole Miss in the fall of 1962. According to Branch, in *Parting the Waters,* King was troubled by President Kennedy's pragmatic actions in resolving the riots through a series of discussions with racist Mississippi governor Ross Barnett.[11]

When the violent Ole Miss protests went from ugly to deadly in the fall of 1962, President Kennedy was forced to send federal troops to the campus to prevent James Meredith from being lynched by an out-of-control racist mob. However, in sending federal troops—ultimately twenty-three thousand soldiers—Kennedy agreed that Negro soldiers should not be allowed to accompany their regular units posted on the campus.[12] According to Branch, King complained privately that President Kennedy had focused only on strict legal considerations and had handled the Ole Miss riots with little concern for the broader civil rights of blacks. King later wrote that the collective actions of President Kennedy and Governor Barnett during the crisis "made Negroes feel like pawns in a white man's political game."[13] In an ironic twist, Kennedy's decision to post only white federal troops at the campus to protect James Meredith was in direct conflict with Harry Truman's goal of integrated armed services, which Truman had ordered fourteen years earlier with Executive Order 9981.

President Kennedy's lack of passion on the civil rights front was further evidenced by the limited action he finally took on November 20, 1962. Realizing that civil rights remained a hot-button issue with Southern voters who could impact the Democratic plurality in Congress, President Kennedy waited until the midterm congressional elections were over before he signed Executive Order 11063—an executive order that was hardly comprehensive in terms of federal civil rights reform as it focused primarily on eliminating racial discrimination in federal housing projects, as well as in housing financed with federal loans.[14]

Earlier in his administration, on March 6, 1961, President Kennedy had issued Executive Order 10925, establishing the President's Committee on Equal Employment Opportunity. Executive Order 10925 combined the President's Committee on Government Contracts and the President's Committee on Government Employment Policy—committees that had their origins in actions taken by President Harry Truman more than a decade earlier. While Kennedy's issuance of Executive Order 10925 was initially heralded by some journalists in the black press as a significant development, it clearly was not the comprehensive federal assault on segregation that black voters, based on President Kennedy's rhetoric in the 1960 presidential campaign, expected.

In contrast to the heated civil rights environment that confronted President

Kennedy in the early 1960s, the political climate when Truman delivered his special civil rights message to Congress in 1948 was largely undisturbed by the kind of violent civil rights upheavals that took place at Ole Miss and in Selma, Alabama. There was a general absence of race riots in the late 1940s and early 1950s, while the violent civil rights upheavals of the 1960s created a nationwide crisis that forced Presidents Kennedy and Johnson to address the widespread civil disobedience that was ravaging urban areas in the North and South.

On February 2, 1948, when President Truman decided to put the Eightieth Congress on public notice that he wanted them to enact sweeping civil rights reform legislation, Truman knew he would get little help from his own party. In today's climate, a president can rely on the well-organized support of the powerful Congressional Black Caucus when working for civil rights reform, but Truman had no coalition of black congressional leaders to lobby for his comprehensive civil rights program. There was no Congressional Black Caucus in 1948, and blacks in the South were still largely disenfranchised.

That black Americans in the South were politically disadvantaged and unable to assert meaningful political pressure was highlighted by the *New York Times* on February 15, 1948. *Times* reporter John N. Popham wrote in an article entitled "Negro in South Still Lags in Political Power" that "white supremacy is unshaken." Just two weeks after Truman sent his ten-point special civil rights message to Congress, Popham reported on the political smugness of white politicians who were confident that Truman's expansive view of civil rights reform would garner little support in a Congress dominated by states' rights Republicans and segregationist Southern Democrats.

> Despite the furor in Southern Democratic ranks in recent months over Federal Administration and court moves to strengthen Negro civil rights, there is nothing to indicate that the Negro has yet become a solid political power in Dixie.
>
> Southerners of every belief and disposition were quick . . . to tear aside the usual veil of protestations that Negroes in the South were not qualified to govern. They admitted freely that President Truman's civil rights program stung because it touched the issues of segregation and social equality.
>
> In the Deep South there are no signs as yet of any political threat from Negroes. Most Southerners are convinced that white supremacy at the polls will remain intact for a long time, and in no community is there any evidence of Negroes' winning elective office. . . .

President Truman's ten-point civil rights program struck at the South's traditional Jim Crow policies in transportation. . . .

Southerners largely are infuriated by these developments. Many liberal Southerners will not go along with proposals dealing with anti-lynching, anti–poll tax, FEPC and abolition of segregation in interstate public conveyances.[15]

Harry Truman, a sage politician, appreciated the often overwhelming impact of the segregationist hurdles confronting black voters throughout the South; he knew that black voters in the South in 1948 were largely unable to vote, let alone exert organized political pressure. But Truman did not need political pressure to act; all he needed to move forward were the documented cases of civil rights abuses that his Committee on Civil Rights had provided him in their report of October 29, 1947.

Citing his Civil Rights Committee's report in his Special Message to Congress on Civil Rights, the president referred to "flagrant violations" of the civil rights of African Americans. And describing the committee's work as "a frank and revealing report," Truman told the members of Congress what most legislators already knew but largely ignored—"There is a serious gap between our ideals and some of our practices. This gap must be closed."[16]

In conveying the same sense of urgency and impatience for prompt civil rights reform that he had expressed in his earlier speech before the NAACP, Truman's special civil rights message of February 2, 1948, reiterated the proactive role that the federal government must play to realize his primary domestic goal of civil rights equality: "The Federal Government has a clear duty to see that Constitutional guarantees of individual liberties and of equal protection under the laws are not denied or abridged anywhere in our Union. That duty is shared by all three branches of the Government, but it can be fulfilled only if the Congress enacts modern, comprehensive civil rights laws, adequate to the needs of the day, and demonstrating our continuing faith in the free way of life."[17] With these words, the president once again publicly embraced the controversial concept of a federal solution to eliminating the continued inequality between the races. By stressing the need for a federal solution based on his sweeping legislative proposals, Truman publicly placed the burden of closing the civil rights gap on the Congress—a Congress whose Republican voting majority could easily be augmented by the votes of Southern Democrats.

New York Times political correspondent Arthur Krock succinctly articulated the disastrous political scenario that was likely if Harry Truman insisted on pushing his ten-point civil rights program. In an analysis that appeared on Sunday, February 15, 1948, just two weeks after Truman sent his special civil rights message to Congress, Krock opined,

> If a determined band of Southern Democrats—many of them more able than their Northern colleagues and most of them former chairmen of the chief committees in the Senate and the House—decides to become a wrecking crew, the party will present a show of bitter disorder which undoubtedly will damage its voter-appeal in the forthcoming campaign. Should this condition persuade the Northern Democratic majority to force by cloture Presidential legislation that is most resented by the South, then there are some states in this region which conceivably will deny their electoral votes to the traditional party.[18]

As Truman had predicted in his February 2, 1948, diary entry, his special civil rights message prompted a violent reaction amongst Southern Democrats in the Congress. *New York Times* reporter C. P. Trussell reported that Southern Democrats were preparing to move against Truman's ten-point civil rights proposals. Trussell claimed in a front-page story on February 20 that Southern Democrats in "the House were planning a new 'Revolt.' . . . They will gather in closed session . . . to organize for cooperation with the Southern Governors' Conference in resisting President Truman's civil rights program."[19]

The *Canton (Ohio) Repository* of February 3, 1948, carried a headline reading "President's Civil Rights Program Angers South." Associated Press reporter Jack Bell focused on a series of electoral options being considered by leading Southern Democrats that were designed to defeat Truman in November 1948.

> Southern Democrats talked bluntly . . . of calling a Dixie convention to split away from President Truman on the civil rights issue.
>
> One Deep South senator told a reporter present plans are to ask the Conference of Southern Governors to call an all-southern convention.
>
> Such a political gathering could pick its own candidate for president. But the main objective would be to work out some way to withhold at least part of the South's electoral votes from Mr. Truman. . . . The southerners are boiling mad over four of those points. They call for (1) a federal anti-lynching law, (2) a permanent fair employment practice commission, (3) an end to Jim Crow rules in transportation and (4) outlawing state poll taxes.

Senator [James] Eastland (D) of Mississippi called these proposals "outrageous."

"The South will have to protect herself in the electoral college," he told a reporter. He refused to be more specific.

But at Jackson, Walter Sillers, Speaker of the Mississippi House, flatly urged a convention call to name a southern presidential candidate.

Mr. Sillers said he favors this course "even if it means throwing the election of president into the House of Representatives."

"Then we can let events take their course," the state lawmaker declared.

Still another course being discussed by some southerners here is to have the state legislatures in Dixie appoint presidential electors who would be instructed not to vote for Mr. Truman.

Those back of this plan think that if they can get 60 electoral votes switched, they might throw a close presidential race into the House. Then they would propose a southern Democrat as a compromise between Mr. Truman and his Republican opponent.[20]

While Truman apparently took little public notice of the threatened Southern revolt, it was, nonetheless, a troublesome political development. That Southern Democrats had decided in February of the 1948 election year to use the Southern Governors' Conference to oppose Truman's presidential candidacy represented a serious threat to his election prospects—particularly since Southern Democratic voters were considered essential in 1948 to any Democrat's chances of winning the White House.

A revolt at the Southern Governors' Conference in 1948 was a particularly unwelcome development since the conference was a potent force led by the popular and racist Governor Strom Thurmond of South Carolina. From February 2 to July 14, 1948, Thurmond's opposition to Truman's civil rights program became so heated that Thurmond was ultimately nominated as the Dixiecrat presidential candidate—an event that was predestined after Truman sent his ten-point Special Message to Congress on Civil Rights to the Congress.[21]

In his autobiography, *Counsel to the President,* Truman White House aide Clark Clifford offered a stark view of the racist Southern Democratic movement to derail the president's ten-part legislative civil rights program. Describing then-Governor Strom Thurmond as the leader of "a political movement based openly and almost entirely upon racism," Clifford described the vehement and nearly instantaneous Southern backlash to Truman's special civil rights message to

Congress: "Immediately, letters began to pour in from all over the South charging that President Truman was breaking up the Democratic party. Most of the letters were bitter, and many of them contained ugly or obscene racial slurs directed at the President, his family, and some of his staff, including me. Arkansas governor Ben Laney branded the civil rights message 'distasteful, unthinkable, and ridiculous.' Mississippi House Speaker Walter Sillers went even further, attacking the civil rights proposal as 'damnable, communistic, unconstitutional, anti-American, anti-Southern legislation.'"[22]

One of the reasons Truman's special civil rights message became such a lightning rod for Southern opposition was the scope and detail of the ten specific recommendations contained in the February 2 message. Not only were the ten points explicitly articulated but the president also urged immediate, not staggered, enactment of the entire ten-point civil rights program. As detailed in the *New York Times*, elements of the program included

1. Establishing a permanent Commission on Civil Rights, a Joint Congressional Committee on Civil Rights and a Civil Rights Division in the Department of Justice.
2. Strengthening existing civil rights statutes.
3. Providing federal protection against lynching.
4. Protecting more adequately the right to vote.
5. Establishing a Fair Employment Practice Commission to prevent unfair discrimination in employment.
6. Prohibiting discrimination in interstate transportation facilities.
7. Providing home rule and suffrage in Presidential elections for the residents of the District of Columbia.
8. Providing statehood for Hawaii and Alaska and a greater measure of self-government for our island possessions.
9. Equalizing the opportunities for residents of the United States to become naturalized citizens.
10. Settling the evacuation claims of Japanese citizens.[23]

For White House aide George Elsey, who helped draft this message for the Congress, Truman's decision to send such a comprehensive plan to the Congress was a clear reflection of Harry Truman's determination to do what was constitutionally right for black Americans. In his 1976 oral history, Elsey commented on Truman's politically reckless but morally correct action as the president finalized the wording of his special civil rights message for Congress and for a country that, for the most part, would not like what Truman had to say: "Truman's determination as President to fight hard for civil rights, and to press, and even going so far as to risk his own nomination in 1948, by the civil rights message of February 2, 1948, which was the most comprehensive all embracing message on civil rights that any President had sent up to that time. He knew very well that this was a great risk, political risk, as indeed it was. It led to a fourth party. But as President, he saw what he thought was his duty, and he went right ahead with it."[24]

While the president's recommendations were primarily designed to improve the civil rights of black Americans, Truman's dominant theme in his civil rights message to Congress was the concept of a more aggressive federal role to enforce the civil rights of all Americans. "As a first stop, we must strengthen the organization of the Federal Government in order to enforce civil rights legislation more adequately and to watch over the state of our traditional liberties."[25] To conservatives and states' rights advocates, who dominated the Congress, Truman's continued advocacy for a greatly expanded federal civil rights role constituted "fighting words"—words that Truman would repeat at the Democratic convention in July 1948 and again in his presidential campaign speech in Harlem during the bleak days immediately before the November election, when Truman's defeat was widely predicted by the nation's press corps.

In addition to outlining his ten civil rights recommendations, Truman's special message also included compelling language focusing on the insidious threat of lynching—a practice that still haunted African Americans who lived in or visited the South. "A specific Federal measure is needed to deal with the crime of lynching—against which I cannot speak too strongly. It is a principle of our democracy, written into our Constitution, that every person accused of an offense against the law shall have a fair, orderly trial in an impartial court. We have made great progress toward this end, but I regret to say that lynching has not yet finally disappeared from our land. So long as one person walks in fear of lynching, we shall not have achieved equal justice under [the] law. I call upon the Congress to take decisive action against this crime."[26] Protecting every citizen's right to vote was also a priority for Truman; he noted that "some whole groups are prevented from voting by outmoded policies prevailing in certain states or communities."[27] As Truman the politician knew, these policies, which led to serious voter interference, were largely concentrated in Southern states and could only be eliminated by congressional legislation.

In asking Congress to act on his comprehensive ten-point civil rights package, Truman fully appreciated how unlikely favorable congressional action was in view of the makeup of the Congress. Nonetheless, in the words of his eventual Supreme

Court appointee, Justice Tom C. Clark, President Truman "was determined to make some progress in this area. Of course, the Congress didn't cooperate too much during the 80th Congress in particular."[28] Like John Kennedy and Lyndon Johnson who followed Harry Truman to the White House more than a decade later, Truman was an experienced veteran of the Senate; he fully understood the powerful leadership role traditionally played by Southern Democrats, such as Senators Richard Russell, Harry Byrd, James Eastland, and John Sparkman.[29] Even when briefly relegated to the minority party in the Congress, Southern Democrats in the Senate remained formidable, and their filibuster threat was poisonous.

Truman's ten-point legislative proposal also drew strong public opposition from Southern Democrats in the House of Representatives, including Congressman Lyndon B. Johnson. Johnson, increasingly frustrated by his decade-long service in the House, was determined to win election to the Senate on election day, November 2, 1948. The last thing the then-conservative Congressman Johnson wanted was his Democratic Party standard-bearer and president publicly advocating a radical civil rights bill that would be repulsive to Texas voters. Not surprisingly, Johnson's frantic campaigning—after which he won the Democratic primary by a mere eighty-seven votes—included Johnson's frequent denunciations of Truman's ten-point civil rights legislative proposal. Ironically, Truman's ten-point civil rights plan was similar to the comprehensive civil rights legislation that President Lyndon Johnson would force Congress to enact in 1964 and 1965.

While President Johnson proved to be the effective and tenacious sponsor of the Civil Rights Act of 1964 and the Voting Rights Act of 1965, Johnson's congressional record confirms that he was a born-again civil rights advocate. In 1948, when Congressman Johnson waged a forceful primary campaign to be the Democratic Party's nominee for a senate seat from Texas, candidate Johnson frequently expressed his public and unequivocal opposition to President Truman's comprehensive ten-point civil rights program, which was formally submitted to the Eightieth Congress by Harry Truman on February 2, 1948.[30]

In a kick-off rally on the evening of May 22, 1948, in Austin's Wooldridge Park, Congressman Johnson declared his views on civil rights—views that were in direct conflict with those expressed by the Democratic president from Missouri, who was seeking his own first election to the White House. In a rousing campaign speech, Johnson declared that Truman's "Civil Rights Program is a farce and a sham—an effort to set up a police state in the guise of liberty. I am opposed to that program. I have voted AGAINST the so-called poll tax repeal bill; the poll tax should be repealed by those states which enacted them. I have voted AGAINST the so-called anti-lynching bill; the state can, and DOES, enforce the law against murder. I have voted AGAINST the FEPC; if a man can tell you whom you must hire, he can tell you whom you can't hire."[31]

During the stormy 1960s when President Johnson was in the White House, his earlier public opposition to President Truman's civil rights program was apparently viewed as so politically explosive that the text of Johnson's May 22, 1948, campaign speech in Austin was closely held by White House staffers, who were instructed by an official notice attached to the speech that read, "DO NOT RELEASE THIS SPEECH—NOT EVEN TO STAFF, WITHOUT EXPRESS PERMISSION OF BILL MOYERS. As background, both Walter Jenkins and George Reedy have instructed this is not EVER TO BE RELEASED."[32]

For Justice Tom Clark, Johnson's lifelong friend from Texas, the legislation that Johnson finally supported in the 1960s had its origins in Truman's radical legislative proposals of 1948. "Mr. Truman took the position that we had to have immediate action on it, and he proposed legislation to the Congress, some of which became law. Eventually, the housing legislation which Mr. Johnson was able to get through in the middle sixties was really a refinement of Mr. Truman's proposals. He also made proposals with reference to voting[,] public accommodations and things of that kind. So, I rather think that [LBJ's 1964–1965 civil rights legislation] had its inception back there."[33]

From the perspective of the 1948 presidential campaign, besides alienating Southern Democratic leaders crucial to his election, President Truman's special civil rights message and its sweeping proposals were clearly out of step with the American public. In fact, a nationwide Gallup poll of fifteen hundred Americans conducted in early March 1948—a month after Truman's special message on civil rights was submitted to the Congress—showed that 82 percent of those surveyed opposed congressional enactment of Truman's civil rights program. Of the 18 percent remaining, only 9 percent supported it.[34]

In the opinion of Walter White, Truman's decisive action on February 2, 1948, in submitting the program to Congress was a courageous—but politically unwise—move. White, one of the country's most experienced civil rights activists in 1948, notes, "If the President wanted to play politics he would have followed the course of his predecessors of evading or postponing action on this most explosive of American issues."[35]

George Elsey said that President Truman "meant absolutely everything he said in his well-known civil rights message of February 2nd, 1948."[36] As the trusted assistant to Clark Clifford during Truman's first term in the White House, Elsey drafted many of the president's speeches and messages, including the landmark Special Message to Congress on Civil Rights. In his comprehensive nine-part oral history of the Truman presidency, Elsey confirmed how involved the president was in the special civil rights message, as well as other presidential pronouncements. "Every statement issued in President Truman's name, I'm confident, was personally approved by President Truman."[37] In the case of the special message of February 2, 1948, there are numerous versions of the message in the Harry S. Truman Library files reflecting the president's intimate involvement in drafting the explosive message.

In reflecting on Truman's commitment to civil rights reform, Elsey provided important insight based on his unfettered, frequent contact with the president during Truman's days in the White House.

> On the matter of civil rights, I think that [the] President's perspective and outlook evolved over a period of time. His outlook on civil rights, just as on many other questions, was not fixed and constant and as he grew in responsibilities through his political career in the State of Missouri, and in the decade in the Senate, then the White House years, the country was changing, times were changing, attitudes amongst the American people were changing, he himself was becoming broader in his understanding and concern, responsibilities, and outlook, and so his civil rights stance was . . . constantly evolving . . .; too, I think he probably had a much broader outlook on these matters after he became President than he had before. I certainly think he meant absolutely everything he said in his well-known civil rights message of February 2nd, 1948. I don't think there was anything phoney about that at all. It wasn't a sham, it wasn't a pretense, it wasn't a lot of hot air *just* for political purposes. I believe that he believed what he was advocating there.[38]

Thus on February 2, 1948, without any nationwide political pressure to act and with the certain knowledge of the serious political risks to his presidential election goals, Harry Truman submitted his comprehensive civil rights message to the Congress. He did so less than four months after the Presidential Committee on Civil Rights completed their exhaustive report, which documented the myriad civil rights abuses in the United States. Based on the report's documentation, members of Congress could, and surely would, disagree with Truman's special message, but they could no longer credibly challenge the underlying factual basis for Truman's message: that widespread racism existed throughout the United States and that racism was the basis for the pervasive abridgement of the constitutional rights of black Americans.

While Truman's special civil rights message expressed the hope that state and local governments would put their own legal houses in order from a civil rights standpoint, Truman was a realist, and his formal message to Congress reflected his deep-rooted belief that the overall remedy for the civil rights abuses detailed by his Civil Rights Committee could only be achieved through a massive federal effort. "The legislation I have recommended for enactment by the Congress at the present session is a minimum program if the Federal Government is to fulfill its obligation of insuring the Constitutional guarantees of individual liberties and of equal protection under the law."[39]

Truman's "minimum program," as articulated in this special message, was comprehensive, touching nearly every aspect of human activity in the United States: voting, housing, employment, protection from lynching, and interstate travel. Consistent with his earlier speech before the NAACP, Truman's special civil rights message once again characterized the civil rights crisis in the United States in 1948 as a moral, rather than a political, matter. In Truman's view, the federal government had a moral obligation to enact the sweeping civil rights legislation he proposed. "We must protect our civil rights so that by providing all our people with the maximum enjoyment of personal freedom and personal opportunity we shall be a stronger nation—stronger in our leadership, stronger in our moral position, stronger in the deeper satisfactions of a united citizenry."[40]

Having told the members of Congress that they had a clear moral obligation to enact his "minimum," yet sweeping civil rights program, President Truman concluded his special civil rights message on a typically frank, optimistic note. Free of frills and flourishes, Truman's closing remarks conveyed a hopeful tone about the serious national challenge that civil rights reform represented in terms of the country's integrity. In Truman's view, it was particularly vital for the United States to have integrity within its own democracy if the president's Marshall Plan and Truman Doctrine were credibly to nurture new democracies throughout a ravaged Europe and a devastated Asia. "If we wish to inspire the peoples of the world whose freedom is in jeopardy, if we wish to restore hope to those who have already lost their civil liberties, if we wish to fulfill the promise that is ours, we must correct the remaining imperfections in our practice of democracy. We know the way. We need only the will."[41]

While Truman no doubt believed that "we need only the will" to make civil rights equality a reality for African Americans, Harry Truman was also a political realist; he shared Tom Clark's gloomy view that, for the upcoming presidential election, the South was lost following his submission of the special ten-point civil rights plan to the Congress. In 1972, Clark confirmed how outraged Southern

Democratic leaders were after release of the February 2, 1948, special civil rights message. Clark, recalling his own appearance before Arkansas Democrats on February 19, 1948, just seventeen days after Truman delivered his explosive civil rights message, spoke about the hostile mood at the Arkansas Democrats' dinner, where Clark was to introduce the president by a live television broadcast. According to Clark, the mood "was terrible. . . . you could feel sort of a coolness, you know, the air was so thick you could almost cut it. . . . The [Arkansas] Governor is going to try to keep us from presenting Mr. Truman through this closed TV circuit, and also, when it comes on—if he is not successful—why, he's got it planned that people will start getting up and leaving the hall."[42]

While Clark was able to abort the planned walkout by Arkansas Democrats determined to publicly embarrass Truman for his radical civil rights program, this incident nonetheless was typical of the widespread political backlash that Truman was subjected to throughout traditional Democratic Party strongholds in the South. As a politician, Truman knew even before his ten-point civil rights message was delivered that it would cost him the South just ten months later. When Clark was asked whether he had discussed his own views with Truman about the president's probable loss of the South because of the ten-point program, Clark replied, "Well, I was satisfied we'd lose the South"; after returning from the Arkansas Democratic Party event, Clark talked to Truman, who "said he thought so, too."[43]

Even though Truman knew that his ten-point federal civil rights program would further anger Southern Democrats, he did what he knew was morally right and necessary on February 2, 1948. Anything less than his explicit declaration for civil rights reform to the Congress would not only further compromise the constitutional foundation of American democracy but would also rob the United States of its ability to serve as a credible global standard-bearer for democracy in a devastated postwar world—a world in which the Cold War had begun as Stalin mounted his aggressive challenge to democracy.[44] For Truman, the time for massive federally led civil rights reform in the United States had come. Without it, the moral integrity of the United States would be compromised both at home and abroad.

After February 2, 1948—and the widespread negative reaction to his special civil rights message to Congress—President Truman had clarity on one fundamental point: to gain the support of a nation in which 82 percent of the voters opposed the sweeping civil rights reform program, Truman had a great deal of work to do in the remaining ten months before the 1948 presidential election.[45]

CHAPTER SEVEN

The 1948 Democratic Party Convention and the Civil Rights Plank: July 14–15, 1948

Everybody knows that I recommended to the [Eightieth] Congress the civil rights program. I did that because I believed it to be my duty under the Constitution.
—HST, July 15, 1948

As President Harry Truman prepared for the National Democratic Party Convention in July 1948, he looked forward to its rough-and-tumble environment, an environment in which he hoped and expected to be nominated for the first time as the party's national standard-bearer.

Just four years earlier, Senator Harry Truman had been extremely reluctant to give up his enhanced leadership position in the Senate for his party's vice presidential nomination. During his ten years in the Senate, Truman had earned the high regard of his congressional colleagues, as well as a growing national reputation, for cracking down on waste and corruption in the nation's industrial wartime effort. Truman's reluctance in the summer of 1944 to be drafted by FDR and a group of party bosses to replace Vice President Henry Wallace on the Democratic ticket was described by Justice Tom Clark in a 1972 oral history. Clark, who was Truman's close friend and appointee, as well as a devoted friend of the Speaker of the House, Sam Rayburn, a fellow Texan, recalled the events of the 1944 convention when Senator Harry Truman was thrust into the presidency. "Here [Truman] was a man that had been in the Senate—he had not had any on the job training, other than as a County Judge which didn't amount to too much; of course, he was the head of a fiscal agency of Jackson County, but that was just one small county, and as you say, it was really a rural community. Here he was catapulted into the Presidency; and didn't want it, didn't want it.

He was for Sam Rayburn for President. He wasn't for Harry Truman. As a matter of fact, he asked me—I was out in Chicago in 1944—he asked me to call Sam up and get him up to Chicago."[1]

By 1948, after serving for almost four chaotic years as president, Truman's genuine reluctance in 1944 about assuming a national leadership position was long gone—and Truman was determined to be elected president of the United States at his party's convention in the City of Brotherly Love. But because of Truman's bold actions in support of civil rights reform during the prior three years, candidate Truman would find that brotherly love was in short supply amongst Southern delegates to the 1948 convention.[2]

For delegates attending the Democratic convention in 1948, the single most serious obstacle to the president's goals for a unified party draft was his stubborn insistence on full equality of opportunity and protection under the law for African Americans. And while friends and political advisers urged that he temper his civil rights program—at least until after the 1948 elections, Truman was unmoved.[3]

For Truman historian and sometime confidant of the thirty-third president Jonathan Daniels, it was a given that Truman would not equivocate on civil rights, even if it put his election chances at serious risk in 1948. In his 1950 book about Truman, *The Man of Independence,* Daniels focused on Truman's consistent commitment to civil rights reform well before his presidency had suddenly begun on April 12, 1945.[4] Based on Daniels's close observations of Truman and discussions with him while Truman served in the Congress and in the White House, Daniels was convinced that Truman's commitment to full civil rights for black Americans was rooted, in large part, in Truman's basic sense of fairness, which sprang from his early life in the rigorous rural world of the border state of Missouri. To support this view of a consistently fair and racially enlightened Truman, Daniels quoted Senator Harry Truman's remarks in 1940 as Truman launched his uphill senate reelection campaign.

At that Sedalia[, Missouri,] rally, with his mother, sitting on the platform before the courthouse, approving what he said, he gave his views on the racial question.

"I believe in the brotherhood of man," he said, "not merely the brotherhood of white men but the brotherhood of all men before [the] law.

"I believe in the Constitution and the Declaration of Independence. In giving the Negroes the rights which are theirs we are only acting in accord with our own ideals of a true democracy."[5]

These words, spoken publicly in 1940 before his "unreconstructed rebel" mother, were articulated again and again by President Truman, long before the 1948 Democratic convention opened in July in Philadelphia. And when Truman spoke about civil rights, whether as senator or as president, his words were consistent: black and white Americans were entitled to the same equality of opportunity and basic civil rights. Daniels was not surprised that presidential candidate Truman would once again articulate his unequivocal call for a federal civil rights program as part of his presidential plank at the 1948 National Democratic Party Convention in Philadelphia. In Daniels's view, Truman's inflexible position on civil rights was morally rooted—and because Truman's views were anchored in his basic sense of fairness, nothing had occurred since 1940 to alter Truman's position on civil rights by 1948.[6]

Daniels's characterization of Truman as a consistently enlightened civil rights proponent, even before he became president, was echoed by the NAACP's executive director Walter White in an article he released to black American newspapers through the *Graphic Syndicate* on February 12, 1948. White, a key force in the NAACP's early efforts over much of the three decades preceding Truman's presidency, stated,

> I can add a personal footnote on the history of the President's position on lynching, disfranchisement, discrimination in employment and segregation. Few men in public life have ever had so consistent a record as has been that of President Truman. As a member of the Senate, long before he or anyone else ever dreamed that he would sit in the White House he voted consistently for anti-lynching legislation and other measures which were included in his memorable address to the Congress on February 2nd. He did this in a quiet, diffident way without fanfare or publicity or boasting.
>
> In his quiet Missouri fashion Harry Truman has demonstrated that he is in earnest when he says that "we must correct the remaining imperfections in our practice of Democracy."[7]

From a civil rights perspective, two significant events that contributed to Truman's civil rights advocacy in 1946 converged in his life in the years following his 1940 Sedalia speech. First, Truman, who as a serviceman experienced firsthand the cruelty of a world war, had become president—a position in which, as commander in chief, he was empowered to act unilaterally through executive branch authority, even if Congress disagreed with him. Second, his presidency occurred at that pivotal time, in terms of U.S. race relations, when black American veterans of World War II were returning home to a postwar society in which the KKK of Truman's Missouri youth was staging a rebirth throughout the South.[8]

In view of the documented increase in racism in 1948, Daniels felt that Truman's presidential actions in the civil rights area were predictable. In Daniels's opinion, the issue of civil rights for Truman was primarily a moral one, and because it was a moral issue, political considerations became largely irrelevant to Truman as he publicly committed himself to ridding the country of its debilitating racism.[9] As Daniels expected, President Harry Truman would not equivocate on civil rights during the 1948 campaign even though he fully appreciated the need to unite his party's three traditional voting groups—the western farmers, big city labor, and Southern states' righters.

THE THREE ESSENTIAL ELEMENTS FOR VICTORY

To win in 1948, Truman knew that he needed the farmers from the western states, labeled *western Progressives;* the unions, commonly called *big city labor;* and the Southern conservatives.[10] These three diverse groups had collectively ensured Franklin Roosevelt's election to the White House in 1932, 1936, 1940, and 1944.

The necessity of maintaining traditional Democratic support from these three demographic groups of voters in 1948 was reiterated to President Truman in a November 19, 1947, memo that White House aide Clark Clifford presented to the president. The Clifford Memo, as it was later called, was largely authored by James Rowe, a legendary political strategist, who had gone to Washington as one of President Roosevelt's bright New Dealers. While the memo cogently presented a comprehensive nationwide political strategy for the 1948 campaign, Truman White House aide George Elsey recalled that Truman never indicated his reliance on it as he waged a campaign that logically focused on the party's traditional strong support from western Progressives, big labor, and Southern Democrats.[11]

In Elsey's opinion, Truman did not need a blueprint from Clifford or from anyone else about the nuances of Democratic Party politics; Truman knew his party well—and whether it was farmers from the key western states, big city labor leaders from America's industrial strongholds, or states' rights Southerners, Truman had his own keen sense of their political needs and aspirations. With America's farmers, Truman evinced a special empathy gained from his own years on the family's Grandview farm in Jackson County, Missouri. He knew about the vagaries of farm life, where nature could wreak economic havoc for even the most able farmer. Truman also knew about the GOP's vulnerability with farmers in 1948; and as the campaign unfolded, candidate Truman would direct some of his harshest campaign rhetoric at the failed GOP policy regarding America's farmers. Truman was also reasonably well positioned with big city labor leaders who realized from Truman's earliest presidential pronouncements, including his twenty-one-point address to Congress on September 6, 1945, that Truman was philosophically as liberal in domestic policy as FDR had been. Even though Truman occasionally took on powerful U.S. labor leaders, such as the bellicose John L. Lewis, who wanted wage increases for coal workers after World War II, Truman generally was viewed as a friend of the unionized working class—the second demographic group essential to Truman's victory on November 2, 1948.

While Truman knew of his relatively positive standing with the country's farmers and urban labor leaders, he also realized that he had put himself on a collision course with the third key element of the Democratic coalition, Southern conservatives. In terms of the essential Southern Democratic voters, President Truman placed his campaign in real jeopardy when he went far beyond FDR's cautious approach to civil rights. By November 1947, Truman had publicly embraced a federal civil rights program that put him in direct conflict with the Southern conservatives, whose states' rights philosophy had effectively served as the legal foundation for racial segregation throughout the South. As a result of Truman's civil rights efforts of 1946 and 1947, the stage was set for a bitter conflict with the all-important Southern wing of the Democratic Party when the Democratic convention convened on July 14, 1948.

As Truman prepared for the July convention, in addition to juggling the often competing policy agendas of the three essential voting groups within the Democratic Party, Truman had to harmonize the fiercely divergent views of several colorful and egotistical leaders of his party. These political prima donnas included the fiery racist Governor Strom Thurmond of South Carolina, who had repeatedly threatened to create a Dixiecrat Party; the impassioned liberal, rising-star mayor of Minneapolis, Hubert Horatio Humphrey, who was hoping to use his liberal record as Minneapolis's mayor to springboard into the Senate in the November election; and Henry Wallace, who as one of the most articulate politicians of the 1940s had established strong ties to the western Progressives while serving as FDR's vice president from 1940 to 1944 and as Truman's commerce secretary until the president fired him on September 20, 1946.[12] For Truman, these three politicians—racist Strom Thurmond, ultraliberal Hubert Humphrey, and progressive Henry Wallace—represented a powerful and complex set of personalities—any of whom could derail his 1948 presidential campaign through intraparty warfare.

In early 1948, Truman also had to diffuse the concerns of the "Draft Eisenhower" group, which included Franklin Roosevelt's three sons, James, Franklin, and Elliot Roosevelt, and other leading Democrats, such as Mayors William O'Dwyer of New York and Hubert Humphrey of Minneapolis.[13] Because of General Eisenhower's enormous popularity in the postwar environment of 1948—popularity akin to the broad-based popular support enjoyed in the 1990s by General Colin Powell—the Draft Eisenhower Democrats politically were a mortal threat to the incumbent Democratic president, who was criticized by some of the Draft Eisenhower leaders for not being liberal enough. From a pragmatic political perspective, many leaders of the Draft Eisenhower movement were simply convinced that Truman was unelectable on November 2, 1948.

In Clifford's view, the Draft Eisenhower effort was a serious threat by a group of prominent Democrats who unfairly overlooked the accomplishments and domestic goals of the incumbent Democratic president from Missouri.

> Ironically, the leading liberal organization in the country, Americans for Democratic Action [ADA], was leading the effort to replace President Truman. Just as he was proposing the most far-reaching civil rights legislation in American history, this group proposed to replace him with General Eisenhower, whose political views were completely unknown, and who, when he finally surfaced four years later, turned out to be a conservative Republican. It may seem hard to believe today, but the ADA's Committee to Draft Eisenhower was strongly backed in 1948 by such influential Democrats as FDR's three sons, Franklin, Elliott, and Jimmy; Alabama's two Senators, John Sparkman and Lister Hill; Florida Senator Claude Pepper; the courageous leader of the United Automobile Workers, Walter Reuther; and a promising young mayor from Minneapolis named Hubert H. Humphrey. This was serious business: it seemed clear that if Eisenhower made himself available, he would be nominated and elected in 1948.[14]

While the efforts of this prestigious group of liberal Democrats eventually collapsed on the eve of the Democratic convention with General Eisenhower's unconditional statement of unavailability, the Draft Eisenhower Committee nonetheless reflected widespread concern within the leadership of the Democratic Party that Truman would lose on election day to the popular moderate Republican governor of New York, Thomas Dewey.

THE GOP'S DREAM CANDIDATE: THOMAS DEWEY

Thomas Dewey, the GOP's presidential candidate in 1948, was a formidable opponent for Truman on several fronts, including the emerging civil rights horizon. As governor of New York, Dewey had enacted a statewide version of the FEPC—a Truman-supported concept that was rejected by the GOP-led Eightieth Congress. Dewey, the moderate, Wall Street–backed Republican, enjoyed widespread support from black newspaper editors who were impressed by his aggressive efforts to bring African Americans into the mainstream of New York's burgeoning postwar economy.[15] In 1948, Dewey's highly visible efforts on behalf of blacks had earned him the gratitude of the growing population of African Americans in New York, where the black vote was no longer the certainty for the Democratic candidate it had been in FDR's four prior presidential elections. In fact, because of Dewey's impressive civil rights record in New York, the GOP in 1948 was beginning to enjoy increased black voter support that harkened back to the pre–New Deal days when black Americans often gave their political allegiance to the Republican Party of Abraham Lincoln.

Dewey's ability to attract black voters was enhanced by the GOP's adoption of a strong civil rights plank at the 1948 National Republican Party Convention meeting in Philadelphia in the third week of June—just three weeks before the fractured Democratic Party would convene in the same steamy Convention Hall in Philadelphia. Dewey's civil rights plank was a powerful political tool because it explicitly proposed antilynching legislation, elimination of the poll tax, and integration of the military—numerous federal reforms already articulated in Truman's Civil Rights Committee report of October 1947 and in Truman's special message to Congress in February 1948.[16]

While echoing Truman's earlier views on civil rights, Dewey's 1948 platform reflected a high degree of GOP sensitivity to the potential black vote—a vote that was maturing into significant, yet underappreciated urban voting blocks in the North and Midwest, where black Americans continued their post–World War II migration out of the segregationist South. This migration had been predicted in an April 8, 1945, *Atlanta Constitution* article entitled "Negro Migration from South Will Follow War, Survey Finds." The *Constitution,* focusing on the results of a survey of thousands of officers and enlisted men who were still on active duty, reported, "Negroes express the intention of moving from the south to the east- [and] north-central states. . . . In general, the survey shows that nine out of every ten white enlisted men intend to remain in the states where they lived before the war, but that one out of every three Negro enlisted men intends to move into another state. And since the majority of these Negroes comes from the south, the indications are, according to this survey, that the southern states will as a result of this postwar migration soon lose approximately one-third of its Negro population."[17]

The migration of Southern blacks to Northern states where voting was possible was "significant" in the view of historians McCoy and Ruetten, who focused in detail on the 1948 campaign in *Quest and Response.*

> The geographical movement of blacks and other minorities during World War II was heavy—and significant. Some 2,729,000[,] or about 20 percent, of the nonwhite population migrated. Of these, 964,000 moved within one state, 578,000 between contiguous states, and 1,187,000 between noncontiguous states. Urban nonwhite population increased by two-and-one-half million. The proportion of the nation's nonwhites living in the South declined from 75 to 63 percent, while the nonwhite population of the Northeast, Middle West, and Far West rose substantially. The significance of these population shifts was to become increasingly clear after the war, in terms of political strength, black aspirations, and intergroup alliances.[18]

Not surprisingly, the postwar black American exodus from the South was particularly evident in New York State, where blacks benefited from Governor Dewey's proven record of developing programs for the new minority residents of the state.

Because of Dewey's well-established civil rights record in New York State, and based on the strong GOP civil rights platform in 1948 on which Dewey would run for president, Truman and his aides were under increased pressure to respond to Dewey's civil rights platform yet, at the same time, to respond in a manner that did not exacerbate the deep tensions already evident in the fractious Democratic Party—a party primarily at war within its own membership over its civil rights plank.

As the 1948 Democratic convention drew near, Truman had plenty on his presidential plate beyond trying to minimize the growing threat of a partisan revolt from segregationist Southern delegates to the Democratic convention. At the top of Truman's list of crises was the very real possibility that Joseph Stalin would start World War III over the divided city of Berlin, Germany. While

Truman was wrestling with intraparty politics as the convention approached, he was also wrestling with the growing threat that Stalin's ambitions represented for the peace and stability of a war-ravaged Western Europe, where Truman's Marshall Plan was just taking effect. To stop Stalin as he sought control of Berlin, Truman on June 26, 1948, launched the massive Berlin Airlift—an airlift that was unprecedented in terms of its resources and precision. For Truman and the country, the Berlin Airlift would end eleven months later with Stalin's backing down and lifting the Soviet's blockade of West Berlin. Just as Truman's stubborn commitment to force civil rights reform on the nation convinced Southern leaders like Strom Thurmond of his resolve, his Berlin Airlift confirmed for Stalin just how determined Truman could be—and that resolve, along with 2,326,204 tons of supplies, flown into Berlin on 277,264 U.S.- and British-piloted flights kept West Berlin open and kept the world free of another World War.[19]

In the early days of July 1948, as the Berlin Airlift became operational, Truman's primary political goal remained preservation of the New Deal coalition of western state farmers, big city labor, and the states' rights Southern voters—a coalition that was increasingly combustible as the bedrock states' rights philosophy of Southern conservatives ran head first into the federal civil rights program envisioned by the party's liberals. In the area of civil rights, Democratic Party liberals had been repeatedly urged on by Truman's words and actions to support an aggressive federal strategy to resolve the country's racial problems. Ironically, while the president sought to promote Democratic Party harmony in the weeks before the 1948 convention, it was Truman himself who created the charged environment for the inevitable collision of states' rights advocates and civil rights activists at the Democrats' Philadelphia convention in July—and it was Truman who ensured that there could be no retreat for the Democrats from his already publicly stated support of a comprehensive federal program for civil rights reforms.

In Truman's view, as evidenced in many of his postwar speeches, it was essential that the Democratic Party continue to hold itself out as the credible protector of Democratic values both at home and abroad in the new global world of the United Nations—a United Nations that Truman had helped to launch just weeks after he became president in the spring of 1945. As Truman repeatedly noted, the United States must promptly put its own civil rights house in order through a Democratic Party–led program of federally protected civil rights for all Americans; if it did not, the United States would have no credibility and greatly diminished effectiveness in the emerging Cold War, in which an expansionist Soviet Union and widespread global instability compelled Truman to advance the Truman Doctrine and the Marshall Plan.[20] For Truman, the volatile domestic political issue of civil rights reform was inextricably tied to the struggle for democracy and human rights in the new world order of 1948.

Beyond his obvious global concerns, Truman's creation of the Committee on Civil Rights in December 1946 and the predictable yet revolutionary report it issued in October 1947 had publicly established the solid evidentiary predicate for civil rights reform. Given that irrefutable record established by Truman's Civil Rights Committee, it was inevitable that a strong civil rights plank would ultimately be adopted when the Platform Committee met at the Democratic convention in July. In addition, Truman's spirited NAACP speech on June 29, 1947, and the president's equally unequivocal special message to Congress on February 2, 1948, guaranteed that the Democratic convention would confront the civil rights issue head-on if Truman were to be the party's presidential nominee.

THE DEMOCRATIC CONVENTION AND
TRUMAN'S CIVIL RIGHTS PLANK

Meeting on July 14, 1948, the Democratic Party Platform Committee confronted three vastly different options for its civil rights plank. On the eve of the convention, the Truman forces were still trying to hold on to some Southern support despite months of public secessionist threats from racist Southern leaders led by then-Governor Strom Thurmond. Accordingly, in a vain effort to avoid a party revolt, the Truman forces proposed civil rights reform language in general terms that captured the basic concept of racial equality based on the Constitution.[21] While Truman in no way retreated from his radical civil rights positions taken in 1947 and earlier in 1948, he and his advisers hoped that the moderate language of their proposed civil rights plank would pass muster with Southern Democrats, just as similar language had been accepted at the 1944 convention.

For liberals in the party, the initial Truman-supported plank was inadequate because it lacked some of the specificity of Truman's February 2, 1948, special civil rights message to Congress. Notwithstanding criticism from liberals, the initial Truman-supported civil rights plank called for a congressionally mandated end to all forms of racial discrimination.

> The Democratic Party commits itself to continuing its efforts to eradicate all racial, religious and economic discrimination.
>
> We again state our belief that racial and religious minorities must have the right to live, the right to work, the right to vote, the full and

equal protection of the laws, on a basis of equality with all citizens as guaranteed by the Constitution.

We again call upon the Congress to exert its full authority to the limit of its Constitutional powers to assure and protect these rights.[22]

To states' rights advocates from the conservative South assembled at the 1948 Democratic Party convention, Truman had already poisoned the political well with his frequent articulation of a federal civil rights program that was totally at odds with their status quo philosophy. Accordingly, the Truman-proposed plank, despite its more moderate language, was still unacceptable to Southern Democrats because it referred to constitutionally based civil rights and advocated congressional actions to enforce those rights.

As a result, the introduction of Truman's constitutionally grounded civil rights plank on July 14 prompted the immediate introduction of a states' rights plank, called the Moody plank, which argued for "the reserved powers of the states . . . to control and regulate local affairs and act in the exercise of police powers."[23] As expected, states' rights delegates from Mississippi, Tennessee, and Texas who supported the Moody plank wanted the Democratic Party to agree that civil rights was a state issue, not a federal concern. The Moody plank also reiterated the principle that each state enjoyed the exclusive right to police itself and its citizens.

The introduction of the regressive Moody plank ignited a broad-based uproar from moderate and liberal Democratic delegates who countered by proposing a substitution called the Biemiller plank. According to Tom Clark, the Biemiller plank was the collective work product of Democratic Party liberals led by Congressman Andrew Biemiller of Wisconsin and Mayor Hubert Humphrey of Minneapolis. Truman's incumbent attorney general, Tom Clark, who was actively involved in the politics of the 1948 convention, recalled, "Biemiller was a good friend of the President's, and a good friend of ours."[24] While mindful of the fact that Truman and his convention team wanted to minimize the threatened Southern delegations' walkout, Biemiller and Humphrey led a growing coalition of liberal and moderate Democratic delegates who demanded more detailed plank language than that used in the initial Truman-supported civil rights plank— language that explicitly urged Congress to enact legislation guaranteeing blacks full and equal political participation, equal employment opportunities, personal protection, if necessary, and integration of the military.[25]

The battle lines were drawn on this volatile issue as it became clear that it was either going to be the radical Biemiller plank or the status quo, states' rights

Moody plank. However, because Truman had already publicly taken his party so far down the public policy road for radical federal civil rights reform, the outcome of the fight over the civil rights plank was predestined. That there could be no retreat for the Democratic Party on civil rights became obvious to the delegates in Philadelphia after the eloquent, thirty-seven-year-old leader of the liberal wing of the Democratic Party, Mayor Hubert H. Humphrey, spoke in support of the Biemiller plank:

> There will be no hedging, and there will be no watering down, if you
> please, of the instruments and the principles of the civil rights program.
>   My friends, to those who say that we are rushing this issue of civil
> rights, I say to them, we are 172 years late.[26]

In supporting the explicit and comprehensive civil rights program articulated in the Biemiller plank, the spirited mayor of Minneapolis told his fellow delegates, which included only 17 blacks out of 1,234 delegates, that he viewed Truman as the genuine pioneering civil rights president.[27] "In unmistakable terms . . . we proudly hail and we courageously support our President and leader, Harry Truman, in his great fight for civil rights in America."[28] For Humphrey and his liberal colleagues, as well as for the moderates gathered in the Convention Hall, Truman's words and actions as president during the prior three years had created both the proactive civil rights record and the legitimate expectations for comprehensive civil rights reform that the Democratic Party could not abandon.

While Truman obviously wanted and needed a unified party supporting him after the convention, he also hoped that the Democratic Party would not reject his federal civil rights program because of the moral implications both at home and in the new global arena. In Truman's view, the Democratic Party's ability—as well as his ability as president—to lead, domestically and globally, with credibility had become tied to the party's stand on civil rights.

In his memoirs, Truman recalled the civil rights platform fight at the 1948 convention and confirmed his personal determination not to back down on the radical civil rights reform program that he had proposed earlier in 1948 to the recalcitrant Congress.

> To me, party platforms are contracts with the people, and I always looked
> upon them as agreements that had to be carried out. That is why I was
> perfectly willing to risk defeat in 1948 by sticking to the civil-rights plank
> in my platform.

There were people around me, of course, who were anxious to prevent any sort of split in the Democratic party, and efforts were made to
soften the approach to the civil-rights issue. I would not stand for any
double talk on this vital principle, however, and insisted on plain language
being used. Members of the Cabinet and others warned me that I was riding to a defeat if I stuck to my FEPC orders and if I did not let up on the
battle for civil-rights legislation. But I wanted to win the fight by standing
on my platform, or lose it the same way.[29]

When the heated convention rhetoric about the civil rights plank ended on
July 14, Truman prevailed when the Democratic delegates, with a 651 $\frac{1}{2}$-to-582 $\frac{1}{2}$
vote, rejected the states' rights–supported Moody plank and immediately adopted
the Humphrey-supported, more expansive Biemiller plank.[30] For the first time
in the history of the country, and more than eight decades after the issuance of
the Emancipation Proclamation by a Republican president, the Democratic
Party's presidential candidate would be a man who publicly and unequivocally
promised that he would take comprehensive federal actions to eliminate the pervasive racial discrimination in the United States.

In his diary, the president noted that "the platform fight [is] in dead
earnest."[31] Truman went on to write that the convention voted down the states'
rights plank and adopted the "Crackpot Biemiller" amendment—an amendment
introduced by his friend Andrew Biemiller—that Truman knew would necessarily cause the Alabama delegation and other Southern delegations to bolt from the
party. In his memoirs, the president recalled that he expected his insistence on
comprehensive civil rights reform would cause a Southern Democratic revolt. "I
was reasonably sure, far in advance of the convention, that there would be a splin-
tering off of the South or at least a portion of it."[32]

As Truman expected, immediately after the July 14 vote on the civil rights
plank, protests from Southern delegations erupted on the crowded convention
floor, and walkouts were led by members of the Mississippi and Alabama delegations. On July 15, only 13 Southern delegates cast their votes for Truman, and
263 Southern delegates voted for the South's "favorite son," racist Senator
Richard Russell from Georgia. Notwithstanding Truman's concerns about the
probable revolt by Southern Democrats, he publicly and enthusiastically
embraced the more expansive language of the Biemiller amendment with his
rousing acceptance speech before the fractured convention delegates on July 15.[33]

William S. White's front-page *New York Times* story, "Truman Is Shunned
in Votes of South," reported, "Eleven States of the old Confederate South gave

only thirteen of their 278 votes."[34] Despite this resounding Southern boycott of his candidacy, Truman was easily nominated by an impressive 947 1/2-delegate-vote margin, and for the first time in his long political career, Truman became the official presidential candidate of his beloved Democratic Party.

TRUMAN ACCEPTS THE NOMINATION AND
GOES ON THE ATTACK

Following his nomination by an overwhelming vote of his fellow Democrats, a dapper Truman, dressed impeccably in a white suit, took the podium at the Convention Hall and delivered one of the most powerful speeches of his long political life. In another front-page *New York Times* story, this one by W. H. Lawrence, the *Times* reported that candidate Truman "set the convention on fire with his acceptance speech, which came at the end of a long, tiring, tumultuous session in which the north-south party split was deepened appreciably."[35] Speaking with the vigor of a much younger politician, candidate Truman proceeded to castigate the do-nothing Republican-controlled Congress, bluntly blasting GOP leaders for every problem in the country, including the sad state of civil rights for black Americans. In an indignant tone, candidate Truman reminded the Democratic delegates, "Everybody knows that I recommended to the Congress the civil rights program. I did that because I believed it to be my duty under the Constitution. Some of the members of my own party disagreed with me violently on this matter, but they stand up and do it openly. People can tell where they stand. But the Republicans all professed to be for those measures, but the Eightieth Congress did not act. They had enough men to do it and they could have had cloture. They didn't have to have a filibuster. There are enough people in that Congress that could vote for cloture."[36]

Relentlessly, Truman focused his Democratic delegates and the country that gathered by their radios on the do-nothing Republican leaders in the Congress who, in Truman's view, were the real culprits keeping the country from embracing federal civil rights reform. Truman, as he acknowledged in his memoirs, deliberately made the GOP-led Congress Exhibit A in his first and only presidential campaign. By focusing exclusively on the Republicans and not on the racist Southern Democratic members of Congress who repeatedly and effectively used their filibuster threat to block even modest civil rights reform, Truman steered criticism away from Southerners in his own party, a tactic he would use repeatedly until election day. Moreover, by making the civil rights issue an explicit priority in his acceptance speech, Truman gained added respect in the emerging black voter strongholds of Illinois and Ohio—states that ultimately proved pivotal to his successful election on November 2.

Truman's electrifying acceptance speech also announced, for the first time, the president's plan to summon the GOP-controlled Congress back to steamy Washington for a special, unavoidably heated session in just eleven days. Referring back to his twelve-hour workdays plowing the fields of his mother's Grandview farm from sunup to sundown, the president announced to the applause of delegates, "On the 26th day of July, which out in Missouri we call 'Turnip Day,' I am going to call Congress back and ask them to pass laws to halt rising prices, to meet the housing crisis. . . . Now, my friends, if there is any reality behind that Republican platform, we ought to get some action from a short session of the 80th Congress."[37]

By focusing so brutally on the legislative omissions of the GOP-led Congress, candidate Truman also added to the dilemma facing Governor Dewey as he campaigned for the urban black vote. While Dewey had legitimately earned a strong pro–civil rights reputation as governor of New York, his Republican colleagues in the Congress had been far less courageous in regards to civil rights reform. In fact, the members of the GOP leadership were unofficial partners with Southern Democrats in blocking Truman's civil rights program.[38] It would prove politically difficult for Dewey to focus on his own stellar civil rights record because, to do so, he would inevitably highlight the fact that Truman was partially correct when he blamed the Republicans in Congress for derailing Truman's civil rights program. If a Republican governor could make meaningful civil rights progress in New York, why had the GOP-led Congress failed to pass the Truman civil rights program? By focusing on his own successful civil rights record in New York, Dewey ran the serious risk of increasing the black voter's appreciation of what Dewey's Republican congressional colleagues consistently failed to do for African Americans.

As a result of the conflicting GOP political track record on civil rights—an impressive record in New York under Dewey, versus a do-nothing GOP record in the Congress—Dewey was stuck. Truman, beginning with his rousing acceptance speech on July 15, 1948, took full advantage of Dewey's painful dilemma during the months leading up to election day.

THE DIXIECRATS REVOLT WITH CANDIDATE
STROM THURMOND

Two days after Truman's formal nomination in Philadelphia, Southern Democrats—who had labeled themselves *Dixiecrats,* gathered for the States'

Rights Party Convention in the heart of the segregationist South—Birmingham, Alabama. As expected, Governor Strom Thurmond of South Carolina was nominated as the Dixiecrats' presidential candidate with fellow racist Governor Fielding Wright of Mississippi being chosen as the Dixiecrats' vice presidential nominee.[39] The party schism that Truman had hoped to avoid over the Democratic Party's civil rights plank was a reality, and because of his public program for federally mandated civil rights reform, Truman was now faced with the real prospect of losing the White House in November because of his party's formalized internal revolt over civil rights.

Governor Thurmond and his States' Rights Party allies throughout the largely Democratic South appreciated the hostility of Southern voters toward Truman as the November election approached. To take the fullest possible advantage of Truman's widespread vulnerability, Governor Thurmond repeatedly sought a public forum throughout his Dixiecrat campaign to personally debate candidate Truman on his radical civil rights plan. Thurmond's zeal to take on Truman was evident in a telegram that Thurmond sent to Truman on October 10, 1948, less than a month before voters would go to the polls.

THE PRESIDENT

THE WHITE HOUSE

AGAIN RENEW MY CHALLENGE TO DEBATE YOU FACE TO FACE ON THE SAME PLATFORM ON YOUR "SO CALLED CIVIL RIGHTS PROGRAM" STOP SUGGEST WE DEBATE IT IN VIRGINIA, TEXAS, OR MISSOURI STOP YOU NAME THE TIME AND PLACE

J. STROM THURMOND STATES RIGHTS DEMOCRATIC PRESIDENTIAL NOMINEE[40]

While Truman and his aides knew that Thurmond's chances of being elected president were virtually nil, they nonetheless appreciated the Democratic Party's vulnerability based on the Dixiecrats' astute strategy—a strategy designed to siphon off enough popular votes in the November election to force the presidential election into the House of Representatives.[41] The possibility of a 1948 presidential election conducted in the House, where states' rights advocates were well positioned, was a particularly attractive prospect to Dixiecrats, who by mid July were confronted with two pro–civil rights presidential candidates—Dewey and Truman—either of whose election on November 2, 1948, would be disastrous for Southern states' righters. And as troublesome as it was for Truman to confront a renegade Dixiecrat presidential candidate in November, his problems would only increase as former Secretary of Commerce Henry Wallace formally decided that he too would become a candidate for the White House.

THE FOURTH AND FINAL CANDIDATE

Three days after the Dixiecrats held their nominating convention in Birmingham, Henry Wallace was nominated as the Progressive Party's presidential candidate in Philadelphia. Wallace, FDR's former vice president from 1940 to 1944 and Truman's fired commerce secretary, was a relentless civil rights activist whose effective advocacy had earned him the esteem of black voters throughout the country.[42] While Wallace had indicated his intention to run in late December 1947, the Progressive Party's formal nomination of Wallace in the wake of the Democratic convention represented another serious threat to Truman's election to the White House on November 2—little more than one hundred days away.[43]

Despite the threat of defeat in November because of Wallace's Progressive Party candidacy and the Dixiecrats' revolt, Truman remained optimistic. Even though he had hoped to prevent a party revolt over his civil rights plank, candidate Truman was positioned after July 15, 1948, to run for the presidency on a civil rights platform that he had stubbornly pursued since the early days of his inherited presidency. For Truman, the battle for civil rights reform was much more than politics—it was a moral fight; and as Jonathan Daniels predicted, because it was morally and constitutionally grounded for Truman, civil rights reform was a battle worth losing the White House over if necessary.[44]

Civil rights reform was also a moral fight for Hubert Humphrey in 1948. After the bitter fight over the civil rights plank concluded, the eloquent Mayor Humphrey spoke once more to the convention's delegates. Humphrey took the convention microphone and reminded his fellow Democratic delegates about Truman's obstinate commitment to a comprehensive civil rights program. Characterizing Truman's vision for civil rights as a "New Emancipation Proclamation," Humphrey reiterated his view that 172 years was too long for black Americans to wait for their constitutionally guaranteed civil rights.[45]

One hundred seventy-two years was too long—but with the adoption of the Democratic Party plank on civil rights, a new era of civil rights activism by the federal government was embraced by the Democratic Party. Walter White, the NAACP's relentless executive director during the Roosevelt and Truman presidencies, told the *New York Times* that adoption of the 1948 civil rights plank by the Democrats "marks the greatest turning point for the South and for America since the Civil War." In White's opinion, "Real Americanism won at Philadelphia," where Truman's civil rights plank represented a "victory for decency."[46]

By his words and actions in 1946, 1947, and throughout the first half of 1948, President Truman showed that he too shared Mayor Humphrey's sense of urgency about civil rights. It was well past time for black Americans to be lifted from second-class status in a segregated United States. And if he won on November 2, Truman assured Democratic delegates and voters across America, he would make sure that there would be no more delay.

In the few months that remained for campaigning after the stormy Democratic convention, sixty-four-year-old Truman would directly take his platform, including his divisive civil rights plank, to voters across the country. It would prove to be a grueling and emotionally challenging campaign in which Truman himself often remained the only hopeful person on his campaign train, the Ferdinand Magellan. But before that train headed west, Truman had several additional civil rights bombshells to drop, and what better place for fireworks than a special session of the Republican-led Eightieth Congress?

CHAPTER EIGHT

The Turnip Day Congressional Session and Executive Orders 9980 and 9981: July 26, 1948

It is hereby declared to be the policy of the President that there shall be
equality of treatment and opportunity for all persons in the armed services
without regard to race, color, religion or national origin.
—HST, July 26, 1948

During his spirited acceptance speech at the 1948 Democratic convention in Philadelphia, candidate Harry Truman announced that he would summon the reluctant members of the Republican-led Eightieth Congress back to a special session; that session began on July 26 in a steamy Washington, D.C.[1] As members of Congress returned to the humid federal city on the banks of the Potomac River—a city where air conditioning was a rare luxury in 1948—the thirty-third president of the United States used the first day of the Turnip Day congressional session to hit the do-nothing Congress with a political two-by-four.

Without warning and in obvious response to gross congressional inaction on the president's civil rights special message, which had been submitted six months earlier, President Truman on July 26, 1948, issued two related executive orders, 9980 and 9981—orders that would forever change the racial landscape of the United States. With the stroke of his presidential pen, Harry Truman unilaterally mandated an integrated federal workforce and simultaneously integrated the vast U.S. armed forces.[2]

For the million-plus African American readers of the *Chicago Defender*, Truman's issuance of Executive Orders 9980 and 9981 was described in articles under banner headlines as "a dramatic and historic move, unprecedented since the time of Lincoln."[3] When he issued these two executive orders, President Truman acted in an environment where the vast majority of Americans were generally comfortable with—or at least acquiescent to—the segregationist laws and traditions that dominated large portions of the United States, including the nation's capital. That most Americans were comfortable with the civil rights status quo in 1948 was evident in Gallup's nationwide poll of fifteen hundred adults in March 1948 wherein 82 percent of those surveyed were opposed to Truman's radical federal civil rights program—a program that was partially implemented by his issuance of Executive Orders 9980 and 9981.[4]

In spite of needing all the popular support he could muster to defeat GOP standard-bearer Governor Thomas Dewey in the coming election, Truman acted without any major national political pressure when he issued these two landmark orders integrating the federal workforce. Moreover, in view of the violent opposition that was expected from Southern voters, many political sages predicted that President Truman's issuance of these two controversial civil rights executive orders would ultimately prove to be an act of political suicide.

President Truman had little, if any, political capital available to blunt the pervasive public antipathy toward his integration of the military, a fact confirmed by another Gallup poll showing that Truman only enjoyed a favorable rating of 39 percent in the crucial weeks before the Democratic Party's July 1948 convention.[5] Nonetheless, this World War I veteran who occupied the White House on July 26, 1948, felt strongly that the time had come to eliminate all racial barriers in federal employment, including the armed services.

As a former member of the Senate, Truman fully appreciated the deep-rooted congressional opposition to his civil rights agenda. Nonetheless, the president ignored the concerns of legislators when he spoke to them in a joint session on July 27, one day after issuing his two civil rights bombshells.[6] Truman undoubtedly knew that he was adding insult to injury to the members of the Congress by issuing these two monumental executive orders on the first day of a special congressional session that the members were literally forced into during an election year recess—a recess when most members needed to be back home campaigning for reelection.

According to a front-page report by C. P. Trussell in the *New York Times* on July 27, 1948, the atmosphere in the Congress was hostile as members reluctantly answered the president's call for a special Turnip Day session issued eleven days earlier. "The Eightieth Congress returned to work . . . in response to the July 15 call of President Truman. It did not come back happily. The first flashes of smiling greetings on reassembly soon wore off. . . . As Dixie Senators planned this afternoon to resist to the last any attempts to get [Truman's Civil Rights] program through Congress, President Truman, [*sic*] fired two more shots along the civil-rights front. In two Executive orders the President called for the abolition of discrimination because of race, creed, color or national origin within the Armed services and in Federal employment."[7] Truman's actions, in Trussell's opinion, were "expected generally to accentuate the bitterness in the Democratic cleavage in Congress."

Truman's Executive Order 9980, Regulations Governing Fair Employment Practices Within the Federal Establishment, explicitly mandated the elimination of discriminatory practices throughout the federal government based on race, color, religion, or national origin.[8] In characterizing Executive Order 9980, the *New York Times* reported that a "little FEPC is created"—an FEPC that Congress refused to enact as part of the ten-point legislative proposal articulated in Truman's special civil rights message to Congress on February 2, 1948.[9] To ensure that fair employment practices would become a reality throughout the vast post–World War II federal bureaucracy, Truman's Executive Order 9980 required that "all personnel actions taken by Federal appointing officers shall be based solely on merit and fitness; and such officers are authorized and directed to take appropriate steps to insure that in all such actions there shall be no discrimination because of race, color, religion, or national origin."[10] By using these explicit words, President Truman served notice on the public at large, as well as on his own federal bureaucracy, that he was immediately eliminating discrimination in federal hiring that was based on anything but "merit and fitness." Federal employers could no longer consider race, color, ethnic heritage, or religion in their hiring decisions. To ensure that this mandate would take effect promptly in a federal employment environment rife with discrimination, the president put the heads of each federal department and agency—in effect, all the members of his cabinet and other presidential appointees—on explicit notice that he would hold each one of them "personally responsible for an effective program to insure that fair employment policies are fully observed in all personnel actions within his department."[11]

This personal accountability within the Truman cabinet was important because Washington, D.C., in July 1948 was a pervasively segregated city. For most members of the federal workforce, except workers at the Department of the Interior, "whites only" and "blacks" or "Negroes" signs prominently designated restrooms, drinking fountains, and cafeterias throughout the sprawling federal buildings of the nation's capital. These important trappings of a segregated society were a perverse part of the legacy of an earlier, seemingly enlightened Democratic president, Princeton professor Woodrow Wilson.

President Wilson's imposition of a policy of racial segregation throughout the federal workplace in early 1913 is rarely noted by historians.[12] Wilson's actions segregating federal employees were challenged in letters sent to President Wilson on August 18 and August 27, 1913, by *New York Post* publisher Oswald Garrison Villard, one of the original founders of the NAACP.[13] In his capacity as chairman of the board of the embryonic multiracial NAACP, Villard wrote President Wilson in courteous yet firm words to inform the president "of the intense dissatisfaction of colored people at their treatment by your Administration thus far." Villard enclosed with his August 18, 1913, correspondence to Wilson a compelling letter from Booker T. Washington, who reported on the "embittered and discouraged" colored people of Washington, D.C., who, as federal workers, were, for the first time, being forced to use segregated facilities that were mandated by members of President Wilson's cabinet. Villard's letters on behalf of the NAACP failed to convince Wilson to reverse his segregationist policy. Over time, the segregated federal facilities initiated during the Wilson presidency contributed mightily to the discriminatory, race-based employment practices that permeated the federal government when Harry Truman became president more than three decades after the Wilson presidency had begun.

The often historically overlooked fact that Woodrow Wilson was a proactive segregationist is discussed by Sean Dennis Cashman in his book, *African-Americans and the Quest for Civil Rights, 1900–1990*. Cashman describes the Wilson presidency from 1913 to 1921 as the most racist presidency since the Civil War.[14] While Wilson did not issue executive orders mandating segregated federal facilities, he did, through surrogates, implement a general policy that resulted in the segregated federal lunchrooms and restrooms that became commonplace in the nation's capital during and following the Wilson presidency. And while President Roosevelt took limited remedial action in June 1941 with Executive Order 8802, which directed that black Americans be accepted in the War Department's job-training programs, little measurable progress had been made in eliminating widespread discriminatory federal employment practices by the time Harry Truman became president on the evening of April 12, 1945. Ironically, while President Roosevelt and his wife, Eleanor, were viewed by black Americans as their champions, according to Alonzo Fields, the African American who served as the chief butler in the White House during the Roosevelt and Truman presidencies, the Roosevelts maintained segregated dining rooms at their Hyde Park estate for their servants.

Separate dining rooms for the white and colored help existed [at the White House] until the Roosevelt Administration ended this by the simple process of eliminating white help in household capacities except for the housekeeper. The gardeners, carpenters and electricians did not have their meals in the White House. However, at Hyde Park, whenever the colored help went there to serve the President, they were not permitted to eat in the dining room for the help. They had to eat in the kitchen. Of course at the White House, with Virginia so nearby, the separate dining rooms could be attributed to the influence of that State's policy, but in New York you did not expect this. So I had my reservations concerning the [Roosevelt] White House as an example for the rest of the country.[15]

When Truman moved into the White House in early 1945, the federal bureaucracy was generally segregated except for workers at the Department of the Interior, where FDR's outspoken interior secretary, Harold Ickes, insisted on an integrated workforce—a workforce that was an anomaly that resulted from Ickes's strong feelings about racial equality. While President Truman and Harold Ickes shared an enlightened view of civil rights, little else united them, and Secretary Ickes, on February 13, 1946, was one of the first departures from the former Roosevelt cabinet that Harry Truman inherited on April 12, 1945.[16]

On July 26, 1948, when he issued Executive Order 9980, President Truman did what FDR would not do: he unilaterally integrated the workforce and the infrastructure of the vast federal government. While FDR for political reasons looked the other way on civil rights reform, Truman knew with certainty how dismal the federal employment situation remained for black Americans. His Civil Rights Committee had methodically documented the grossly discriminatory practices that were commonplace throughout the federal workplace. Harry Truman also knew that meaningful progress could not be made until each cabinet officer and senior federal official was held individually responsible to the president for civil rights progress in his department or agency. To emphasize this unprecedented degree of personal accountability at the cabinet level, Truman's Executive Order 9980 instructed each federal department head (i.e. cabinet officer) to designate a fair employment officer who would be given "full operating responsibility, under immediate supervision of the department head" for carrying out the detailed mandate of Executive Order 9980.[17] In focusing on the explicit requirements in both Executive Orders 9980 and 9981, the *New York Times* on July 27, 1948, reported, "The presidential orders, which require no Congressional sanction, specified in detail the machinery that would be employed to monitor both anti-discrimination programs."[18]

Some of the machinery mandated by Executive Order 9980 included new procedures whereby employees would have knowledge of and access to their new appellate rights. To achieve this goal, a two-part appellate procedure was established in which aggrieved federal employees, or would-be employees, could directly appeal the decisions of a department's fair employment officer to the cabinet officer heading that department.[19] This presidentially mandated appeal provision essentially empowered a federal employee to go directly to members of Truman's cabinet for relief if they felt that the decisions of the newly created fair employment officer were unjust.

This unheard of appellate right for federal employees or prospective employees was merely the first of two independent vehicles of appeal available. Executive Order 9980 also established a seven-member Fair Employment Board within the Civil Service Commission. The board was authorized to review the employment decisions of any cabinet officer in the Truman administration. Moreover, if the Fair Employment Board ruled against a cabinet officer and that department head refused to reverse his action, the board was afforded direct access to the president himself.[20] By establishing this kind of multitiered appellate infrastructure for federal employees, President Truman immediately empowered black Americans seeking employment in the burgeoning postwar federal bureaucracy to obtain relief if they felt they were the victims of discrimination. Whether the head of a cabinet department or the chairman of a federal agency, Executive Order 9980 applied specifically to all federal employers throughout the United States.

The broad scope of Executive Order 9980 was obvious in paragraph seven of the order, which also mandated relief when inaction resulted in federal workplace discrimination: "The term 'personnel action' as used herein shall include failure to act. Persons failing of appointment who allege a grievance relating to discrimination shall be entitled to the remedies herein provided."[21] This language expanded the basis for appellate relief to include those African Americans who might not be able to establish a case of actual harm due to federal employment practices but who nonetheless suffered a more subtle form of discrimination due to the omission of action by federal employers. The inclusion of this concept in Executive Order 9980 was important because it legitimized employment complaints of black Americans who could not produce hard evidence of discrimination but could show harm by the inaction of a federal supervisor or a potential federal employer.

To ensure the most prompt and robust implementation of Executive Order 9980, Truman named a multiracial panel of seven respected Americans to the newly created Fair Employment Board. Included on the board were two nationally known black Americans: civil rights activists Jesse Mitchell, president of the Industrial Bank of Washington, and the Urban League's Eugene Kinkle Jones.[22]

For African Americans seeking to gain employment in the volatile U.S. marketplace in 1948, President Truman's issuance of Executive Order 9980 represented tangible progress, not mere political rhetoric, for black Americans seeking federal employment. Executive Order 9980 not only mandated the immediate elimination of race-based discrimination in the federal bureaucracy but also established the specific procedures for blacks to follow to gain fair and open access to jobs long denied them. If they were denied fair access to meaningful federal employment, black Americans were, for the first time in the country's history, provided two independent federal appellate vehicles to address and remedy discriminatory employment practices. After July 26, 1948, black Americans were put on a new legal footing of equality with white citizens working for or seeking to be employed by the federal government; moreover, based on the explicit wording of Executive Order 9980, it did not matter whether a cabinet secretary or a federal agency chairman violated their rights to federal employment, black Americans now had two legal means of appeal to protect their equal access to employment in the federal workforce.

Not surprisingly, Executive Order 9980 prompted negative reactions from many federal officials, particularly throughout the South. Truman historians McCoy and Ruetten noted the mixed reaction prompted by the executive order. "Obviously, the program would take time to implement; and there would be variances in departmental operating procedures, although at least eighteen agencies had established such procedures by the end of the year. There were also outright refusals to obey the presidential order. On September 17, for example, Mortimer Jordan, Collector of Internal Revenue in Alabama, informed Secretary of the Treasury John Snyder that he had no intention of following the directive. Jordan was subsequently removed."[23]

While Executive Order 9980 immediately opened up federal employment opportunities—and federal "whites only" cafeterias—to black Americans, Truman's more profound civil rights bombshell, dropped on July 26, 1948, was his issuance of Executive Order 9981, which integrated the vast, segregated armed services. With this executive order, Truman set into motion the integration of the black soldiers and sailors into the then overwhelmingly white man's armed services of the United States.[24] While the massive military buildup triggered by the Korean War was still two years off, the armed services in 1948 remained a major employer in the U.S. postwar economy, which was still trying to absorb and employ the twelve million veterans who had returned after V-J Day and V-E Day.

When asked about the impact of Executive Order 9981, Dr. Height, the respected civil rights advocate who served for four decades as the president of the NCNW, explained, "Harry Truman's integration of the armed services represented the most significant institutional advance for the civil rights of black Americans since President Lincoln issued the Emancipation Proclamation." Height, who succeeded civil rights pioneer Mary McLeod Bethune at the council, recalled how Truman's decisive take-charge action in integrating the military provided a much-needed example for U.S. corporate leaders, who often were reluctant to force integration of their employees in the same bold manner that the commander in chief had used in integrating the U.S. military.[25]

In issuing Executive Order 9981—clearly one of the most controversial actions of his presidency—Harry Truman reiterated his belief that the country's democratic principles had to be extended to the armed services. "It is essential that there be maintained in the armed services of the United States the highest standards of democracy, with equality of treatment and opportunity for all those who serve in our country's defense."[26] As commander in chief and, importantly, as a World War I veteran who observed firsthand the high degree of sacrifice rendered by America's fighting men, President Truman appreciated the overarching need for equality within the fighting units. Moreover, based on the compelling statistics provided by his fifteen-member Committee on Civil Rights in their October 1947 report, Truman had ample documentation of how profoundly segregated the various branches of the U.S. military remained in 1948. The statistics contained in the committee's report confirmed that all branches of the military had actively pursued unspoken policies that kept black Americans largely relegated to menial jobs. For example, in the Marine Corps in 1946, the report noted that blacks could only enlist in the stewards' branch. In the U.S. Army, the committee reported that there was a ceiling that limited "Negro personnel to 10% of the total strength of the service," and only one black in seventy was a commissioned officer in 1946, compared to a ratio of one white commissioned officer for every seven enlisted white men. Likewise, racially based employment ceilings existed in the U.S. Navy and the Coast Guard, with black Americans making up only 4.4 percent of the U.S. Navy and 4.2 percent of the Coast Guard in 1946.[27]

With his issuance of Executive Order 9981, President Truman ordered his military leaders, many of whom came from privileged and often Southern backgrounds, immediately to begin to integrate all service branches. As a former army officer who was familiar with crowded military barracks and transport ships, Truman knew that the executive order would cause consternation throughout the upper echelons of the military. However, as commander in chief, he must have been stunned by the public outburst from four-star General Omar Bradley, Truman's military chief of staff and one of the nation's most beloved World War II heroes. The *Washington Post* reported in a front-page article on July 28, 1948, that General Bradley publicly expressed his opposition to Executive Order 9981 by declaring, "The Army is not out to make any social reforms. The Army will put men of different races in different companies. It will change that policy when the Nation as a whole changes it."[28]

On the following day, the *Washington Post* reported Walter White's angry reaction to General Bradley's public refusal to adhere to the president's unequivocal mandate in Executive Order 9981. "This statement by the Chief of Staff less than 24 hours after the Commander in Chief of the Army, Navy and Air Force had issued an executive order to eliminate racial discrimination and inequality in the armed services is unbelievable. It is another illustration of how men who have been isolated in the Army for many years from contact with the outside world are unable to understand or even be aware of the growth of enlightened public opinion."[29]

General Bradley subsequently apologized to his commander in chief—who awarded Bradley his fifth star in 1950—but the general's public tantrum was a reliable indication of the firestorm that Truman's issuance of Executive Order 9981 created throughout the elitist leadership of the U.S. military.[30] Echoing General Bradley's spontaneous public outcry, Southern politicians also quickly voiced their public opposition to the order. In a front-page story in the July 27 edition of the *New York Times,* political journalist Anthony Leviero reported that Executive Orders 9980 and 9981 "were expected to have a thunderbolt effect on the already highly charged political situation in the Deep South, a situation which is expected to be aggravated further . . . when Mr. Truman makes his omnibus call on Congress for action. The message . . . is expected to go down the line for his ten-point civil rights program, which last February started the deep fissures in the Democratic party."[31]

While Truman anticipated the concerns of military leaders who felt that Executive Order 9981 might adversely impact the morale of the segregated armed services, the president nonetheless ordered that the integration be accomplished as soon as possible. "It is hereby declared to be the policy of the President that there shall be equality of treatment and opportunity for all persons in the armed services without regard to race, color, religion or national origin. This policy shall be put into effect as rapidly as possible, having due regard to the time required to effectuate any necessary changes without impairing efficiency or morale."[32]

Using a procedural vehicle similar to the commission that had been mandated in Executive Order 9980, Executive Order 9981 created a special seven-member committee that was empowered to ensure that the integration of the massive U.S. military would become a reality in the near term. Modeling this new committee's membership after the racially diverse makeup of the President's Committee on Civil Rights of 1946, Truman named a high-powered, multiracial committee of seven men to the President's Committee on Equality of Treatment and Opportunity in the Armed Services. The seven-member committee, which later became known as the Fahy committee, was chaired by the former solicitor general of the United States, Charles Fahy, and included two respected black leaders, Lester Granger, the executive secretary of the Urban League and editor John H. Sengstacke.

Truman's appointment of John Sengstacke to the Fahy committee was particularly noteworthy because Sengstacke, as editor of the *Chicago Defender,* was an activist who enjoyed widespread credibility amongst the newspaper's black subscribers. During the 1940s, Sengstacke had become a powerful force in the black American community, where his *Chicago Defender* informed a million readers each week. Under Sengstacke's forceful leadership, the *Defender* became a popular editorial force throughout the country, advocating the rights of black citizens, particularly in the U.S. military. While only thirty-five years old in 1948 when he was tapped by President Truman to serve on the committee, John Sengstacke enjoyed enormous influence within the African American press. In 1940, Sengstacke had formed the Negro Newspaper Publishers Association, which would elect him as its president five times. Truman's appointment of an outspoken man of Sengstacke's talents, energy, and influence within the African American community added further credibility to the president's actions in issuing Executive Order 9981. For military leaders in the United States who were frequently harangued by the *Defender*'s editorials during the war years, Sengstacke's appointment to the Fahy committee was sobering additional proof of Harry Truman's deep commitment to integrating the military.

John Sengstacke publicly acknowledged Truman's genuine commitment to civil rights reform by honoring him with the Robert S. Abbott Memorial Award in a ceremony on May 25, 1949. In view of Sengstacke's harsh editorial criticism of the segregated U.S. military throughout the 1940s, it was significant that the publisher of the *Chicago Defender* would honor Commander-in-Chief Harry Truman for his dedication to the fight for equality for all black Americans.[33]

When reflecting on the president's rationale for issuing Executive Order 9981, Clark Clifford knew from his unguarded conversations with the former

Captain Truman that the president was intensely troubled by the corrupting influence of continued segregation within all branches of the military. Clifford, a former naval officer, recalled in his autobiography,

> President Truman believed segregation in the armed forces undermined American values and acted against the nation's best interests. He thought it was outrageous that men could be asked to die for their country but not be allowed to fight in the same units because of their color. He knew that in the military, where arguments over equipment and privileges were a way of life, white soldiers inevitably took precedence over blacks.
>
> I had seen the effects of segregation in the Navy. Discrimination went far beyond anything that could be imagined today; I thought the Navy at times resembled a Southern plantation that had somehow escaped the Civil War. Blacks swabbed the decks, shined shoes, did the cooking, washed the dishes, and served the food. Virtually no other jobs were open to them. The Army, after establishing a postwar board of inquiry into the "utilization of Negro manpower," had established a quota for black Americans in the Army of 10 percent—a policy Army leaders actually thought of as progressive. They trained with white troops but lived in segregated barracks, shopped at segregated stores, rode on segregated trains, and served in separate units.[34]

The genuineness of Truman's commitment to the intent of Executive Order 9981 is further evidenced by Harry Truman's less-public actions to ensure that U.S. military leaders were moving rapidly and forcefully to integrate all branches of the armed services. At a January 12, 1949, meeting called by the president for his Joint Chiefs of Staff, Harry Truman, in typically blunt language, told the recently named secretary of the air force, Stuart Symington, and the other military secretaries, "I want concrete results—that's what I'm after—not publicity on it. I want the job done."[35] Reflecting on that meeting fifty years later, James Symington, the son of the late Senator Stuart Symington, recalled his patrician father's admiration for Harry Truman's stubborn determination to see the armed services of the United States integrated *now*.[36]

For Air Force Secretary Symington, integration had been a way of life for his privileged family decades before Truman issued Executive Order 9981. In fact, as a child growing up in Baltimore at the turn of the twentieth century, young Stuart Symington observed his mother, Emily Harrison Symington, as she provided food and shelter for needy freedmen and their families living in Baltimore. As a young industrialist, Stuart Symington moved to St. Louis, Missouri, in 1938, where he assumed the presidency of Emerson Electric—a company whose professional work force Symington integrated prior to World War II, well before Executive Order 9981 was issued. For Stuart Symington, it was particularly gratifying to see his fellow Missourian Harry Truman advance the civil rights of black airmen in a U.S. military establishment that had, until Truman's issuance of Executive Order 9981, generally relegated black servicemen to a demeaning secondary status.[37]

Symington's commitment to a fully integrated air force was noteworthy amongst his often less committed peers who held leadership positions in other branches of the vast post–World War II military infrastructure. In the army, serious anti-integration sentiment was still evident in the early days of the Korean War in a meeting between NAACP counsel Thurgood Marshall and a reluctant General Douglas MacArthur. Their meeting in Tokyo in early 1951 took place only after Marshall personally petitioned President Truman. Truman agreed to facilitate a meeting with MacArthur. Following his discussion with MacArthur, Marshall was convinced that the general was a racist whose views adversely affected the treatment of black Americans serving under him in the Korean War.[38] By contrast, the air force under Stuart Symington tolerated no delay in immediate integration following Truman's issuance of Executive Order 9981. Symington's son, James, a former member of Congress, recalled his father's no-nonsense approach fifty years earlier when integrating the air force—an approach that was directly conveyed to the leadership within the air force when Symington called his senior staff together and said, "We're going to integrate the air force now—okay, let's go do it."[39]

Although other military leaders in the Truman administration were less enthusiastic than Symington about integration, they were nonetheless subjected to the intensive oversight of the seven-member Fahy committee as it fashioned its final report, *Freedom to Serve*. The Fahy committee's report, submitted to President Truman on May 22, 1950, confirmed the complex problems triggered by Truman's Executive Order 9981.[40] In formally accepting the Fahy committee's report, President Truman issued a statement that praised the committee members for

> working quietly to find ways and means to bring about true equality of opportunity for everyone in military service.
>
> I have followed its work closely, and I know that it has probed deeply into the problem, which is not a simple one, and has been careful to keep uppermost the need for military efficiency.

As the Committee explored personnel practices in the Armed Services, the members of the staff worked in the closest possible consultation with the Army, the Navy and the Air Force. In fact, the consultation was so close and continuous that the Committee's recommendations grew naturally out of the joint discussions. The Services have accepted all of the Committee's recommendations.

It is, therefore, with a great deal of confidence that I learn from the Committee that the present programs of the three Services are designed to accomplish the objectives of the President; and that as these programs are carried out, there will be, within the reasonably near future, equality of treatment and opportunity for all persons in the Armed Services, with a consequent improvement in military efficiency.[41]

For future black servicemen and -women, Executive Order 9981 represented a monumental step forward that never would have occurred if President Truman had sought the approval of the Eightieth Congress. Significantly, Executive Order 9981 created a profoundly different and open legal environment in the rigidly segregated U.S. military of 1948, and this altered environment provided a workplace in which brilliant African Americans, such as General Colin Powell, could begin realistically to hope to assume top leadership positions well before the end of the twentieth century.

Clark Clifford, who helped draft Executive Order 9981 and who later served as President Johnson's secretary of defense, believed that this landmark action by Harry Truman paved the way for General Powell to become President George Bush's chairman of the Joint Chiefs of Staff in 1989. Executive Order 9981

was a milestone in American history, similar to Jackie Robinson breaking the color barrier in baseball the previous year. . . . That point was illustrated in the most dramatic fashion when General Powell became Chairman of the Joint Chiefs of Staff in 1989. Powell had an outstanding thirty-one-year career in the Army, with service in Vietnam, Korea, West Germany, and the White House (where he was National Security Assistant to President Reagan). A natural leader and a man of great intelligence and strength, Powell was ideally qualified to be the top military officer in the U.S. He also happened to have been born in Harlem, the son of black immigrant laborers in Manhattan's garment district. As I watched him standing next to President Bush on the day of his appointment, I thought back to 1948, and another President who had ignored words of caution from many of his advisers and the Pentagon itself because he felt that it was time to take action. I could not avoid a feeling of pride that the long road started by President Truman had reached if not its end, an important new plateau.[42]

In 1948, Clifford's "plateau" was a long way off in view of the segregationist mind-set that was pervasive in the military's infrastructure. For the black service-men traveling from New York to Washington who were routinely denied access to restaurants, motels, and even restroom facilities, Truman's integration of the armed services was profoundly important—and profoundly disconcerting to many whites, who realized that their sons, brothers, and husbands would now be sharing all of the country's military facilities with blacks. Whether assigned to duty on board navy or Coast Guard vessels or on army, air force, or Marine bases throughout the world, black and white servicemen would now work and live side by side as equals.

For African American leaders like Dr. Height, Truman's issuance of Executive Order 9981 triggered a deep cultural change in the country. "It was the seminal event in regards to eliminating institutional racism in America in 1948—and because the president took total control over the military establishment with his issuance of the executive order integrating the U.S. armed services, the president provided an example for enlightened civil rights leadership in the corporate community."[43]

As Height noted, in 1948, racism was institutionalized throughout much of the United States. While segregated housing, eating, and restroom facilities were commonplace and a generally accepted way of life in the South, these trappings of racism could often be found in the North as well, including in Washington, D.C. Proof of the segregationist attitude that dominated Washington during this era was reflected in a *Washington Post* article on January 5, 1947, which reported on the 83-to-2 vote by the Federation of Citizens Association in Washington "to accept a special committee report favoring separation of the races as the most logical relationship at the present time. This stand was aimed against a recent race relations survey which called for an end to 'arbitrary segregation.'"[44] The *Post* article went on to confirm that the nearly unanimous vote of the prestigious Federation of Citizens Association in the nation's capital reflected the Federation's view that "changes [in a segregated society] . . . cannot be brought about by excited demagogues, nor drastic action." The *Post* also reported that, on January 4, 1947, during the federation's "discussion, two other organizations came under fire as working against the best interests of the community. They were the Washington Urban League and the Washington Housing Association."

For many ordinary residents of the rigidly segregated nation's capital, as well as for citizens throughout the segregated Southern states, the reaction to Executive Order 9981 was prompt and often harsh. Almost immediately after July 26, 1948, Harry Truman was inundated with letters and telegrams of protest from angry citizens around the country. An indication of the widespread vitriolic reaction to Executive Order 9981 and Truman's broader civil rights plan was contained in a telegram the president received on his campaign train on September 30, 1948, from citizen Howard Uriah Omohundro:

PRES HARRY S TRUMAN=
=THE PRESIDENTIAL TRAIN DUE AM 30TH STL=

YOU AND YOUR CIVIL RIGHTS HAS [*sic*] COST YOU THE ELECTION[.] I HAVE ALWAYS VOTED FOR A DEMOCRAT NOW I AM VOTING FOR THURMAN [*sic*]. WHY DON'T YOU KNOW THAT THE SOUTHERN MAN WILL NOT TOLERATE A NEGRO LOVER[?] HARRY YOUR [*sic*] THROUGH. YOU'VE DONE NOTHING SINCE YOU'VE BEEN IN THERE BUT TRY TO PUT MY DAUGHTER IN THE SAME CATEGORY AS A SOUTHERN NEGRO. I'LL BE GLAD WHEN NOVEMBER FOURTH [*sic*] COMES SO I CAN PROTEST YOU OUT OF THE WHITEHOUSE [*sic*]. YOU'LL NEVER NEVER [*sic*] AGAIN BE RESPECTED IN THE SOUTH. WE SOUTHERN MEN ARE VERY EASY TO GET ALONG WITH WHEN WE LIKE [*sic*]. I'LL CONTINUE VOTING DEMOCRAT BUT I'LL VOTE FOR THURMAN [*sic*] TO PROTEST. YOU WON'T BE BACK IN WASHINGTON AFTER JANUARY. YOU SHOULD READ THE HISTORY ABOUT THE SOUTHERN PEOPLE. IF YOU HAVEN'T READ ABOUT THEM WELL. IF YOU GO ANY FURTHER SOUTH YOU'LL HELP DEWEY. I REPEAT WE SOUTHERN MEN DON'T LIKE YOUR CIVIL RIGHTS. PERSONALLY I AM VERY BROADMINDED BUT I HAVE SOME DECENCY=

HOWARD URIAH OMOHUNDRO=[45]

Not all of the public reaction to Executive Order 9981 was negative. For civil rights advocate Sadie Tanner Alexander, who had served as one of the fifteen members of the president's multiracial Committee on Civil Rights, President Truman's Executive Order 9981 was exactly what she and the other members of the Civil Rights Committee had recommended. In her view, Truman's actions were so momentous that this leading black American woman issued the following statement to the Associated Negro Press (ANP):

The frame work of a democratic army has been established by President Truman's Executive Order. Its realization depends upon the people of

America using their power to secure the appointment of and action by a
Committee that recognizes the Army as a living symbol of Democracy
and not dissipating our strength in arguments as to whether the President
intended by decreeing equality in the Armed Services to eliminate segregation as recommended in the Report of the President's Committee on
Civil Rights. I am convinced that the President has as his purpose an army
representative of our great American heritage of equality.[46]

Alexander was a tough-minded woman who was rightfully skeptical about
political rhetoric not backed up with definitive presidential action. It was both
remarkable and gratifying to her and to the other members of the President's
Committee on Civil Rights that their recommendation of October 29, 1947—
that the U.S. military be integrated—became a reality less than a year after they
completed their report. However, while Sadie Alexander rejoiced, many
Democratic Party leaders anguished about the fact that the president integrated
the military at the most politically precarious time, on July 26, 1948—just three
months before Harry Truman would need every vote he could muster to be
elected president on November 2, 1948.

Another black leader who applauded President Truman's issuance of
Executive Order 9981 was Percy Sutton. More than fifty years after its issuance,
Sutton recalled with clarity how Truman immediately changed the racial landscape within the armed services. Even though Sutton had served with distinction in a segregated military during World War II, in Italy and North Africa, he
volunteered for a second tour of duty when the Korean War broke out during
Truman's second term. In the intervening years, between 1945 and 1950, Sutton
had used his time well, completing his law school studies at Brooklyn Law School
while also working on civil rights reform, including mobilizing the black vote in
the 1948 campaign. Equipped with a law degree in 1950, Sutton entered an
entirely different U.S. military—an integrated service in which African Americans
were put in leadership positions with jurisdiction over both white and black servicemen. In a 1999 interview, when asked if there was a noticeable difference in
the military, as a black American, from 1945 to 1950, Sutton confirmed that it was
"dramatically different."[47]

The dramatic difference that Percy Sutton experienced in Truman's integrated armed forces was evident in 1950 by the assignment that young attorney
Sutton received as chief legal officer at the Andrews Air Force Base outside of the
nation's capital. And Sutton's appointment was no anomaly; his fellow officers
at Andrews included a black dental officer and a black medical officer. It was

indeed a dramatically different armed services by the early 1950s: African Americans were finally allowed to serve as officers in positions of authority.

When Harry Truman issued Executive Order 9981 on July 26, 1948, he brought about this profound structural change—structural change that impacted African Americans throughout the United States and at U.S. military installations around the globe. The integrated military that Percy Sutton and his fellow black officers experienced at Andrews Air Force Base in the early 1950s became the norm—and years later, because of Truman's politically perilous actions on Turnip Day 1948, the next generation of black officers would include such brilliant military leaders as General Colin Powell.

Truman's audacity on Turnip Day made July 26, 1948, unquestionably the most memorable day of the predictably unproductive special Turnip Day congressional session. And while it was unproductive from a legislative standpoint, the special congressional session provided a dramatic media stage for candidate Truman to remind black Americans that he, not the GOP-led Congress, was the one who delivered on civil rights reform. Having demonstrated once again that the Republican Congress was a do-nothing body, candidate Truman returned to Independence, Missouri, where he would spend a few weeks enjoying the company of his wife, Bess, and their daughter, Margaret, before the 1948 presidential campaign started in earnest on Labor Day weekend.

As Truman headed west to his beloved Independence, politicians of both parties knew that regardless of who won the White House in November, things would never be the same in the United States. By virtue of Truman's actions on July 26, 1948, the country's racial landscape was suddenly and permanently altered. Taken collectively, Executive Orders 9980 and 9981 guaranteed for the first time in American history equality of opportunity for all workers in the federal government. As Dr. Height noted, Harry Truman had effectively assaulted the institution of racism in the United States as it had not been attacked since Abraham Lincoln issued the Emancipation Proclamation.

CHAPTER NINE

The Great "Comeback" Campaign and Truman's Harlem Speech: October 29, 1948

Our determination to attain the goal of equal rights and equal opportunity
must be resolute and unwavering. For my part, I intend to keep moving
toward this goal with every ounce of strength and determination that I have.
—HST, October 29, 1948

When the special Turnip Day session of the Eightieth Congress concluded in early August 1948, weary legislators from both parties left the nation's capital wilted from Washington's oppressive heat and humidity; they also left convinced that Harry Truman would be moving out of the White House by the time the Eighty-first Congress convened in January 1949.

Even though candidate Truman had effectively used the Turnip session to publicly slam the do-nothing GOP leadership of Congress, Truman's presidential campaign was bogged down at the outset with a host of nearly fatal problems, not the least of which was the serious financial crisis that confronted the Truman forces.[1] In contrast to the flush and confident Dewey campaign, which enjoyed the active support of Wall Street and big business across the country, Truman's campaign was viewed by journalists and political pundits as a losing proposition. In politics, then and now, smart money goes to the likely winner; and in the 1948 presidential race, the odds-on favorite was Governor Thomas Dewey of New York. This gloomy prognosis was confirmed in an October 11, 1948, *Newsweek* poll of the nation's fifty leading publishers—all of whom predicted that Dewey would win the White House on election day, November 2, 1948.[2]

Most of Truman's closest friends and advisers also thought he would lose in November—a loss that was predictable in view of his stubborn refusal to equivocate on his pledge to bring about major, federally enforced civil rights reform.

That most of Truman's close friends thought his campaign was doomed was confirmed by Stuart Symington, Truman's first secretary of the air force. In a May 29, 1981, oral history provided to the Truman Library, then-Senator Stuart Symington (D-Mo.) admitted, "I honestly did not think he would win. . . . I remember only two of my friends who believed strongly that he would win; Clark Clifford and Bob Hannegan."[3]

While most around him—and the national press—expected the president to lose his first presidential campaign—Truman was confident of victory. His determination to win, despite the devastating *Newsweek* poll of October 11, was witnessed by his aide Clark Clifford, who traveled by train across the United States with the president on his nonstop campaign. In his autobiography, Clifford shared his firsthand observations of President Truman's reaction to the sobering results of the *Newsweek* poll.

Newsweek magazine decided to query fifty of the leading political journalists in America, and run the results in their October 11 issue. We awaited this article anxiously, since it included some of journalism's brightest names, men like columnists Marquis Childs of *The St. Louis Post-Dispatch,* Arthur Krock of *The New York Times,* and Raymond Moley, former New Dealer turned *Newsweek* columnist.

Early on the morning that the issue of *Newsweek* was due on newsstands, I slipped off the train at the first stop and found it. I opened the issue and found a big black headline: ELECTION FORECAST: 50 POLITICAL EXPERTS PREDICT A GOP SWEEP. That Dewey would be favored hardly surprised me, but the shocker was the vote: fifty to *nothing*. Not even one pundit out of fifty was willing to buck conventional wisdom and predict a Truman victory.

I had to pass through the President's car to get back to my own cabin. He was sitting on a sofa reading a newspaper, so I tucked *Newsweek* into my jacket and tried to slip by, but he stopped me. "What does it say, Clark?" he asked.

"What does what say?" I said, trying to look innocent.

"What have you got under your coat, Clark?"

"Nothing, Mr. President."

"Clark. I saw you get off the train just now and I think that you went in there to see if they had a newsstand with a copy of *Newsweek*. And I think maybe you have it under your coat."

I hated to be the bearer of bad news. Reluctantly I handed it over.

He looked at the article for a while, and then handed the magazine back to me, seemingly unperturbed. "Don't worry about that poll, Clark," he said. "I know every one of those fifty fellows, and not one of them has enough sense to pound sand into a rathole."[4]

Notwithstanding the dismal prospects of his winning on election day, Truman remained a steady optimist throughout his vigorous eight-week campaign, which officially started with a Labor Day speech in Detroit, Michigan. Traveling nearly thirty-one thousand miles on the Ferdinand Magellan, his campaign train, Truman relentlessly attacked the GOP-led Eightieth Congress at nearly every train station as he crisscrossed the United States.[5] According to George Elsey, who traveled aboard the train with Truman as his prolific speechwriter, Truman was determined to get to the people directly at the local level; to do this, Truman relied each day on a variety of hard-hitting, often pithy speeches that kept the press corps scrambling to file the new stories emanating from Truman's 142-ton, specially equipped Pullman train car.[6] Elsey later explained,

Each day the President's itinerary, as developed, would call for eight, ten, twelve, sometimes as many as fifteen simple, rear platform or whistlestop speeches, in addition to one major address. For the dozen, plus or minus a couple, whistlestop speeches, we would have, we would propose that the President speak on a different topic at each of the Whistlestop speeches so that during the course of a day he would have touched on most of the issues of the campaign in this simple whistlestopping informal off-the-cuff manner. Further, that he not talk on the same subject more than once in any one day and that insofar as was possible to do so we would try to pick a whistlestop topic that was pretty close to the hearts of the people in the community where we were going to be. . . . By the time that we set out on our first cross country whistlestop campaign tour, September 17, 1948, I was armed with reference material on every community we were going to visit and some background about the town, about the history of it, about the leading personalities, about the congressional incumbent, whether he was Republican or Democrat made no difference, and his challenger of the other party, of course.[7]

With this campaign format in place, Truman was at his pugnacious best as he crisscrossed the nation's railways and hammered away at the do-nothing Republican Congress—a Congress that he constantly blamed for local problems.

When focusing on local problems, Truman was particularly effective because he could personally relate to any audience with empathy based on his own varied life experiences. Whether Truman's audience was predominantly made up of farmers, merchants, or veterans, he could genuinely touch a responsive chord with voters because, at some point in his long life, citizen Truman had experienced firsthand the vagaries of life on a farm, financial survival as a small-town merchant, and human survival as a World War I veteran.

Truman's homespun campaign speeches, sometimes just a few minutes in length, were typically delivered from the rear platform of the Ferdinand Magellan. Even when there were fifteen whistle-stops in a given day, Truman varied his message at each stop, thereby creating "news" for reporters at every stop along the campaign trail. Ironically, even though the traveling press corps generally believed Truman would lose to Dewey on November 2, 1948, Elsey reported on the keen attentiveness of the traveling press corps and the daily media frenzy that resulted from Truman's varied campaign messages.

> By giving him a different subject at each of the whistlestops during the course of the day, he intrigued the newsmen. The newspapermen would pile off the train and go back because they wouldn't know what the President was going to say next and they had to listen to him. And they did listen to him. And all during each of the whistlestop days there would be a continuous flow of traffic from the newsmen and the news media off the train. So, by the time the story was written in the *New York Times* the next day or what have you, the story wouldn't be just about one speech Truman made but would have comments on a half a dozen subjects that he'd covered.[8]

While Truman focused on the dominant local problems confronting voters along the campaign trail, his itinerary during the 1948 campaign deliberately omitted a big chunk of the South—a South that had supported FDR four times but that would fragment its traditional Democratic vote in 1948 because of Truman's civil rights crusade. Thus, because of the predictably harsh reception that Truman would receive there, and because of severe financial constraints facing the Truman presidential campaign, the Ferdinand Magellan's route took the president primarily to urban voters in the industrial states of the North and Midwest, to rural voters throughout the farm belt, and to big electoral vote states, such as California and Texas.[9]

On September 27, 1948—a typical day during the president's four-day campaign swing through Texas—Truman, a notorious early riser, gave new meaning to that term when he started the day in San Marcos at 6:40 A.M. with a brief campaign speech from the rear platform of the Ferdinand Magellan. Taking note of the hearty crowd of early well-wishers from San Marcos, President Truman said,

> It certainly is a pleasure to see so many people up so early in San Marcos. . . .
>
> I hope, I sincerely hope, that every one of you will study the issues in this campaign, and I'm sure that—as my friend down here said—99 percent of you will vote the right way.
>
> I can't tell you how very much I appreciate this turnout at this time of day. It's a wonderful thing that you want to meet your President bad enough to get up before breakfast.
>
> I'm sorry that my family, my wife and daughter, do not get up so early. They had a terrific day yesterday and the day before, and the day before that, and I'm so sorry to say I can't introduce them to you because they're not up.
>
> But I do thank you most sincerely for the turnout.[10]

At 7:35 A.M., the president joined Governor Beauford Halbert Jester and city officials in Austin, Texas, the state capital, where Truman reminded voters that he had appointed Texan Tom Clark as attorney general of the United States. Truman also used his Austin speech to remind voters of his Texas relatives— "cousins and uncles and aunts." But the core of the president's Austin speech— and the theme of most of Truman's spirited campaign speeches from Labor Day until the Harlem civil rights address in the final days of the campaign—was the omissions of the do-nothing Republican-led Congress.[11]

To the Austin voters gathered around the platform of the massive Ferdinand Magellan early that morning, the blunt-speaking president hit a nerve when he warned Texas voters,

> This Republican 80th "do-nothing" Congress would like to turn the Colorado River and its power projects over to the public utilities so they could cut your throat with prices if they had a chance. They are trying to do that all over the West, in Texas and everywhere else.
>
> Now, you can't afford, you simply can't afford to renew the 80th Congress.
>
> Now, these gentlemen who head the Republican Party are trying their best to direct your attention away from the issues in this campaign.

They want to talk about home and mother and what a beautiful country this is. They don't want you to get interested in this campaign for the simple reason that the Democrats are right and they're wrong, and that's the reason we're going to win.

I have only one request to make of you—and I don't think I have to make that request in this district of Texas. I want you, on election day, to get up as early as you did this morning and go to the polls and vote a straight Democratic ticket—Governor and Senator and President and everything else—and then the empire of Texas and the Great Republic of the United States will be in safe hands for another 4 years, and I won't have to be worried by the housing problem—I'll still live in the White House.[12]

Truman's remarks in Austin, echoed throughout his campaign swing through Texas, are noteworthy for two reasons. First, they reflect the political toughness of the president's campaign rhetoric—frank, yet simple rhetoric that made it clear what Republicans would do if reelected to a leadership role in the Eighty-first Congress. Truman's warning that Republicans would "cut your throat with prices if they had a chance" was an ominous threat that was characteristic of Truman campaign speeches. In an earlier speech to farmers on September 18, in Dexter, Iowa, Truman played equally tough political hardball when he accused the GOP-led Eightieth Congress of sticking "a pitchfork in the backs" of America's farmers.

Second, Truman's Austin comments urging his audience to get up early on election day so that they could vote a straight Democratic ticket are significant because the Democratic senatorial candidate, Congressman Lyndon B. Johnson, was traveling throughout Texas telling voters that he vigorously opposed President Truman's civil rights program. Washington political journalists Rowland Evans and Robert Novak in their biography, *Lyndon B. Johnson*, quote Congressman Johnson in his notoriously close 1948 senatorial campaign as stating publicly, "My feelings are well known in my district and in Washington. And Harry Truman knows I am against him on this [civil rights] program. I just don't think Congress should try to cram his program down the throats of Southern states."[13] Despite Johnson's public opposition to the president's civil rights program, Truman—the party's standard-bearer—repeatedly urged Texas voters to elect Johnson to the Senate—an election that occurred after a razor-slim eighty-seven-vote Democratic Party primary victory that would forever tag him as "Landslide Lyndon."

Notwithstanding tensions over his civil rights position with fellow Texas Democrats like Congressman Johnson, carrying Texas was an important goal for Truman—a goal that he aggressively sought throughout the balance of the day as he roared on through Texas, from Austin to Georgetown, from Temple to Waco, from Hillsboro to Fort Worth, and from Grand Prairie to Dallas. In Dallas, the president left the train and made a major campaign address at 4:30 P.M. in Rebel Stadium, where he told a multiracial audience,

> I came to Texas because I am engaged in one of the toughest political fights with which this country has ever been faced, and I wanted the people of Texas and the people of California and the people of all the States in the Union to understand just exactly what that fight means. . . . The interests in this campaign go far beyond the election. They go to the very core of American life. . . . The Democratic Party stands for the people. . . . The Republican Party is concerned with the rights of the selfish and wealthy interests, and they demonstrate this by taking the fight of the privileged few against the people every time they get a chance. . . . I wish I had time to read you the record of that good-for-nothing, "do-nothing" Republican 80th Congress.[14]

In typical Truman campaign polemics, he told voters in Dallas that it wasn't just a Republican versus Democratic contest in which they would cast their vote on November 2, 1948; it was an election about the very "core of America," its values and future. Incredibly, Truman's willingness to address a multiracial audience in Rebel Stadium—a stadium named to honor Southern soldiers of the Civil War—was such a significant, precedent-setting event that it prompted front-page attention in the September 28, 1948, edition of the *Dallas Morning News*. The *Morning News* reported that "President Harry S. Truman stood just back of the pitcher's box . . . and fired three political fast balls at his Republican opponents. . . . The crowd had begun to gather before noon. By the time the President arrived, the stands were full. . . . There was a heavy sprinkling of Negroes, and the crowd was not segregated. Night Chief Flay Nelson of the police department made a rough guess that the Negroes made up 30 per cent of the audience."[15]

While Truman's multiracial Dallas audience generated front-page news in Texas, African Americans were welcomed everywhere along the Truman campaign trail. General Donald Dawson, who handled the advance work for Truman from September 1, 1948, through election day, noted that the integrated audience in Rebel Stadium on September 27, 1948, was the norm and not an anomaly for audiences to whom Truman personally carried his partisan message of hope. When later asked to confirm that the Dallas rally was integrated, General Dawson replied, "That's true, but all of our rallies were integrated from the standpoint that we welcomed the participation of everybody and discriminated against nobody."[16] General Dawson emphasized the fact that all of the Truman campaign events were open to all Americans, regardless of race. "We wanted everyone to hear Harry Truman's message and we never even thought of our audiences in terms of black or white. We knew that once the people heard directly from the president they'd vote with us on election day."[17]

While Dawson's boss insisted on a colorblind admissions policy for the campaign audiences, Truman's decision to address integrated audiences proved to be unpopular in the South, where Truman had burned all his political bridges with the racist Dixiecrats. Even though Truman wanted to attract every Southern vote to defeat Dewey, Truman risked the wrath of the voting South to do what he knew was right—and that included welcoming blacks to every Truman campaign event. For the Dixiecrats in Texas and throughout the South, Truman's civil rights program made him unacceptable, and their best hope was to throw the presidential election of 1948 into the House of Representatives where a compromise candidate might not support the dreaded federal civil rights program that was a core element of Truman's campaign.[18]

Truman's tireless campaign efforts were possible, in large part, because of his amazing physical stamina. Though most sixty-four-year-old men would have been exhausted after the rigorous day of campaigning that preceded the president's campaign speech in Dallas's Rebel Stadium, Truman delivered several more speeches and shook hundreds of additional hands before his day ended. From Dallas, the Ferdinand Magellan moved eastward to Greenville, Texas, for a brief 6:20 P.M. whistle-stop speech, then on to Bells, followed by a stop in Bonham.[19]

This exhausting Texas tour in late September, like much of Truman's 1948 campaign, exhibited not only Truman's physical endurance but more importantly his skill of connecting with voters. Truman had not been gifted with the rhetorical skills of FDR or John Kennedy, and presidential campaigning in 1948 had not yet become the broadcast media phenomenon that would compliment the impressive verbal skills of future presidents Ronald Reagan and Bill Clinton. Nonetheless, Truman had an engaging empathy, an honesty, and a basic decency that he personally conveyed to voters throughout the country. That sense of decency was evident during a brief stop in Waco, where the *Dallas Morning News* reported in its September 28, 1948, edition that the president was booed by a disgruntled voter who took offense when Truman graciously greeted and shook the hand of "a Negro woman" who walked across the rear platform of the Ferdinand Magellan to meet her president.[20] That Truman ignored the heckler and treated this woman exactly as he had other voters demonstrated Truman's basic decency as a candidate—a candidate who attacked the GOP mercilessly while retaining his basic common touch with voters.

Earlier in 1948, before he was the official standard-bearer of the Democratic Party, Truman had shown this same decency to another black woman, Alice Allison Dunnigan, a reporter for the ANP who was traveling with Truman as the first accredited black female reporter in the presidential press corps. During a visit to Cheyenne, Wyoming, as part of the fifteen-day, nine-thousand-mile trip on the Ferdinand Magellan she was grabbed by a racist military guard while walking with white reporters following the president in a parade. After hearing about this incident, the president "surprised" Dunnigan by stopping by her compartment on the train to inquire about her treatment on the trip. "When I answered affirmatively, he said, 'That's good. But if you have any further trouble let me know.' Needless to say that my ego was inflated by the thought that the president of the United States would show personal interest in an insignificant newspaperwoman, and would take time out to express this concern. This, to me, was a true indication of a great man."[21]

Truman's conduct in publicly greeting the black female supporter in Waco and in seeking privately to comfort Alice Dunnigan after the ugly incident in Cheyenne demonstrated Truman's public and private sensitivity to black Americans. That consistent concern and the president's impatience with those who would not abandon their antiquated racial bigotry was confirmed in a series of letters between Truman and the president's longtime friend from World War I, Ernest W. Roberts.

"Ernie" Roberts wrote to the president shortly before the 1948 campaign commenced to urge his Missouri friend to moderate his politically risky position on federal civil rights reform. Writing "Dear friend Harry" on the Saturday night following the end of the special congressional session, Roberts advised the president, "You can win the South with *out* the 'Equal Rights Bill' but you cannot win the South—*with* it. Just why?? Well You, Bess and Margaret, and shall I say, myself, are all Southerners and we have been raised with the Negros [*sic*] and we know the term 'Equal Rights'. Harry, let us let the South take care of the

Niggers, which they have done, and if the Niggers do not like the Southern treatment, let them come to Mrs. Roosevelt. . . . Harry, you are a Southerner and a D—— good one so liston [*sic*] to me. I can see, you do not talk domectic [*sic*] problems over with Bess. ????? You put equal rights in Independence and Bess will not live with you, will you Bess[?]"²²

Truman's August 18, 1948, letter responding to his lifelong friend, just weeks before the official start of the grueling presidential campaign, speaks volumes about Truman's personal views on segregation.

Dear Ernie:

I appreciated very much your letter of last Saturday night from Hotel Temple Square in the Mormon Capital.

I am going to send you a copy of the report of my Commission on Civil Rights and then if you still have that antebellum proslavery outlook, I'll be thoroughly disappointed in you.

The main difficulty with the South is that they are living eighty years behind the times and the sooner they come out of it the better it will be for the country and themselves. I am not asking for social equality, because no such thing exists, but I am asking for equality of opportunity for all human beings and, as long as I stay here, I am going to continue that fight. When the mob gangs can take four people out and shoot them in the back, and everybody in the country is acquainted with who did the shooting and nothing is done about it, that country is in a pretty bad fix from a law enforcement standpoint.

When a Mayor and a City Marshal can take a negro [*sic*] Sergeant off a bus in South Carolina, beat him up and put out one of his eyes, and nothing is done about it by the State Authorities, something is radically wrong with the system.

On the Louisiana and Arkansas Railway when coal burning locomotives were used, the negro firemen were the thing because it was a back-breaking job and a dirty one. As soon as they turned to oil as a fuel it became customary for people to take shots at the negro firemen and a number were murdered because it was thought that this was now a white-collar job and should go to a white man. I can't approve of such goings on and I shall never approve it, as long as I am here, as I told you before. I am going to try to remedy it and if that ends up in my failure to be reelected, that failure will be in a good cause.

I know you haven't thought this thing through and that you do not know the facts. I am happy, however, that you wrote me because it gives me a chance to tell you what the facts are.

Sincerely yours,
Harry S. Truman

[Note in longhand:] This is a personal & confidential communication and I hope you'll regard it that way—at least until I've made a public statement on the subject—as I expect to do *in the South.*

HST[23]

This letter, written more than two years after Sergeant Isaac Woodard was blinded by a racist sheriff in Batesburg, South Carolina, and after another veteran, George Dorsey, and his wife, Mae, and two of their friends were murdered by being shot more than sixty times during a racist mob attack in Walton County, Georgia, provides powerful proof of the continuing impact that racial violence directed at black veterans had on the president. The lasting impact of the horrendous racial abuse that President Truman wrote about to his friend was still evident more than fifty years after World War II. On June 1, 1999, the *New York Times* reported on a Memorial Day ceremony honoring army veteran Dorsey, whom Truman had referred to in his letter to Ernie Roberts. The *Times* noted, "Back in 1946, the [Dorsey] killings made national headlines and led to a six month investigation by the Federal Bureau of Investigation. In the end, a federal grand jury of 21 whites and 2 blacks listened to 100 hundred witnesses and came up with no indictments."[24] This incident and others like it clearly weighed heavily on the president, as is evident in his letter to Roberts. While written as a private communication, Truman's letter to his World War I friend is significant because it also confirms how the president was unwavering in his commitment to forcing federally mandated civil rights reform on the South—a South that the president accused of living "behind the times": "the sooner they come out of it the better it will be for the country and themselves."[25]

When he wrote this letter on August 18—just seventy-six days before election day—Truman had already ruptured the Democratic Party with his uncompromising stand on civil rights. In response to Truman's civil rights proposal, Southern Democrats had elected their own Dixiecrat presidential candidate, racist Governor Strom Thurmond. Yet despite this disquieting political development and its very serious implications for his chances of being elected for the first time to the White House, Harry Truman privately chided a beloved colleague from his World War I days about his unenlightened racist views.[26] Truman also made it clear to Roberts that he was "going to try to remedy it"—that is, work for equality for African Americans under the Constitution—even if it meant he would lose the election.[27]

Truman's letter to Roberts is also instructive on the issue of Truman's view of social equality for blacks. In blunt Trumanesque language, the president told his veteran friend that he was not demanding true social equality, "because no such thing exists." Truman was demanding "equality of opportunity for all human beings."[28] While modern readers may conclude that Truman was evidencing a seg-regationist attitude, it is important to note how rigidly segregated much of the country, including Washington, D.C., was in 1948. The report of the President's Civil Rights Committee documented the pervasive racism that reached far beyond the South, even into elitist colleges and universities of the North.[29] Thus Truman's view that social equality did not exist and would not exist for the foreseeable future is not surprising in view of the realities of the times.

In formulating an accurate view of how Truman felt about and related to African Americans during his life, particularly in his White House years, the first-hand observations of Alonzo Fields, White House chief butler, are illuminating. In his book, *My 21 Years in the White House,* Fields discusses his professional days at the White House from October 1931 through February 1953. Fields's insights about Truman provide an insider's personal view of a president who cared deeply about the well-being of those around him, regardless of their race. Thus while Truman expressed the view to Roberts that he was not talking about social equal-ity, Fields documents a consistent thread of egalitarian conduct on the part of Truman and his family when dealing with the blacks they met routinely within the privacy of the White House living quarters. For example, in acknowledging that neither President Herbert Hoover nor President Franklin Roosevelt took note of black servants in the White House, Fields recounts his obvious shock when President Truman introduced him to family members who visited the White House shortly after Truman suddenly became president on April 12, 1945.

> Shortly after the family moved into the White House the President's brother, Mr. Vivian Truman, came to visit. The first time he appeared in the dining room the President, before he took his seat, said, "Fields, this is my brother, Mr. Vivian Truman."
>
> This was something new for a President to acquaint a member of his family with servants. We were soon to meet all the Wallaces and Trumans in this manner. The President and Mrs. Truman knew each servant by

name and at any time a new man was taken into the dining room I would go along and say to the President and Mrs. Truman, "This is —— We are trying him out as a butler."

The President, if seated, would rise and shake hands and say, "Now don't be disturbed by me. You just do what Fields tells you and I know we will be glad to have you aboard." This would at once relieve the tension that faces any waiter or butler who had never been in the presence of the President before.[30]

In addition to reporting on Truman's personal graciousness in dealing with black employees while president, Fields wrote of his warm relations with Truman after both men had left the White House. Once again, his recollections are instructive because they show a man who obviously felt a personal bond to another man who had loyally served him during his often lonely days at the White House.

When [former] President Truman is in Boston I always go to call on him. I make no appointment. I merely find out what hotel he will be stopping at and his time of arrival and place myself in a position where he might see me. And he always does. He will call out to me amidst all the people he is with, "Hello there, Fields," and make his way to me and shake hands. Then he will say, "Come on up. I want to talk to you." I felt when he first came to Boston that he would expect to see me and would appreciate my sincere desire to see him.

I would not have dared to assume that President Roosevelt would expect to see me anywhere and recognize me in public. Of course it has been so long since I have seen President Hoover that I doubt that he would even remember my name.[31]

That Alonzo Fields was a black man was irrelevant to this former president who was reared six decades earlier in a rural Missouri environment where black people were definitely second-class citizens.

When reflecting on his relations with the three presidents whom he served, Fields also noted in his memoir that the populist Truman best understood him as a man—an assertion that provides further support for the conclusion that the thirty-third president's private and public attitude toward African Americans was consistently fair and caring.

So if the question is, "Which one of the Presidents did I understand and which one did I think understood me as a person?" I must say that the answer is President Truman. I always felt that he understood me as a man, not as a servant to be tolerated, and that I understood that he expected me to be a man, sincere in my duties and trying to do what is right at all times.

President Roosevelt was genial and warm but he left one feeling, as most aristocrats do, that they really do not understand one. As if to a less fortunate human being, they extend a charitable, human tolerance, but never permit the right to understand them.[32]

While the Fields–Truman relationship sheds light on the president's interpersonal, nonpublic dealings with African Americans, the men's relationship also provides evidence of Truman's belief that blacks should enjoy full economic equality of opportunity. Truman's belief, expressed privately to Ernie Roberts, that economic opportunity should be equally available to all Americans, black and white, is affirmed by the following note in Fields's memoir: "I want to express my deepest appreciation to former President Harry S. Truman for the encouragement he gave me when I told him that I was going to write a book about my experiences in the White House."[33]

Here a former black servant from the White House during a time when Washington, D.C., was a rigidly segregated city with "whites only" restrooms and drinking fountains publicly confirms that President Truman encouraged him to break into the ranks of the white male–dominated U.S. publishing world in the late 1950s. Mindful of that reality, author Alonzo Fields expressed his appreciation to Truman because he knew all too well how extraordinary it was for a black butler at the White House to become a bestselling author. For Truman, it was simple: Why shouldn't Alonzo Fields have his story told and profit from it, bringing added economic wherewithal to his family?

Another indication of Truman's basic openness and social comfort level with African Americans was provided by a Truman appointee, the chief judge of the Third Circuit Court of Appeals, William H. Hastie. Hastie, a respected black legal scholar and academician who earned degrees from Amherst College and Harvard Law School—schools that had been out of reach for Truman—described a very relaxed and approachable Truman when the two men spent several days together in February 1948 when the president visited then-Governor Hastie in the Virgin Islands. In describing his contacts with the president during Truman's three-day visit to the Virgin Islands, Judge Hastie stated,

I don't know how many hours I spent with the President during that period of time. Obviously at the times of his public appearances when he was driving around, I was at his side. He and I had numerous opportunities to talk both about the Virgin Islands' matters and socially, just the two of us. My regard for Harry Truman, both as a human being and as the head of our Government, grew tremendously during that three-day experience of being with him a great number of hours in an informal way where he relaxed and pretty obviously, to me, felt he could be Harry Truman the human being, and not have to be as reserved as the President, and as much on his guard as to what he said as he would ordinarily be.[34]

Based on Hastie's direct contact with Truman—both during their days together in the Virgin Islands and in subsequent dealings during the Truman presidency and when Truman was simply a citizen—Judge Hastie saw no evidence of a lack of genuine commitment on Truman's part to full equality for African Americans. Hastie was unequivocal in his belief that Truman really cared about the well-being of blacks. In his 1972 oral history, Hastie concluded,

There's no question in my mind that this was a deep personal commitment as distinguished from a political maneuver. This is not just an impression from talking with him. It's perfectly clear, I think, that many of his advisors counseled him against this [civil rights] position on the grounds that it would be politically catastrophic, that it would alienate the southern leadership and a lot of the southern electorate, and might well cost him re-election. I'm sure he went into [the 1948 campaign] with his eyes open, that there was danger in it. And it was largely because of that, as well as because of the way he had helped and supported me in the work of the Virgin Islands, that with the election coming up, during the summer of '48, I went up to Washington. I had asked for an appointment with him, and I told him that, as he knew, I had never participated in party politics, but it seemed to me that what he had done in this particular regard was of the greatest importance to the country, because I felt that once a President had taken the position that he did, both in endorsing the report of the [President's Civil Rights] Commission, and in the program that he sent to Congress, that no President thereafter would be able, that as a matter of political reality, to repudiate that, that a President might drag his feet, might not move vigorously, but that he had dramatically and in a very important way, taken new and higher ground for the Federal Government that would not be lost.[35]

Hastie knew that this ground gained in the civil rights area would pave the way for eventual social equality in some parts of the United States—but only after the full impact was felt from Truman's actions in integrating the U.S. armed services and pushing amicus briefs in the U.S. Supreme Court to end restrictive covenants and seriously erode *Plessy v. Ferguson's* separate-but-equal doctrine.[36] Truman was a realist about the long road to social equality in a racist America, and he knew that social equality would only derive from total equality of opportunity for black Americans.

While total equality for African Americans was Truman's ultimate goal, his immediate goal in the fall of 1948 was the White House. And despite pressure to temper his campaign comments on civil rights reform, Truman refused to back down. This stand was clear in the final days of the tumultuous 1948 presidential campaign—a campaign in which Truman continued to be viewed by the vast majority of the nation's press corps as the certain loser to the GOP candidate, Governor Thomas Dewey. Notwithstanding the press's gloomy prognosis of certain defeat, and despite political pressure on Truman not to exacerbate further the tensions with states' rights voters, the president put civil rights for black voters prominently at the center of his campaign with a rousing campaign visit to Harlem in New York on October 29, 1948.[37]

Speaking in Governor Dewey's political backyard just four days before the presidential election, Truman greeted an enthusiastic Harlem audience gathered at 3:50 P.M. in Dorrance Brooks Square in the heart of Harlem. After receiving the Franklin Roosevelt Award from Dr. C. Asapansa-Johnson, who headed the Interdenominational Ministers Alliance, the president delivered a comprehensive civil rights address that made it explicitly clear to the sixty-five thousand Harlem residents in his audience that Truman remained stubbornly committed to earning their full civil rights under the Constitution.[38]

For White House staffer Philleo Nash, drafting Truman's Harlem speech provided a rare opportunity to interface directly with President Truman. In his extensive oral history for the Truman Library, Nash recalled the meeting in which the president reviewed a final draft of the Harlem speech. The speech had undergone six revisions involving Truman counsel Clark Clifford and other White House aides senior to Nash.[39]

> So Clifford signaled to me that I should do the speaking so I just said, "Mr. President, I brought up a draft of a speech on civil rights for the Harlem rally."
> And he said, "Well, I've been waiting for a long time to get this taken

care of. We should have done it sooner." I didn't, of course, argue with that. He said, "Let's see what you've got." So he read it all the way through once without stopping, read it aloud, paragraph by paragraph. And when he got through he said, "Well, anybody who isn't for this, ought to have his head examined," I don't think he meant the speech particularly. I just think he meant the subject of civil rights and so forth. There was then some discussion, and I've forgotten just who took part in it, but there were the usual "nervous Nellies" who said, "Well, you know, we're in very close elections in Tennessee, and Kentucky, and the border states and so on, and we have to do this and so on." And the President just rode them all down and said, "Of course we have to do it. We should have been doing it all along."[40]

At this critical point in the final stage of the campaign, Truman was not going to back down on his radical civil rights program, even if it meant losing the South and border states, including his own Missouri. As he told his racist friend Ernie Roberts in August, he would not equivocate—and by the time he got to Dorrance Brooks Square in Harlem on October 29, 1948, the president was eager to reiterate his absolute commitment to full civil rights for all Americans.

While election day was just four days off, the crowd of mostly African Americans who jammed into Dorrance Brooks Square acted more like participants in a religious revival meeting than voters at a campaign rally. Philleo Nash, who accompanied the president to Harlem, described the unusual behavior of the sixty-five thousand people in Truman's audience as follows:

So I had my back to the crowd and when it was time for the President to get up and speak, after they'd had the ruffles and flourishes and invocation and a rather lengthy prayer, I heard—there was applause—and then I heard the CCNY [City College of New York] students saying and shouting, "Pour it on, Harry," "Give 'em hell, Harry," and then all of a sudden the cry wasn't being taken up by anybody and it was sort of fading away, and then they felt they didn't have any support for what they were saying, so they became silent, and all of a sudden, there was a big crowd, but a silent crowd.

Well, this is rather ominous, rather frightening. I had my back to the crowd and I just wondered whether I'd been wrong in urging that this be done. . . . So, I finally turned around and faced the crowd and then I saw why they were silent, it wasn't ominous. Almost everybody in that crowd was praying, either with his head down or actually was kneeling. They were quiet because they were praying, and they were praying for the President, and they were praying for their own civil rights. And they thought it was a religious occasion.

So that was my first real face-to-face indication of the depth of feeling that the people who were most intimately concerned with civil rights had about Mr. Truman, and I think ought to have served to a good many people as an indication of what was going to happen with the Northern Negro vote—well, with the Negro vote, because there wasn't much Southern [Negro] vote in those days.[41]

When Truman began to speak after the prayerful introduction by Asapansa-Johnson, the president reminded his predominantly black audience, which included Eleanor Roosevelt and Mayor O'Dwyer of New York, that October 29 was a particularly significant date; just one year earlier, on October 29, 1947, the President's Committee on Civil Rights had issued its final report detailing the civil rights challenges facing the country. Using his Harlem address to praise the members of his Civil Rights Committee for their courage in frankly stating their troublesome conclusions, Truman stated, "I created the Civil Rights Committee because racial and religious intolerance began to appear after World War II. They threatened the very freedom we had fought to save."[42]

Truman's use of the word *we* before his audience of black Americans was significant. During his own days as an army officer in World War I, Truman had learned firsthand about the significance of the collective *we* when a whole nation went to war, with its young men of various ethnic heritages fighting together for their common goal. By choosing inclusive words like *we* before his Harlem audience, Truman demonstrated his empathy and his personal appreciation of the fact that all Americans—black and white—had recently joined together and sacrificed collectively and mightily in World War II; and because of that joint sacrifice, Truman let his audience feel his personal repulsion about recent and increasing outbreaks of racial intolerance that had victimized returning black veterans.

No audience better appreciated the terrible, pervasive reality of continued racial intolerance in the United States than the black voters gathered that autumn afternoon at 135th Street and St. Nicholas Avenue in Harlem. As the President's Civil Rights Committee report confirmed, widespread racial discrimination permeated every segment of life in the South where the prospect of lynching remained as real a threat in 1948 as it had been decades earlier.[43] Truman's Harlem audience also appreciated better than most Americans how the poll taxes continued to impede full black voter participation throughout much of the South in 1948.[44] For this audience, it was indeed a momentous event for an incumbent president to journey to Harlem—the urban heartland of black America—to deliver a speech that frankly acknowledged the panoply of civil rights abuses that continued to restrict their lives and the lives of their relatives throughout the country.

Equating the voluminous report of his Committee on Civil Rights to the Declaration of Independence and the United States Constitution, Truman explained to his Harlem audience how the committee's report provided an explicit and comprehensive blueprint whereby the federal government, working together with state and local governments, could make the principle that all men are created equal a reality. "When every American knows that his rights and his opportunities are fully protected and respected by Federal, State, and local governments, then we will have the kind of unity that really means something."[45]

Unity with white Americans was a far-fetched concept for many in this audience who had themselves been denied their civil rights—whether in restaurants while traveling throughout the South or in the employment lines of major corporations in both the North and the South. Nonetheless, Truman spoke of unity as an attainable goal—one that could be achieved if the next, preferably Democrat-led, Congress would do what the GOP-led Eightieth Congress had failed to do: enact the sweeping recommendations of his Committee on Civil Rights.

> The job that the Civil Rights Committee did was to tell the American people how to create the kind of freedom that we need in this country.
>
> The Civil Rights Committee described the kind of freedom that comes when every man has an equal chance for a job—not just the hot and heavy job—but the best job he is qualified for. . . .
>
> The Committee described the kind of freedom that comes when every citizen has an equal opportunity to go to the ballot box and cast his vote and have it counted.
>
> The Committee described the kind of freedom that comes when every man, woman, and child is free from the fear of mob violence and intimidation.[46]

Mincing no words, Truman's empathy resounded throughout his speech. He bluntly acknowledged the unfair prospects for black Americans, the unequal chance for black boys and girls to gain an education, and the common occurrences where black Americans voted without having their ballots actually counted.[47] While these gross inequities were commonplace for blacks in 1948, it was nonetheless unprecedented for Truman's Harlem audience to hear a U.S. president talk so frankly, and with such obvious passion, about their struggle for equal rights and the need for full protection under federal laws.

Dr. Height recalled in a 1998 interview how frank and genuine Truman was when he spoke about civil rights reform. Height suggested that the president's ability to connect with African Americans in Harlem and elsewhere was particularly evident in the way black voters responded to him with unprecedented voter support just four days after his Harlem speech.[48]

By deciding to go to Harlem at the close of his presidential campaign, Truman publicly reaffirmed his belief that individual civil rights for all black Americans would not be realized until the federal government assumed a new and much more aggressive leadership role in the civil rights arena. Reminding his Harlem audience that the vehicle for achieving full civil rights protection for all Americans was his proposed ten-point civil rights legislation, which was languishing before the GOP-led Congress, President Truman concluded his remarks by reassuring the huge audience of his personal commitment to their civil rights. "Our determination to attain the goal of equal rights and equal opportunity must be resolute and unwavering. For my part, I intend to keep moving toward this goal with every ounce of strength and determination that I have."[49]

For the people gathered in Dorrance Brooks Square that day, and for the larger audience of black Americans that read the next day's newspaper accounts of this presidential foray into Harlem, President Truman's words of empathy and determination to reform civil rights in the United States were electrifying. In Percy Sutton's opinion, October 29, 1948, was "a momentous day" for Harlem's residents, who knew that Truman believed what he said about the long-overdue promise of full equality for all Americans.[50]

Judge William Hastie shared Percy Sutton's view about Truman's credibility and impact with black voters when the president made his spirited Harlem speech. Hastie, who was serving as Truman's governor of the Virgin Islands in 1948, traveled to New York shortly after Truman received an "enthusiastic response" from the sixty-five thousand Harlem residents. In 1972, Hastie confirmed that, by the time Truman made his Harlem Speech on October 29, 1948, "Certainly there is no doubt that throughout the country, the black population came to appreciate, and I think they did appreciate, that he had done something important and sensational in the interests of the advancement of the Negro."[51]

Even Mayor O'Dwyer, who just three months earlier had been a leader in the Draft Eisenhower effort, was moved to express his deep admiration for President Truman's refusal to compromise on his civil rights program. Mayor O'Dwyer further endeared candidate Truman to voters gathered in Harlem when he recounted his firsthand observations of President Truman's reaction to the Southern Democrats' threatening to bolt from the Democratic convention. O'Dwyer quoted Truman at the Democratic convention as saying about the racist, states' rights Southern Democrats, "Let them go. I'm not going to change my opinion."[52]

Just as he had done in his address to the NAACP at the Lincoln Memorial sixteen months earlier, President Truman used the Harlem speech to reassure African Americans in Harlem and throughout the United States that he was fully committed to making their federal government live up to the Constitution's guarantee of equality for all Americans. Truman was once again publicly outspoken on this basic point, and he in no way softened his proactive civil rights stance even though his remarks could be expected to adversely impact his already shaky standing with voters throughout the traditionally Democratic Southern states—states that Truman desperately needed to achieve the impossible in defeating Governor Dewey on November 2.[53]

For Truman, the Harlem speech was both a gutsy move and a politically savvy thing to do. Presidential strategists in 1948 did not have the demographic data that modern political consultants utilize to determine likely voter reaction to a presidential candidate's views. In the 1948 election, there were no scientific surveys that could reliably predict black voter turnout: while the black migration from the South had accelerated during and after World War II, political analysts and pundits simply could not accurately measure the black voters' influence on the outcome. Thus it was indeed a high-risk—but ultimately politically rewarding —decision for Truman to make a major civil rights address in the heart of Harlem just days before voters would elect their next president. As White House aides and reporters confirmed, Truman's Harlem speech—impassioned as it was, had a spiritual dimension as Truman obviously connected with his prayerful and energized audience of sixty-five thousand African Americans. The profoundly spiritual nature of Truman's address in Harlem was referenced by journalist Carleton Kent in a postelection *Chicago Sun-Times* analysis.

> Every time I hear casual or cynical (or wishful Southern) doubt expressed over President Truman's earnestness in campaigning for enactment of his civil rights recommendations, I like to remember the Harlem meeting.
>
> It occurred the Saturday afternoon before [the] election, at an open-air stand around which scores of thousands of New York Negroes had been praying and singing for hours as they waited [for] the President.

The occasion was to present Mr. Truman the annual medal awarded by a Greater New York committee of Protestant Negro ministers—and to afford him a sounding board for an appeal for Negro votes.[54]

When Philleo Nash was asked about the *Chicago Sun-Times's* characterization of Truman's Harlem speech as a prayerful campaign event, Nash confirmed that the *Sun-Times* journalist "had the mood of the occasion all right."[55] Nash also recalled a subsequent meeting with the black press who thought that Truman's speech "was tremendous, and caught the full meaning of it, the full impact, right away. This was a one-issue press, these are one-issue specialists, and they don't need any help in interpreting exactly what's going on."[56]

For a presidential candidate who took his quiet religious beliefs very seriously, Truman's visit to Harlem proved to be as special for him as it was for the sixty-five thousand Harlem residents who prayed openly for this president who cared so deeply about their civil rights. White House staffer Nash confirmed that Truman was deeply moved by his Harlem audience and described a chance, late-evening encounter with Truman just hours after the Harlem campaign appearance.

> Everybody, of course, was exhausted from the night's work, and then the day's work, and was resting getting ready for the night appearance, and the start of the trip to St. Louis and then on to Independence, the final broadcast being from St. Louis Monday night. So I hadn't had any sleep either, but I was still pretty steamed up, so I was just walking down the hall when along came Mr. Truman. He had been working harder than anybody else, but he was lonesome, he was looking for somebody to talk to. So we talked about the [Harlem] meeting and he said, "Well, that was the high point of the campaign. That was emotional, that was really from the heart."[57]

For Percy Sutton, who was in law school and graduate school in New York City when Truman visited Harlem on October 29, 1948, Truman's campaign address was a "marvelous event." "We plastered signs all over the city telling black voters that President Truman would be coming to Harlem. By that time blacks knew that this president meant what he said about civil rights—and they turned out in a big way to let Harry Truman know how they felt."[58]

In a front-page *New York Times* story on October 30 focusing on the Harlem speech, journalist Anthony Leviero reported, "President Truman re-committed himself . . . to the full measure of his ten-point civil rights program, pledging to work for it 'with every ounce of strength and determination I have.'" Leviero went on to report that "the Chief Executive lifted the controversial issue that has split the Democratic party out of . . . limbo. . . . In words that appeared to foreclose any possibility of compromise between Mr. Truman and the States' Rights Democrats Mr. Truman rededicated himself to the program in Harlem, the largest big-city Negro community in the world."[59]

The *New York Times* article further predicted that the president's address before black Americans would have "immediate and far-reaching repercussions" in the South, less than one hundred hours before the presidential election of 1948. Continued political repercussions were likely because Truman confirmed for his Harlem audience, as well as for the white voters in the South, that if elected, full, prompt, and federally protected civil rights would remain a top priority.[60]

Despite Truman's risking further destruction of remaining Southern support for his election in four days, the issue of civil rights remained primarily a moral one for Truman. Not surprisingly, on election day, Truman lost Alabama, Louisiana, Mississippi, and South Carolina as Southern Democratic voters expressed their repulsion at the vision of racial equality that Truman articulated in Harlem.[61] While Truman lost these four traditionally Democratic stronghold states to Dixiecrat presidential candidate Thurmond, the president won election to the White House by an electoral vote of 303 to 189 over Dewey. The popular vote, which the country's fifty leading journalists had unanimously predicted would go to Dewey, ended up at 24,105,695 votes for Truman; 21,969,170 for Dewey; 1,169,021 for Thurmond; and 1,156,103 for Wallace. Though Henry Wallace drained off enough black votes for Governor Dewey to prevail over Truman in New York, the president enjoyed strong black voter support in California, Illinois, and Ohio—states that effectively ensured his election to the White House.[62]

Truman had further offended Southern Democrats and segregationists throughout America with his October 29 campaign speech in Harlem, but the presidential election results, analyzed in the weeks following the election, confirmed that the president's Harlem speech helped to energize African Americans who voted in unprecedented numbers in urban areas throughout the industrial states, especially Illinois, Pennsylvania, and Ohio. The *New Republic,* in a November 22, 1948, article entitled "The Negro Prefers Truman," focused on the popularity of Truman's Harlem message of equality with black voters around the country when it reported,

Negro voters more than justified the increased voice in Democratic Party affairs their leaders are now demanding from them. Final returns from the major centers of Negro population show that in spite of concentrated Wallace-party appeal for their votes, Negroes backed Harry Truman as strongly as they ever backed Franklin Roosevelt.

The pattern of Negro voting nationally ran better than 75 percent for Truman. In Negro wards in Philadelphia, Chicago and Pittsburgh, the public preference of Truman to Wallace was overwhelming. Nine out of every 10 Negro voters in Philadelphia cast their ballots for Truman.

Chicago's second ward, where Representative William Dawson (slated to become the first Negro committee chairman in the new Congress) is ward committeeman, gave Truman more votes than did any other ward in the city.

Seventy-five percent of the Negro vote in Pittsburgh went to Truman, local officials estimate, while only two percent fell into the Wallace column.

Even in California, the picture was the same. The West Coast *Daily Worker (People's World)* had to report that a sampling of precincts in the bay area indicated "that Negro voters piled up heavy pluralities for Harry Truman, shunned Henry Wallace, and all but ignored Thomas E. Dewey."

In Harlem the vote was 90,000 for Truman, 25,000 for Dewey and 21,000 for Wallace.[63]

The surprisingly strong turnout of African Americans who supported President Truman's 1948 presidential bid just days after his rousing Harlem speech established clearly for the first time the new political potency of black voters in urban America. It also demonstrated for future presidential candidates of both parties how one could effectively use blunt, uncompromising words to energize a growing and disenfranchised segment of the population.

For the first time in American history, black voters found their very substantial collective political voice—a voice they used effectively to help elect Truman president on November 2, 1948. Black voters throughout the key industrial states knew by election day that Truman had risked everything during the prior three years of his inherited presidency to bring true equality to African Americans, a group who had been left largely on their own by each U.S. president since Abraham Lincoln had freed the slaves throughout the rebellious South eighty-five years earlier.

When reflecting on the importance of Truman's Harlem speech and the earlier public actions taken by Truman in the civil rights arena, Philleo Nash explained, "Civil rights was the touchstone of the Truman election in 1948. It was via the civil rights route that he first showed he was master of his own party. . . . It showed that he could get the nomination in spite of his strong stand on civil rights. . . . It was his position with the liberals that was most in question, and this made it possible for the liberals to support him."[64]

For the African Americans who gathered at the Truman rally in Harlem, and for the black voters across the country, it was clear that this president really meant what he said. They also knew that election day 1948 was payback time, and black voters did just that with their overwhelming pro-Truman vote on November 2, 1948. Happily for black voters who helped candidate Truman achieve his spectacular surprise victory of 1948, President Harry Truman would remain their resourceful ally during his next four years in the White House.

George Elsey in train yard. Princeton- and Harvard-educated George Elsey *(facing camera)*, one of President Truman's most industrious and respected assistants, drafted Truman's unprecedented February 2, 1948, special message to the Eightieth Congress in which the president proposed a revolutionary ten-point civil rights program. *Courtesy of the Harry S. Truman Library.*

Mary McLeod Bethune. The founder and first president of the National Council of Negro Women, Mary McLeod Bethune *(seated next to President Truman at the White House)* publicly heralded Truman for his "courage . . . and forthright stand in proposing his ten-point civil rights legislation." *National Park Service–Mary McLeod Bethune Council House NHS, Washington, D.C.*

Berryman's cartoon. The *Washington Evening Star's* renowned political cartoonist C. K. Berryman portrays a stubborn Truman in a March 14, 1948, cartoon focused on the politically ruinous consequences of the president's controversial civil rights program during election year 1948. © 1948, The Washington Post. *Reprinted with permission.*

HST as candidate in 1948. Dressed impeccably in a white linen suit, a combative sixty-four-year-old candidate Truman skewered the "do-nothing GOP Congress" as he accepted his party's presidential nomination in the steamy, smoke-filled Philadelphia convention hall in the early hours of July 15, 1948. *Haberman/FPG International LLC.*

HST's 1948 Harlem speech. Just four days before Truman's spectacular come-from-behind presidential election victory on November 2, 1948, a smiling candidate Truman was given a hero's welcome by sixty-five thousand African American voters in Harlem. *Al Gretz/FPG International LLC.*

Dewey victory headline. The *Chicago Daily Tribune* —in its 1948 postelection special edition—and fifty of the country's leading political analysts polled in October 1948 got it all wrong when they predicted Harry Truman's defeat on November 2, 1948. *By permission of the St. Louis Mercantile Library at the University of Missouri–St. Louis.*

HST and William H. Hastie *(on Truman's right)* in the Virgin Islands. During a visit to the U.S. Virgin Islands early in his presidency, Truman took a strong personal liking to then-Governor Hastie—a man who subsequently was appointed by Truman to be the first African American judge on the federal court in the continental United States. *Courtesy of the Harry S. Truman Library.*

G. W. McLaurin. Incredible as it may seem to current law students and M.B.A. candidates, during most of Harry Truman's presidency, women and men of color were forced to attend segregated graduate schools or, in the case of doctoral degree candidate G. W. McLaurin *(shown above)*, to sit in a "coloreds only" section in classrooms at the University of Oklahoma's graduate school. This form of racism ended in the United States after the Vinson Court ruled on June 5, 1950, that segregation in higher education was unconstitutional. *Courtesy of the Library of Congress.*

HST and Thomas J. Lennon. During the extensive restoration of the White House from late 1949 to the spring of 1952, the Trumans lived in Blair House and hosted state dinners at the nearby Carlton Hotel. The young general manager of the Carlton, Thomas J. Lennon (shown greeting President Truman), years later recalled how consistently gracious the president was to everyone, "whether visiting royalty or black waiters at the Carlton." *Courtesy of Theresa Lennon Gardner.*

HST at Key West, Florida. Truman frequently escaped to Key West where he relaxed with loyal aides, some of whom were asked to join the fearless president when he went swimming despite shark sightings. Shown above *(second from right)* is one of the president's favorite young secret service agents, Rex Scouten, who would serve ten presidents, concluding his distinguished government service in 1997 as White House curator. *Courtesy of the U.S. Navy and the Harry S. Truman Library.*

Beryl Hastie and Mary McLeod Bethune protest Washington, D.C., segregation. Beryl Hastie *(left)*, wife of Truman's appointee to the Third Circuit Court, Judge William Hastie, is joined by civil rights pioneer Mary McLeod Bethune in a protest outside a "whites only" Washington drug store that was popular in the late 1940s and 1950s. *Courtesy of the Moorland-Spingarn Research Center–Howard University Archives.*

HST's address to the Howard University class of 1952. Howard University graduates heard a spirited civil rights speech from lame-duck President Truman on June 13, 1952. *Courtesy of the Moorland-Spingarn Research Center–Howard University Archives.*

Washington, D.C., protest by black Korean War veterans. Despite their service in integrated U.S. armed forces during the Korean War, black veterans often returned home to confront stubborn racism even in the nation's capital. The peaceful protesters *(shown above)* in 1952 outside a segregated Washington, D.C., restaurant were determined to gain the full equality that Harry Truman publicly supported from the early days of his presidency. *Courtesy of the Moorland-Spingarn Research Center–Howard University Archives.*

HST with widow of navy flyer. Truman is shown here at a White House ceremony on April 13, 1951, presenting the nation's highest award for bravery, the congressional Medal of Honor, to Lieutenant Thomas J. Hudner. Truman honored navy pilot Hudner *(right)* for extraordinary bravery when he crash-landed his plane behind enemy lines in Korea in a futile effort to save his colleague, the navy's first African American aviator, Jessie Leroy Brown. Brown's young widow, Daisy Pearl, is at Truman's immediate right. *Reprinted by permission of Corbis Images.*

CHAPTER TEN

Civil Rights Progress Despite a Recalcitrant Congress: 1949–1952

Riding on the coattails of Truman's spectacular come-from-behind victory on November 2, 1948, the Democratic Party regained control of both the Senate and the House of Representatives.[1] Truman's successful campaign had worked not only for the president but also for congressional Democratic candidates around the country, who now enjoyed solid control of the country's legislative apparatus in the newly elected Eighty-first Congress.

During the 1948 campaign, the tireless Truman had hammered the do-nothing GOP leadership of the Eightieth Congress for their legislative short-comings, including their failure to take action on Truman's civil rights program, which he had sent to Congress earlier that year. Day after day during his nonstop campaign—a campaign so intense that Truman made at least 126 speeches during the first sixteen days of his famous whistle-stop train tour—candidate Truman relentlessly attacked congressional Republicans.[2] Wisely, when Truman raised the explosive civil rights issue, he artfully failed to mention the real reason that civil rights reform was stalled—the well-organized Southern Democrats who successfully filibustered any civil rights legislation that would have empowered the federal government to circumscribe their states' rights policies.

Ironically, Truman's spectacular success during the 1948 campaign in restoring the Democrats' majority position in both the House and the Senate did nothing to improve his chances of getting the new Congress to pass civil rights legislation. Whether it was the GOP-led Eightieth Congress or the Democratic-led Eighty-first Congress, Truman was confronted with the same insurmountable coalition of Southern Democrats and states' rights Republicans, a coalition that simply would not tolerate any legislatively mandated change in the racism that permeated much of America in the late 1940s. This reality became apparent very early in the Eighty-first Congress, just weeks after President Truman delivered his state of the union address to the new Congress on January 5, 1949. Yet despite this reality, a determined Harry Truman used his cabinet and executive-branch prerogatives to achieve a range of civil rights reforms during the four years from inauguration day 1949 until his presidency ended on January 20, 1953.

The Eighty-first Congress that Truman's spectacular victory helped to shape was led by Truman's dear friend, the powerful House Speaker, Sam Rayburn of Texas and by Senate Majority Leader Scott Lucas of Illinois. Importantly, from a civil rights perspective, Lucas could not have secured his leadership position in the Senate without support from racist Georgia Senator Richard Russell.[3] Russell, who would later promote Lyndon Johnson for senate Majority Leader, controlled a formidable coalition of Southern Democrats who bitterly opposed Truman's federal program for civil rights reform.[4]

Despite the predictable negative reaction of Southern Democrats and conservative states' rights Republicans in the Eighty-first Congress, Truman was unequivocal on January 5, 1949, in reiterating his support of full civil rights for all Americans when he spoke to Congress. Reminding congressional members of the racism that permeated American society in 1949, the president said, "Our democratic ideals are often thwarted by prejudice and intolerance." Truman went on to remind the new Eighty-first Congress that they could not escape consideration of the same comprehensive civil rights legislation that he had submitted in vain to the Eightieth Congress.

> The driving force behind our progress is our faith in our democratic institutions. That faith is embodied in the promise of equal rights and equal opportunities which the founders of our Republic proclaimed to their countrymen and to the whole world.
>
> The fulfillment of this promise is among the highest purposes of government. The civil rights proposals I made to the 80th Congress, I now repeat to the 81st Congress. They should be enacted in order that the Federal Government may assume the leadership and discharge the obligations clearly placed upon it by the Constitution.
>
> I stand squarely behind these proposals.[5]

Truman spoke passionately in his first state of the union address as an elected president about his proposed comprehensive civil rights legislation, but as a seasoned politician and former member of the Senate, he knew how unlikely legislative action on civil rights reform was in the Eighty-first Congress.

148

Truman's attorney general in early 1949, Tom Clark, confirmed in 1972 just how hostile Southern Democrats in the Congress were to any form of civil rights legislation—including even routine appropriations that might help advance Truman's radical civil rights program. "Of course, all those southerners [in the Congress] were very conservative, and it's like pulling eyeteeth to get anything through[.] We'd have to hide the money for this little old Civil Rights Section [at the Department of Justice] under another name or it would never get out of the Committee."[6] Clark further explained that, while Truman "tried his best as President" on civil rights legislation, its enactment was an impossibility because of the unholy alliance of Southern Democrats and conservative Republicans in the Senate. "It was difficult to pierce [the congressional alliance against Truman's civil rights legislation]; and that Southern bloc would go along with a sufficient number of Republicans to have a sufficient number of votes to block liberal legislation."[7]

While Truman confronted Southern Democrats on January 5, 1949, with his state of the union pledge to wage another civil rights battle with Congress, he was also at work planning this country's first integrated inaugural celebration in the segregated capital. To the shock of many Washingtonians, Truman used his inaugural ceremonies to break down many of the segregationist policies of hotels and restaurants in the capital. The president's daughter, Margaret Truman, in her collection of memories of her father, recalled that his 1949 inaugural was the first inaugural at which "black Americans were admitted to all official and unofficial functions." She also noted that "Walter White, head of the NAACP, praised Dad for 'recognizing the new place of all ordinary Americans.'"[8]

The unprecedented participation of African Americans in the 1949 presidential inaugural celebration was detailed by journalist Alice Dunnigan in her autobiography, *A Black Woman's Experience*. According to Dunnigan, "Much ado was being made about the inclusion of Negroes in all of the festivities," including the establishment of the National Participation Subcommittee, headed by the respected black attorney William L. Houston. Blacks were also appointed to all thirty-eight subcommittees of Truman's Inaugural Committee, and prominent black entertainers, including Lena Horne and Lionel Hampton, performed at Truman's only inauguration celebration.[9]

Shortly after Truman's inaugural address, in which he again claimed that "all men have a right to equal justice under [the] law and equal opportunity to share in the common good," he met with a delegation of black American leaders that included Mary McLeod Bethune.[10] Bethune was nationally known as the founder and president of the eight-hundred-thousand-member NCNW. While the

Eighty-first Congress was initially unresponsive to the president's call for civil rights reform, Bethune was encouraged, and after her meeting with the president, she issued the following statement praising Truman for his courage: "You have thrown down the gauntlet to all those at home and abroad who would challenge the essential spiritual nature of democracy—the sacred integrity of every individual soul. The Klansman in his cowardly robe and the false lords of the Kremlin will shiver alike in this cold glaring light of truth."[11]

Bethune and her NCNW colleagues passionately supported the president's civil rights program. Southern Democrats in the Eighty-first Congress, however, remained adamantly opposed to any civil rights legislation. In an effort to limit the effectiveness of the Southern Democrats' filibuster on his civil rights legislation, Truman, in late February 1949, informed Senate Majority Leader Lucas that he wanted to meet the filibuster's stranglehold on the Senate head-on by attempting to modify Rule 22.[12] Rule 22, Precedence of Motions, was an arcane procedural device in the U.S. Senate that kept an issue from being considered "when a question is pending" before the Senate.[13] Until Rule 22 was modified, states' rights Republicans and segregationist Democrats in the Senate could collectively prevent Truman's civil rights legislation from reaching the point of a Senate vote. Without repeal or significant modification of Rule 22, there was no realistic possibility of the future successful cloture votes that were needed to terminate Southern Democrats' filibusters. As William S. White reported in a page-one *New York Times* article on March 1, 1949, Truman decided to muster the forces needed to repeal the Senate's Rule 22. White viewed Truman's battle to end the southerners' continued use of the filibuster as the "greatest struggle of their history to preserve the ability of the Senate minority to kill bills by unlimited debate—by filibusters making it impossible to reach a vote, such as those with which they have always prevented action on President Truman's civil rights program."[14] White, one of the country's foremost political journalists, reported that a determined senate Majority Leader Lucas emerged from a meeting with the president "to say that the President's decision was that the issue had to be met 'head-on,' and now. Asked whether President Truman had accepted the implication that other legislation might have to be put aside, Senator Lucas replied: 'Yes.'"[15]

While Lucas would urge his fellow senators to join him in modifying Rule 22, the Senate ended any possibility for that change with a 46-to-41 vote on March 11, 1949.[16] Several days later, Lucas publicly proposed dropping divisive civil rights legislative proposals "for the time being" so that the Eighty-first Congress could focus on other important priorities, including creation of NATO, the continued Berlin Airlift, and the growing communist menace in Eastern Europe and China.[17]

A *New York Times* article of March 18, 1949, that seemed more like an obituary notice than a public policy news story, focused on the failure of Truman's proactive civil rights forces in the Eighty-first Congress to muster the necessary votes to modify Rule 22. The *Times* story reported that it seemed

> the Senate was giving funeral honors to the President's civil rights program. If, as Republican leaders were suggesting, this was not the case, that will be this year's outstanding surprise. Last November, Governors Thurmond and Wright, running on the States [*sic*] Rights ticket, received about 2[1/2] per cent of the votes cast for President. It might seem odd that their followers should be the winners in the first test of strength in the Senate. But the oddity is not wholly in what the Southern Senators have been able to do. No one doubted where they stood. In the language of the national game, they couldn't have got to first base without Republican help—most respectable Republican help. They have assented to a rules change which might permit the Senate to take swift action if the nation were attacked or some other emergency not sectional in character were to arise, but which will make it hard if not impossible to enact any legislation the Southerners don't approve of. In the matter of federal action on civil rights we will continue to be ruled from Birmingham.[18]

The *New York Times*'s predictions proved accurate, and by the middle of March 1949, President Truman's civil rights program was effectively dead as the political powers of Southern Democrats in the new Congress were tested and confirmed—powers that were enhanced by the Democrats' regaining control of the Congress thanks in part to Truman's coattails.

Notwithstanding this early debacle in 1949, the president's comprehensive proposal for civil rights reform was formally introduced in the Eighty-first Congress by Democratic Senator J. Howard McGrath (D-R.I.) on April 28, 1949. The Truman package included an omnibus civil rights bill modeled on the recommendations of the October 29, 1947, report of Truman's Civil Rights Committee, as well as an antilynching bill, an anti–poll tax bill, and legislation calling for the establishment of a permanent federal FEPC.[19] Truman, who realized the probable terminal fate of his comprehensive civil rights legislation in the Democratic-controlled Eighty-first Congress, looked to other opportunities both in the executive branch and in the federal courts to move forward on civil rights reform.

One of the first things Truman did was to demonstrate in a dramatic fashion his vision of a colorblind judicial system when he nominated a black lawyer to the country's all-white federal court system. This landmark event occurred on October 15, 1949, when he nominated the former dean of the Howard University Law School and his appointee to the governorship of the U.S. Virgin Islands, William H. Hastie, to a seat on the Third Circuit Court of Appeals, an important federal court encompassing Pennsylvania, New Jersey, Delaware, and the Virgin Islands.[20] Truman's actions in nominating Hastie to the federal bench, while routine today, were extraordinary in 1949 and profoundly significant to African American lawyers throughout the United States.

Truman's decision to nominate William Hastie was provocative and unprecedented and in time would prove to be inspired. Hastie, born on November 17, 1904, in Knoxville, Tennessee, had superb credentials and a distinguished record of service as dean of the Howard University Law School. With his impressive background as a lawyer who had argued before the Supreme Court with Thurgood Marshall, Hastie was an important symbol of professional success in the black community in the 1940s.[21] President Truman had been personally impressed with Governor William Hastie during his presidential visit to the Virgin Islands, where Hastie had demonstrated strong leadership skills, as well as an affable personality.[22] President Roosevelt had appointed Hastie to an obscure district court in the Virgin Islands for two years in the late 1930s, but President Truman took the unprecedented action of appointing Hastie to the federal appellate bench—an action that represented the first black American appointment to the federal bench in the continental United States.[23]

Truman's high regard for Hastie was evident in the president's letter to Hastie, released by the White House on November 19, 1949, wherein the president formally accepted Hastie's resignation from the governorship of the Virgin Islands, a predicate to Hastie's being seated on the bench.

Dear Governor Hastie:

Your letter of November fourteenth submitting your resignation as Governor of the Virgin Islands in order to take office as a judge of the Third Circuit Court of Appeals, has been received with decidedly mixed feelings.

I am gratified that you are to assume the important position of a judge in one of our highest courts. To you as a member of the legal profession and a public spirited citizen few fields of service could offer a greater challenge or more satisfying rewards.

On the other hand, your departure from the difficult and highly responsible post of Governor of the Virgin Islands is a matter of real regret. As the first Negro to be appointed Governor of one of our territorial areas, you have been in a conspicuous position. You have rendered fine service to the people of the Islands. . . .

Your service as Governor as well as other phases of your career may well serve as a symbol of that opportunity for high achievement which must always be open in increasing measure to all our citizens.

Very sincerely yours,
HARRY S. TRUMAN[24]

Hastie's appointment to the prestigious Third Circuit was an encouraging and significant symbolic development for African Americans but especially for black attorneys. In 1949, black lawyers often had to confront gross abuses throughout the U.S. judicial system, particularly in the South, where all-white juries typically remained the exclusive vehicle for determining every defendant's guilt or innocence. Truman's appointment of Hastie subsequently proved to be a substantive addition to the federal judiciary as Judge Hastie later became chief judge of the Third Circuit Court of Appeals.[25]

When asked more than two decades later about the significance of his appointment to the federal appellate bench, the typically modest chief judge concluded that his lone appointment by Truman in 1949 was symbolically more important for civil rights advocates than the subsequent numerous appointments of blacks to the federal bench made by Presidents Kennedy and Johnson. "Well, certainly in comparison with what Presidents Kennedy and Johnson did, the number of blacks appointed [by Truman] to high office was relatively small. I suppose that breaking a taboo has a significance in itself, and it's hard to compare that with the quantitatively larger things that were done after this taboo was broken. In that sense, I think my appointment to this bench twenty-two years ago, had a value and importance, perhaps greater than the appointment of several Negroes later."[26]

In his 1972 oral history, Chief Judge Hastie also expressed his perspective on Truman's role in America's long and unfinished civil rights journey. Truman's "accomplishments in the field of race relations and the treatment of the Negro by the Government were in my view precedent-making; they paved the way for, and made very much easier the things that the President[s] that succeeded him did. . . . I'm convinced that he will be remembered and recorded as one of the great Presidents, one of the outstanding Presidents of the United States."[27]

Two months after Hastie's nomination to the federal bench, another unprecedented civil rights initiative was undertaken by Truman's Justice Department on December 12, 1949, when the solicitor general announced that the Federal Housing Administration (FHA) would refuse to provide financial aid to projects that discriminated against African Americans. A page-one, December 16, *New York Times* report by respected journalist John D. Morris focused on the Truman administration's groundbreaking use of the FHA's financial might to force integrated housing in America. The *Times* reported that this novel approach to FHA financing was viewed with alarm by "some real estate interests [who] still feared that Federal insurance would be used either under the new regulations or future revisions as a lever against segregation in housing carrying Federal loan insurance. . . . Apprehensions of real estate men and some others stemmed also from reports that the new policy was the outcome of representations by the National Association for the Advancement of Colored People, which filed a brief with the Government arguing that 'the full integration of minority groups into American life is an essential part of the national housing program.'"[28]

In an earlier administrative action taken by Truman's appointees to the Civil Aeronautics Administration (CAA), an important symbol of racism just across the Potomac River from the nation's capital was eliminated when restaurants at Washington National Airport were integrated. As noted in the *New York Times*, December 28, 1948, "The government . . . ordered a complete end to racial segregation at the Washington National Airport, which lies on Virginia soil across the Potomac River. The Civil Aeronautics Administration, which operates the huge field, ruled that henceforth there should be no 'discrimination or segregation as to race, color, or creed' in any of the airport facilities. Heretofore, a CAA spokesman said, Negroes had not been admitted to the terrace restaurant or to the airport coffee shop. Both are operated by a private concessionaire. Negroes could eat at a small snack bar or use a restaurant in the basement of the Administration Building."[29]

While actions taken by Truman, such as naming Hastie to the federal bench, integrating the restaurants at Washington National Airport, and using the FHA to promote integrated housing, have received little attention from civil rights historians, they confirm Truman's consistent commitment to civil rights reform even when he was completely blocked by a recalcitrant Congress. Instead of abandoning civil rights reform once it was clear that the new Democratic-led Congress would reject any civil rights legislation, Truman and the cabinet that he energized tenaciously pushed forward on a number of civil rights fronts. Through the unilateral presidential actions taken by Truman in 1949, he was able to make some civil rights progress—progress that simply was not possible if left to the Eighty-first Congress, where Southern Democrats retained disproportionate influence.

Despite the congressional impasse over civil rights reform, President Truman continued publicly to express his radical civil rights views following his election to the White House. In a presidential address on November 15, 1949, before Mary Bethune and the membership of the NCNW, President Truman told his audience, "All of us who are here tonight have a deep interest in a great enterprise—the extension of freedom of opportunity to all our citizens without racial or religious discrimination. The people of this country have made and are making progress in this cause. We are awakened as never before to the true meaning of equality. We will continue to advance in our program of bringing equal rights and equal opportunities to all citizens. In that great cause there is no retreat and no retirement, and I know Mrs. Bethune is going to stand by me as she has from the beginning."[30] Truman's address to the NCNW represented another public indication of the president's unwavering commitment to civil rights reform; but because the NCNW and the NAACP were organizations in 1949 that lacked the nationwide political leverage they would later enjoy, their support for Truman's civil rights proposals had little impact on the sitting Congress.

When the second session of the Eighty-first Congress officially opened in Washington on January 4, 1950, President Truman repeated his public support for the Fair Deal, including civil rights reform, in his state of the union address. He reiterated his now-common theme about "the moral imperative to do justice." "As we go forward in achieving greater economic security and greater opportunity for all our people, we should make every effort to extend the benefits of our democratic institutions to every citizen. . . . I again urge the Congress to enact the civil rights proposals I made in February 1948. These proposals are for the enactment of Federal statutes which will protect all our people in the exercise of their democratic rights and their search for economic opportunity."[31] Not surprisingly, despite Truman's repeated pleas for enactment of his stalled comprehensive civil rights legislation, the second session of the Eighty-first Congress, like the earlier session, offered virtually no hope for passage of even modest civil rights legislation.

However, 1950 would prove to be a significant year for civil rights reform in the judicial arena, in part because of actions taken over two years earlier by President Truman's Justice Department. In addition, while civil rights legislation remained stuck under the segregationist thumb of Southern Democrats in the Senate, the Truman administration scored a small but symbolic victory in a heated local civil rights battle that involved segregated Washington public swimming pools, some only a few blocks from the shaded green lawns of the White House.

The local battle between segregationists and liberals in Truman's official backyard over the integration of Washington's public swimming pools was not surprising: Truman had made it abundantly clear to his cabinet and appointees to federal agencies and commissions that, notwithstanding congressional opposition, he wanted everything possible done to eliminate racial discrimination wherever the federal government had leverage. [32] As part of Truman's mandate to his cabinet to integrate all facilities under their jurisdiction, Truman's Interior Department tried to force the integration of the District of Columbia's segregated public swimming pools—pools that were popular recreational facilities for residents during Washington's notoriously hot and humid summers. The continued segregation of Washington pools was discussed in a June 15, 1949, memorandum from White House staffer Stephen J. Spingarn to Clark Clifford. [33] A frustrated Spingarn reported on the District of Columbia Recreation Board's recent five-to-two vote in which the prominent members of that committee ignored the Interior Department's strong urging for an end to the local government's racist policy regarding swimming pools.

For many current residents of Washington, D.C., such a rigid segregationist policy is as repulsive as the apartheid-era environment in South Africa, before Nelson Mandela was elected president. But in reality, Washington, D.C., in the 1940s and 1950s was in many respects as segregated as Selma or Little Rock. The cruel reality of racism in Washington was captured by the *New York Times* in a May 14, 1948, front-page story about fifty-one New York City schoolboys.

RACE BIAS IN WASHINGTON DEPRIVES 51 YOUNGSTERS OF TRIP TO CAPITAL

Long-cherished dreams of passing a few hours among the tokens of freedom and historical attractions of the nation's capital were shattered . . . for fifty-one New York children by Negro segregation and discrimination rules as practiced in Washington. All of the youngsters were medal winners in the safety patrol contests in the New York metropolitan area. . . .

Among the youths designated to share in the safety honors were four Negro children. . . . When the Automobile Club sought accommodations for them with their white companions, the Washington hotel doors were closed to them. This action caused cancellation of the junket. [34]

For Truman's cabinet members, as well as for his appointees in federal agencies and commissions, racism remained an ugly reality in 1950 in Washington,

D.C., and throughout much of the United States; moreover, Truman's appointees knew from the president's public and private actions that he expected each of them to take whatever legal actions were available to eliminate the humiliating trappings of racism wherever they existed, whether at Washington's public swimming pools or at Washington National Airport across the Potomac River in segregated Virginia.

With this mandate from his president, Secretary of the Interior Oscar L. Chapman persisted and ultimately succeeded in 1950 in opening Washington's public pools to black families. The secretary of the interior's victory in integrating Washington's public swimming pools earned guarded praise from the *Washington Post,* which editorialized on September 10, 1950,

> The completion of the first full year of nonsegregated swimming at six Washington pools controlled by the Interior Department affords an appropriate opportunity for sober reexamination of what has been an overheated community issue. Total attendance at the six pools during the summer months of 1950 was 235,533; of this number, about 90,000 swimmers were colored and 146,000 were white. No disturbance or unhappy incident of any kind occurred in the course of the season. . . . The record demonstrates conclusively that nonsegregated swimming can be handled safely and harmoniously in Washington provided the leadership is sympathetic and sensible. Trouble is likely to arise only if, as was the case in 1949, some organized group attempts to foment it. . . . The one defect in the record is that attendance at the six pools was 28 percent lower than during the previous summer. . . . The lesson of the summer's experience, in our judgment, is that nonsegregated swimming is here to stay; that it can be conducted safely and harmoniously under level-headed leadership.[35]

While 1950 marked large and small civil rights victories—ranging from integrating Washington's public swimming pools to major rulings from the Vinson Court—by late 1950 the American public was increasingly focused on the troublesome events in Korea that had ripened into a war. Many Americans, including the president, felt that the Korean War was destined to become World War III just five years after World War II had ended.[36] With the country fixated on Korea, civil rights reform became an even more remote concern for most Americans. Not surprisingly, with the Eighty-second Congress's election in November 1950, Truman's prospects for any legislative progress on his stalled civil rights program grew even dimmer. Both Houses of the Eighty-second Congress remained controlled by Democrats, with the Southern wing of the Democratic Party retaining numerous key leadership positions.[37]

Despite the unlikely passage of civil rights reform legislation, and just weeks after two hundred sixty thousand Chinese joined North Korea in the escalating Korean War, Truman went before the new Eighty-second Congress on January 8, 1951, and delivered a state of the union address in which he once again explicitly called for civil rights reform.[38] The president necessarily focused the bulk of his 1951 state of the union message on a ten-point wartime program to mobilize the country for the escalating Korean conflict—a multilateral conflict in which the United States would provide most of the vast resources and fighting men for the United Nations effort on the Korean Peninsula.[39] Despite the public's understandable fixation on the Korean War effort, Truman used the national media forum of his 1951 state of the union speech to reiterate his belief that the Congress must protect the civil rights of all Americans. "Above all, we must remember that the fundamentals of our strength rest upon the freedoms of our people. . . . We must assure equal rights and equal opportunities to all our citizens."[40]

In submitting his budget message to the Eighty-second Congress, just weeks after his state of the union address, President Truman once again called for a federal fair employment practices committee—a concept that remained totally unacceptable to the Southern Democrats who now exercised even greater influence. Nonetheless, Truman persisted in his call for a permanent FEPC as the country underwent the inevitable massive mobilization effort required by the growing Korean conflict.[41] Based on his earlier experiences as the senator who chaired a committee that uncovered gross waste in the segregated World War II mobilization effort, President Truman knew that African Americans more than ever needed federally protected access to the expanding U.S. workplace; in Truman's view, his FEPC proposal would help ensure that access.

Despite the president's repeated calls for a permanent FEPC, and despite civil rights progress resulting from the ongoing implementation of Executive Orders 9980 and 9981, the president felt that more needed to be done to ensure that black Americans would have equality of opportunity, especially in regard to their fullest possible involvement in the defense mobilization effort. To help achieve this goal, the president relied once again on his unilateral powers and issued, on February 2, 1951, Executive Order 10210, which created civil rights employment protections under the War Powers Act of 1941. Among other things, Executive Order 10210 explicitly prohibited any race-based discrimination under the War Powers Act that was activated as part of the Korean War buildup. "There shall be no discrimination in any act performed hereunder against any person on the ground of race, creed, color or national origin, and all contracts hereunder shall contain a provision that the contractor and any subcontractors thereunder shall not so discriminate."[42]

Although frustrated by entrenched congressional opposition to his call for civil rights reform, the president's civil rights team nonetheless remained vigilant in the Congress, and their vigilance paid off when the Truman forces uncovered and blocked an obnoxious, but seemingly innocuous, piece of segregationist legislation passed by the Eighty-second Congress. In a little-noted action on November 2, 1951, President Truman vetoed a controversial states' rights piece of legislation, H.R. 5411, which could have undone some of the modest progress that the Truman administration was making in the civil rights area.[43] While the *New York Times* would simply report on November 3, 1951, that the president on the prior day had "killed a federal aid bill for local school construction," the president actually vetoed H.R. 5411 because it was creatively designed by Southern racists in the Congress to mandate segregated schools on federal military installations throughout the South.[44] If not vetoed by President Truman, H.R. 5411 would have required integrated schools on federal property to conform to the segregationist requirements for schools in seventeen Southern states.

In a presidential memorandum of disapproval issued by the White House on November 2, 1951, after the president vetoed H.R. 5411, the president explained,

> This proposal, if enacted into law, would constitute a backward step in the efforts of the Federal Government to extend equal rights and opportunities to all our people. During the past few years, we have made rapid progress toward equal treatment and opportunity in those activities of the Federal Government where we have a direct responsibility to follow national rather than local interpretations of non-discrimination. . . . We have assumed a role of world leadership in seeking to unite people of great cultural and racial diversity for the purpose of resisting aggression, protecting their mutual security and advancing their own economic and political development. We should not impair our moral position by enacting a law that requires a discrimination based on race. Step by step we are discarding old discriminations; we must not adopt new ones.[45]

The perverse legislative intent of H.R. 5411 had become symbolically important to Southern leaders of the Eighty-second Congress; nonetheless, it died with the determined stroke of President Truman's veto pen. Unfortunately, Truman could generally only impact civil rights issues in the Eighty-second Congress through the negative influence of a presidential veto or through the creative use of executive orders and amicus briefs before the Vinson Court. When reflecting in 1959 on the president's controversial veto of H.R. 5411, Carl Rowan characterized Truman as "Mr. Civil Rights"—a reputation that was "solidly established" by 1951 because, in Rowan's opinion, President Truman "continued to hammer away on the [civil rights] issue, in both public utterances and in messages to Congress," including his response to the particularly unpleasant H.R. 5411.[46]

While racist members of the Congress were still reeling from Truman's veto of H.R. 5411, the president took additional unilateral action on December 3, 1951, to reinforce the civil rights goals of Executive Order 10210, which the president had issued earlier in 1951. Executive Order 10210 was important in guaranteeing equality for black Americans in the expanding Korean War effort, but the president issued an additional executive order, 10308, which mandated nondiscrimination in the hiring practices of all vendors doing business with the federal government during the frantic Korean War mobilization effort.[47] Referring to the increased federal outlays under the Defense Production Act of 1950, the president issued Executive Order 10308 to put new legal teeth into federal antidiscrimination efforts. Among other forms of increased oversight of federal contractors, Truman's issuance of Executive Order 10308 immediately established a multidepartmental committee that

> shall confer and advise with the appropriate officers of the various contracting agencies and with other persons concerned with a view toward the prevention and elimination of such discrimination, and may make to the said officers recommendations which in the judgment of the Committee will prevent or eliminate discrimination. When deemed necessary by the Committee it may submit any of these recommendations to the Director of Defense Mobilization, and the Director shall, when he deems it appropriate, forward such recommendations to the President, accompanied by a statement of his views as to the relationship thereof to the mobilization effort. The Committee shall establish such rules as may be necessary for the performance of its functions under this order.[48]

As with his earlier issuance of Executive Orders 9980 and 9981, Truman once again used his presidential powers to make sure that the nation's military infrastructure was colorblind. And like these prior orders, Executive Order 10308 provided for the bureaucratic accountability that would ensure that federal contractors could not exclude black Americans from participating fully in the employment boom resulting from the Korean War mobilization effort.

As the stalled Korean War raged on, taking a tremendous toll on young Americans, Truman went before the Congress on January 9, 1952, and delivered his seventh state of the union address. The president's popularity was at an all-time low: only 25 percent of the American public approved of his performance in the White House.[49] Truman's miserable rating in the polls was due in part to a furious nationwide public outcry following Truman's decision the prior April to fire the beloved but egomaniacal General Douglas MacArthur. The president's refusal to ignore MacArthur's insubordination was rooted in Truman's reverence for the constitutional imperative that the president and not a legendary general was the only legal commander in chief. That belief so anchored Truman that he subjected himself to public calls for his impeachment in 1951 when he relieved the aging MacArthur of his control over the frustrating Korean effort.[50]

Despite his low popularity and the repeated rebuffs of his civil rights proposals by Congress over the prior four years, President Truman remained undaunted in his 1952 state of the union address, where he once again urged the Congress to make civil rights a reality for all Americans.

> As we build our strength to defend the freedom in the world, we ourselves must extend the benefits of freedom more widely among all our own people. We need to take action toward the wider enjoyment of civil rights. Freedom is the birthright of every American.
>
> The executive branch has been making real progress toward full equality of treatment and opportunity—in the Armed Forces, in the civil service, and in private firms working for the Government. Further advances require action by Congress, and I hope that means will be provided to give the Members of the Senate and the House a chance to vote on them.[51]

For Truman, now in the twilight of his presidency, the issue of federal civil rights reform—a relatively unimportant issue for most Americans—remained a vital part of his agenda. And although it was painfully clear in early 1952 that civil rights legislation was a hopeless prospect for enactment by the Eighty-second Congress, President Truman persisted on the civil rights front.

While the nation took little note of the president's continued admonitions for congressional action on civil rights, Truman's persistence earned him the gratitude of notable civil rights leaders. That gratitude was evident when a leading group of civil rights advocates met with Truman at the White House on March 8, 1952, to urge him to seek reelection to the presidency.

> Twenty-one Negro leaders urged President Truman . . . to run for re-election in November and asked for a continuance of his civil rights and anti-communism policies.
>
> Assemblyman Elijah L. Crump of Manhattan's Twelfth Assembly District made public a joint statement by the leaders requesting Mr. Truman to stand for election. The statement stressed the concern of Negroes over the civil rights issue and contended that American prestige abroad had been diminished by racial intolerance at home.[52]

The feisty sixty-eight-year-old president subsequently decided not to seek reelection to the White House, but he remained an ardent and outspoken advocate for civil rights reform for the balance of his presidency. In speeches in 1952, including his commencement address at Howard University on June 13, 1952, and his campaign speech on behalf of Governor Adlai Stevenson in Harlem on October 11, 1952, this president from slave-owning ancestors reiterated his uncompromising public call for civil rights equality in a war-distracted United States. And in those final civil rights addresses, the president focused with understandable pride on the significant judicial actions that had been occurring since 1948 at the Supreme Court—a court headed for most of Harry Truman's presidency by his trusted friend and appointee Chief Justice Fred M. Vinson.

CHAPTER ELEVEN

Truman and the Vinson Court

"Separate but equal" is a constitutional anachronism which no
longer deserves a place in our law. . . . It is neither reasonable nor right
that colored citizens of the United States be subjected to the humiliation
of being segregated by law.
—Brief for the United States as Amicus Curiae,
Henderson v. United States, December 1947

When Harry Truman became president at the age of sixty, he had experienced
the vagaries of life in and out of politics. Whether working with hired hands on
his mother's farm at Grandview, leading the rowdy men of Battery D, or man-
aging road contractors as Jackson County judge, Truman knew how to size up
the men around him. This uncanny insight stayed with him when he went to
Washington in 1934 as the junior senator from Missouri; and while his sense of
confidence may have been tested in his early days in the U.S. Congress, he never
lost his basic good judgment about the quality and integrity of the men with
whom he worked.

One man who clearly impressed the green Senator Harry Truman was
Congressman Fred M. Vinson, a Kentuckian, six years younger than Truman
who nonetheless preceded Truman to the Congress by a full decade. While
Vinson's congressional service was interrupted for one term by a GOP landslide
in 1928, Fred Vinson was a seasoned and respected representative from the Eighth
District of Kentucky by the time Truman was elected to the Senate in 1934.

Tom Clark recalled in an oral history that Vinson and Truman "were old
friends. I think they knew one another when Fred was in the House. He was on
the Ways and Means [Committee]. I'm sure they did."[1] And good friends they
were—two men from border states where slavery had been a way of life for their

grandparents before the Civil War. In fact, Kentucky in 1860, with a total population of 1.15 million citizens was home to more than a quarter of a million slaves; with nearly 20 percent of its 1860 population consisting of indentured black Americans, Kentucky had more than double the number of slaves living in nearby Missouri, where 114,931 slaves were recorded by the U.S. Bureau of the Census on the eve of the Civil War.[2]

Truman's and Vinson's direct exposure as young men to the harsh remnants of America's discriminatory slave society was part of a shared intellectual bond. Through their entire lives, these men evidenced many similarities. Both were products of hardworking families that sent their sons to public schools. Both were from white, Anglo-Saxon, Protestant heritages; Truman attended the Baptist Church, Vinson the Methodist Church. Both were devoted to their wives, who were their life partners and the full-time no-nonsense mothers of their offspring. And both Truman and Vinson relaxed together for hours each week from the mid 1930s until Truman's departure from the White House on January 20, 1953, playing poker with a group of mutual friends, leaders in the capital. And while Truman relished the relaxation and good companionship of these weekly games, White House aide General Donald Dawson explained that the "Boss never would host his poker games at the White House since he felt strongly that a game involving money was off limits for that great House."[3]

With the White House off limits, the legendary Truman–Vinson poker games were held on the presidential yacht, at a local hotel, or at the home of his counsel, Clark Clifford. In his memoir, Clifford, one of President Truman's closest White House advisers, described the famous Truman poker games on the presidential yacht, the *Williamsburg,* where Chief Justice Vinson was the president's "favorite poker companion." Clifford wrote that Truman "loved an eight-handed poker game, and played with a core group of regulars, including George Allen, Stuart Symington, and Secretary of Agriculture (later Senator) Clinton Anderson. His favorite poker companion was Fred Vinson, his Secretary of the Treasury, and later Chief Justice of the United States."[4]

Truman's fondness for his "favorite poker companion" is evidenced both in his diary entries and in close friends' later reflections. It is abundantly clear that Truman and Fred Vinson shared much more than their early memories of life in border states. They also shared an intimate bond of friendship that was evident both at the card table and, importantly, in the public expressions of trust that President Harry Truman bestowed again and again on his friend Fred Vinson. Naming Vinson secretary of the Treasury Department in 1945, when the United States was facing one of the greatest economic challenges in its history, and then appointing Vinson to the lifetime position of chief justice of the Supreme Court were ample proof of the depth of the respect and friendship shared by these two men. And yet the by-product of this special relationship between a president, heading the country's executive branch, and the chief justice of the country's co-equal judicial branch is routinely overlooked by many historians of the Court and of the civil rights movement.

When the Vinson–Truman friendship is carefully analyzed, it is clear that a by-product of their close personal and professional relationship is a judicial record at the Vinson Supreme Court that greatly advanced President Truman's civil rights goals. Despite a recalcitrant Congress that refused to address Truman's civil rights reform proposals throughout his entire presidency, the Vinson Court was keenly attentive to the president's concerns about civil rights reform. As a result of the Court's and of Vinson's special receptivity, Truman was able to realize profound advances in regard to the civil rights of African Americans— advances that were simply impossible to achieve with the Democrat-controlled Congress that Truman was saddled with after 1948.

When Vice President Harry Truman became president on April 12, 1945, he was sworn into office by Chief Justice Harlan F. Stone, who had been appointed to the Court two decades earlier by President Calvin Coolidge. Simultaneous with Truman's hasty swearing in, the country began its deep mourning for Franklin Roosevelt, the father figure who had occupied the White House for twelve tumultuous years and had led the nation through the Great Depression and almost to the end of a world war that radically altered life in the United States. While the country was traumatized, Truman was not. Truman was a man of action, and he felt strongly at the outset of his presidency that he should have his own team around him, his own cabinet. In sharp contrast to Lyndon Johnson, who retained John Kennedy's cabinet after he suddenly became president in 1963, Truman moved with dispatch to name respected friends to cabinet posts.

By the end of July 1945, Truman had already begun to reshape his cabinet, and one of his first appointees was Fred M. Vinson, who was sworn in as Truman's secretary of the treasury on July 23, 1945. During this critical early period in his presidency, Truman had a great deal on his plate. He was preparing to meet with Stalin and Churchill for the first time and deciding to hasten the end of the war in the Pacific by using the awesome atomic bomb—a weapon largely unknown to Truman until becoming president. In this chaotic and challenging environment, Truman wanted a few trustworthy men around him, and he knew full well that they did not get much more trustworthy than Fred Vinson.

Truman's diary of June 17, 1945, reflects his trust in Vinson; in a brief entry made as the president relaxed going down the Potomac River on the USS *Potomac*—later called the *Williamsburg*—the president's yacht that became the venue for many of the endless presidential card games with Fred Vinson, he notes, "Went down the river today on the Potomac to discuss plans, issues, and *decisions*. Took Charlie Ross, straight thinker, honest man who tells me the truth so I understand what he means; Matt Connelly, shrewd Irishman, who raises up the chips and shows me the bugs, honest, fair, 'diplomatic' with me; Judge Fred Vinson, straight shooter, knows Congress and how they think, a man to trust."[5]

It was during this critical early period in his presidency that Truman realized that his vision of an effective United Nations, only a few months old, could not be achieved if the United States failed to serve as the credible global role model for the would-be democratic governments that were now emerging in the war-ravaged world. Many countries that were just liberated from the tyranny of Hitler and the Japanese Empire were now free to choose the form of government they wanted for their people. Based on their nearly daily association during this time, Secretary of the Treasury Fred Vinson knew firsthand how important Truman's goals for the United Nations were to a healthy, war-free United States. Vinson also knew that Truman's vision of the United States as the global role model of a true democracy lacked credibility as long as African diplomats stationed at the United Nations in New York could not travel to Washington by car or train without enduring the humiliations of "whites only" restrooms, dining cars, water fountains, and so on.

While these indignities were commonplace and known to the president, Truman was initially focused after becoming president on global issues, including expediting the end of the brutal war in the Pacific and limiting Stalin's greedy landgrab throughout Eastern and Central Europe. With his attention focused on these priorities, Truman did not formally act on civil rights until December 5, 1946, when he created his multiracial special Committee on Civil Rights by executive order. Before taking that bold, formal, presidential action, Truman was becoming increasingly troubled about civil rights abuses, particularly the gruesome and haunting racial violence directed at returning veterans, such as Sergeant Isaac Woodard. Truman also knew that the ugly KKK of his youth was on the move again, determined to reign in the "uppity" black American veterans who were returning to their homes throughout the South. And while there appears to be no lasting record of conversations between President Truman and Fred Vinson during this early postwar period, it is more than probable that these two close friends from similar backgrounds addressed the societal evils attendant on the emboldened KKK—a KKK that inspired increased racism in an America struggling to regain its economic equilibrium in 1946.

That Truman was aware of and deeply troubled by racial discrimination was confirmed by Tom C. Clark, who recalled late-night conversations during this period with the president aboard the *Williamsburg*. In recollecting a typical night of dinner and card playing on the yacht, Clark stated,

> We would eat dinner. We would usually start [playing cards] before dinner, and then we would have dinner, and then we would play until about 2 o'clock. The President and I used to go up and just lay down on the deck. I never saw anybody like him, he'd go to sleep right on the deck, wouldn't have any headrest or anything. You know this was summertime—it was good boating time. In the winter we'd play at our respective houses. He would just—sometimes we'd get to talking and he would tell me about, how when he was growing up—about the discrimination against the blacks, and how they couldn't get to first base, and everybody used them and things of that kind, you know. He was going to try to do something about it, that's what he told me.[6]

Clark's recollection of his conversations with Truman about the pervasive problem of racial discrimination in America is instructive. Based on the president's concern, it is not surprising that when Truman made his first major public declaration as president about civil rights to the NAACP on Sunday afternoon, June 29, 1947, he asked his chief justice of the Supreme Court, Fred Vinson, and his attorney general, Tom Clark, to accompany him to the steps of the Lincoln Memorial when he issued his civil rights Magna Carta.

But even before his friend Fred Vinson would leave his job as secretary of the treasury to become Truman's chief justice, the president began to shape the Supreme Court on September 19, 1945, when he named Republican Senator Harold Burton, his friend and senate colleague from the Truman committee, to the Court. Truman's appointment of Burton to the Supreme Court was mind-boggling to many Washington politicos because President Truman, who had been vilified for years for his Democratic partisanship and earlier ties to the infamous Thomas Pendergast machine, named a respected Republican senator from Ohio as his first appointee to the Court. But as Truman's subsequent three appointments to the country's highest court would confirm, Truman's priority was not political; his top priority was appointing men to the Court in whom he placed the highest trust—trust in each case built on years of professional and personal dealings. In evaluating Truman's appointment of Republican Senator Burton to the Supreme Court, the *Washington Post* editorialized,

> For his first nominee to the Supreme Court, President Truman has chosen one of the ablest and best-loved men in the Senate. Senator Harold Hitz Burton has an enviable record of public service. He is a man of unquestioned integrity and devotion to the public welfare. Although he has never been on the bench, his fairness and his judicious attitude toward problems that come before him for decision are ingrained characteristics.
>
> So far as his personal qualifications are concerned, the fact that Senator Burton is a Republican is of little significance. Politics sit lightly on this son of Ohio. As Mayor of Cleveland from 1935 to 1940 and as a member of the Senate since 1940, his reputation has not been won as a Republican fighting partisan battles. Rather it has been made as an efficient administrator and a thoughtful legislator who is eager to hear all the facts and to base his ultimate judgment on considerations of the public welfare.[7]

Truman's opportunity to place a trusted friend at the helm of the U.S. Supreme Court came with Chief Justice Harlan F. Stone's death on April 22, 1946. Truman seized this important opportunity by naming Fred Vinson on June 6, 1946, as his choice for chief justice of the Supreme Court of the United States. In nominating Vinson to the highest court in the land, Truman was essentially making Vinson his constitutional equal as head of the country's judicial system. As an avid student of American history, Truman knew that he was appointing Fred Vinson to a lifetime position with extraordinary potential to impact the life of every American.

Obviously, with Vinson's appointment as chief justice of the Court, as was the case with Senator Burton, President Truman knew exactly what type of person he was appointing. To Chief Justice Vinson's son and namesake, the president's motive in naming Vinson chief justice was rather obvious: "Well, at the time Dad was appointed to the Supreme Court, as everyone who is interested in history knows, they were having 'knock down, drag out' fights, very unseemly remarks by one justice directed at another. There were perhaps some of those involved in some of the personality conflicts who were running for chief justice. One quality that my father had was as a mediator, as a healer of wounds; he had a knack of getting people to work together who many [*sic*] not have been natural stablemates, and I'm sure that was a factor in President Truman's choice."[8]

Another informed insight about Truman's rationale for moving his trusted secretary of the treasury from the Treasury Building, just a stone's throw from the Oval Office, and putting him at the other end of Pennsylvania Avenue was offered by a close Vinson friend from the early 1920s in Kentucky, Judge Mac Swinford from the Eastern and Western Districts of Kentucky: "I think that the reason President Harry Truman appointed Fred Vinson as chief justice was because they were so much alike. I think that Harry Truman was intellectually honest and I think Fred Vinson was intellectually honest. I think that was the cementing tie of their friendship and their mutual respect for each other. I think of all things that Harry Truman would want as a judge or as chief justice was a man with intellectual integrity. And he recognized that characteristic in Fred Vinson."[9]

Such people as Judge Swinford who knew Fred Vinson and others who knew Truman well from his earliest days in politics appreciated the fact that Vinson and Truman were kindred spirits. Fred Vinson was intellectually and morally in touch with Truman, and Truman was intellectually and morally in sync with Fred Vinson. That special bond explains why it was not all that surprising to close friends of both men that Truman would take the secretary of the treasury away from his vital duties in the midst of the country's challenging postwar economic crisis and name him chief justice of the Supreme Court.

At the helm of the often bitterly divided Court, Truman's new chief justice tried to use his easygoing Kentuckian ways and his quiet persuasive skills to bring a new degree of harmony to the Court's contentious conferences. And with incredible good luck—luck that eluded several presidents in the twentieth century—Truman was able to help Chief Justice Vinson develop a majority coalition by subsequently appointing two additional men to the nine-member Supreme Court. Through these appointments, President Truman empowered four men of similar views to work collectively to shape the judicial agenda for America as it emerged successfully from a global war that had its ideological roots in racial and ethnic discrimination.

The current chief justice of the Supreme Court, William H. Rehnquist, in his book *The Supreme Court*, focused on chief Justice Vinson's "extensive experience in government," experiences that "undoubtedly gave him (Vinson) a feeling for the way government works that some of his colleagues did not possess."[10] Rehnquist had an unfettered view of Chief Justice Vinson and the Vinson Court during his clerkship in 1952 for Associate Justice Robert Jackson.

In discussing Vinson's attitude regarding the sometimes controversial actions of the Truman administration, including Truman's seizure of the steel mills in 1952, Rehnquist suggested that Vinson's prior experiences in government would have conditioned Vinson to think "that the Courts therefore should bend over backward to uphold his 'best effort' in this difficult situation (the Steel Seizure Case)."[11] Rehnquist, who became chief justice of the Court in 1986, noted that "rumor had it that Vinson remained an intimate crony of the President and participated in regular poker games at the White House."

Taken collectively, Rehnquist's observations are noteworthy because they reflect his informed, firsthand assessment of Chief Justice Vinson, a man who in Rehnquist's view was conditioned by his prior professional experiences to afford the chief executive maximum deference when Truman was caught in difficult situations. When it came to Truman's failed efforts to get his ten-point comprehensive civil rights program through the Senate, Vinson saw that his dear friend was in a very difficult and frustrating situation. Truman was literally locked in a legislative vise, with stubborn racist Southern Democrats on one side and equally uncooperative states' rights Republicans on the other. Neither side of this unholy senate coalition was willing to give Truman any chance for enacting the sweeping civil rights reform legislation that he knew was vital to the domestic and international interests of the United States.[12]

Truman's third appointee to the nation's highest court was Tom C. Clark. While Clark was Truman's only appointee to the Supreme Court who had not served with him in the Congress, Truman had worked closely with Clark when the Texan had served as President Roosevelt's assistant attorney general for both the Antitrust Division and the Criminal Division of the Justice Department. The men first met in 1937 when Clark arrived in Washington. Clark had been taken under the mentoring wing of his fellow Texan, House Speaker Sam Rayburn, one of Truman's closest friends in the Congress. Truman thought so much of Rayburn that in 1944 then-Senator Truman tried to persuade Rayburn to throw his hat into the vice presidential race—a race that the reluctant noncandidate Truman won when FDR finally settled on him as his vice presidential nominee.[13] Based on Truman's frequent dealings with Clark, particularly during the Justice Department's investigations supporting the Truman committee's efforts to eliminate corporate fraud in the war effort, President Truman initially recruited Clark on June 15, 1945, to be his first attorney general. Thus, within the first two months of his presidency, Truman's close friends, Fred Vinson as secretary of the treasury and Tom Clark as attorney general, were heading two of the administration's most important departments—departments that would help to mold a new America as the war came to a close in the Pacific on August 14.

As Truman's attorney general, from June 15, 1945, to August 24, 1949, Clark quickly cemented his relationship of trust with Truman. In the matter of civil rights, Clark appreciated Truman's goals for major federally led reform and clearly impressed the president with his quiet ability to make significant progress despite the rigid status quo attitude of most Southern Democrats and states' rights Republicans in the Congress. In recalling President Truman's instructions when naming him attorney general of the United States, Justice Clark said,

> He told me, and you'll find a slight reference to this in his book, that he thought that there were many injustices being visited upon many of our people, and that he wanted me to see if we couldn't bring a more effective justice home to the average man in the courts—not only Federal but state. And he seemed to be very much impressed with the idea of perhaps the Attorney General could in some extracurricular way, as well as officially, be a catalyst in that area. Then he told me, I remember well, he said, "Also I want you to pick out somebody for Solicitor General who, in the event you go, I'll have another man—I won't have to look all over the country and wait around to get me another man to be Attorney General."[14]

Clark's recollection of this key discussion with the president is instructive in several ways; it confirms the president's concerns about pervasive injustices throughout American postwar society; it also confirms Truman's determination to have a proactive attorney general who would use the substantial resources of the Justice Department forcefully to fight those injustices at both the federal and the state level. Clark's oral history, provided in 1972, also suggests that Truman had already decided in 1945 that Clark, like Fred Vinson, may have to exit Truman's cabinet for a new assignment on the U.S. Supreme Court.

However, before Tom Clark moved to the Supreme Court from the sprawling Justice Department Building at Ninth and Pennsylvania, Attorney General Clark aggressively followed President Truman's admonition that he attack the many injustices, including racial discrimination, that were confronting the people of America. In reflecting on his days as Truman's attorney general, Clark said,

> While I was Attorney General the President talked to me about discrimination, about like problems in the labor field. We brought some actions in that area. He also talked to me about restrictions in voting on the basis of color. He, of course, was interested in these basic discriminations during his entire public life. He recognized that the one power politicians recognized was the right to vote. And where a fellow didn't have a vote he

wouldn't get his rights protected and he wouldn't get any of the benefits of our society; and, so, he was anxious to wipe out such discriminations; that's why we pushed prosecutions in the labor and voting area. We found we would be able to successfully prosecute cases like Smith and Allwright, Plessy and the like; when the Government joined in the cases [through amicus curiae briefs,] it gave the case emphasis necessary for an expedited decision. The processes of investigation were so slow and cumbersome; all of the spade work had been completed. Why bring separate cases yourself when all of the points involved were already in the courts, private parties had already started them and the usual delay had already occurred, why not just join in and try to do it. I think our joining those cases were [*sic*] really more effective than if we had filed them ourselves.[15]

The hard-hitting amicus curiae briefs that were filed by Attorney General Clark and his successors at Truman's Justice Department proved to be important catalysts for change in several landmark civil rights rulings that the Vinson Court rendered as it systematically dismantled the separate-but-equal doctrine of *Plessy v. Ferguson*—a doctrine that had legitimized and anchored the segregated lifestyle of much of America since 1896. When Attorney General Tom Clark moved to the Supreme Court in 1949, Truman's next attorney general, Senator J. Howard McGrath, a Democrat from Rhode Island, continued to utilize Clark's effective amicus curiae brief strategy, as well as his own oral arguments before the Vinson Court in crucial civil rights cases.

The momentum for civil rights reform through controversial rulings of the Vinson Court was fueled further on September 15, 1949, when Truman named his fourth appointment to the Supreme Court, a former United States senator from Indiana and federal appellate judge from the Seventh Circuit, Sherman Minton. Like former senator Justice Harold Burton, Judge Minton had worked closely with Senator Harry Truman in the Senate; both had joined that body in 1934. Their friendship was heightened by their similar midwestern backgrounds. In Justice Tom Clark's view, Truman and Minton

> were close friends and Minton was on the Truman Committee [in the Senate]. But I think his experience as a judge from '41 to '49 was very strong—had emphasis in Mr. Truman's mind.
>
> Mr. Truman had gone, as you know, to law school at night for one year, but he did not have a law license.[16]

Harry Truman's own undergraduate and law school ambitions were frustrated throughout his life by family demands and financial problems; in 1923, Truman attended Kansas City School of Law at Kansas City for two years but had to put his nighttime law studies aside to focus on earning a livelihood for his wife and daughter.[17] After arriving in Washington as Senator Truman in 1935, he planned to finish his degree at the old Georgetown University Law School—but like his earlier law school experience, his law studies at Georgetown eluded Truman because of his professional demands—this time, the demands of serving in Congress. While Truman never earned a law degree, his no-nonsense, direct way of thinking and his studies during two years at law school, where he did quite well, equipped Truman with a solid understanding of the law and the role it could play in altering segregated life in the United States.

As illustrated by his four appointments, Truman was also a solid judge of intellectual competence and integrity. And with Minton's addition to the Vinson Court, Truman set the stage for what proved to be a spectacular series of civil rights decisions that would forever change the lives of blacks living and working in a racist America.

While Truman had the good fortune of naming four professional colleagues and friends to the Supreme Court, he also took advantage of his executive branch prerogatives by using the Justice Department to forcefully reiterate his views on civil rights to the very Supreme Court that he had shaped. In this regard, the rulings of the Vinson Court reveal the determined effort made by all three of the Truman administration's attorneys general to utilize an aggressive amicus brief strategy to explicitly and compellingly advocate a radical course of conduct for the Court in a wide range of civil rights cases. Pursuing this strategy of filing hard-hitting amicus briefs before the Supreme Court, Attorney General Clark had nearly four years at the helm of the Justice Department, where he contributed to the Truman administration's success in advancing its civil rights agenda.[18] In a later recollection about the Justice Department's amicus curiae strategy, Clark said that it "gave the [civil rights] case [the] emphasis necessary for an expedited decision. . . . I think our joining those cases were [*sic*] really more effective than if we [at the Department of Justice] had filed them ourselves."[19] This strategy, which Clark described as unprecedented, contributed to a series of fundamental civil rights rulings by the Vinson Court that collectively paved the way for the inevitable landmark ruling by the Warren Court in *Brown v. Board of Education*.

The first civil rights cases where the amicus strategy of Truman's Justice

Department had a noticeable and profound impact were *Shelley v. Kraemer* and *Hurd v. Hodge*—cases argued before the Vinson Court on January 15 and 16, 1948, by Philip Perlman, Truman's solicitor general. Speaking for the Truman administration, Perlman used his time before the Court directly to attack *Plessy v. Ferguson*'s separate-but-equal doctrine in an argument in which he was joined by one of the petitioner's attorneys, Thurgood Marshall. *Shelley v. Kraemer* dealt with the issue of whether the equal protection clause of the Fourteenth Amendment was violated when state courts, in this case courts in Missouri and Michigan, enforced private agreements that prevented African Americans from buying homes in certain "restricted" neighborhoods. *Shelley*'s companion case, *Hurd v. Hodge*, involved judicial enforcement of restrictive covenants in the nation's capital. While the immediate issue before the Court in *Shelley* and *Hurd* dealt with the racial discrimination inherent in restrictive covenants that impacted black petitioners, the restrictive covenants of the 1940s typically targeted not just African Americans but also Jewish citizens and other minorities. Several months before the *Shelley* and *Hurd* cases were argued, the report issued on October 29, 1947, by Truman's Civil Rights Committee highlighted the fact that restrictive covenants were widely enforced throughout the United States, not just in the segregated South.

In the Justice Department's amicus brief in *Shelley v. Kraemer,* filed in December 1947, Solicitor General Perlman, who was the third ranking official in the Justice Department under Attorney General Clark, emphasized the importance of Truman's civil rights goals to the members of the Vinson Court. Wasting no time on procedural niceties, the Justice Department's amicus brief in *Shelley* immediately reminded the Court of Truman's recent, unequivocal rejection of federal- and state-based racial discrimination. Using Truman's own words from his earlier speech before the NAACP at the Lincoln Memorial—a speech attended by Chief Justice Vinson, who had accompanied Truman to the steps of the Lincoln Memorial—the Justice Department's amicus brief made the following argument:

> The Federal Government has a special responsibility for the protection of the fundamental civil rights guaranteed to the people by the Constitution and laws of the United States. The President of the United States recently stated:
>
>> We must make the Federal Government a friendly vigilant defender of the rights and equalities of all Americans. *** Our National Government must show the way.

The Government is of the view that judicial enforcement of racial restrictive covenants on real property is incompatible with the spirit and letter of the Constitution and laws of the United States. It is fundamental that no agency of government should participate in any action which will result in depriving any person of essential rights because of race or color or creed. This Court has held that such discriminations are prohibited by the organic law of the land, and that no legislative body has power to create them. It must follow, therefore, that the Constitutional rights guaranteed to every person cannot be denied by private contracts enforced by the judicial branch of government—especially where the discriminations created by private contracts have grown to such proportions as to become detrimental to the public welfare and against public policy.

Residential restrictions based on race, color, ancestry, or religion have become a familiar phenomenon in almost every large community of this country, affecting the lives, the health, and the well-being of millions of Americans. Such restrictions are not confined to any single minority group. While Negroes (of whom there are approximately 13 million in the United States) have suffered most because of such discriminations, restrictive covenants have also been directed against Indians, Jews, Chinese, Japanese, Mexicans, Hawaiians, Puerto Ricans, Filipinos, and "non-Caucasians." . . .

Racial restrictive covenants on real property . . . have already expanded in large cities from coast to coast. They are responsible for the creation of isolated areas in which over crowded racial minorities are confined, and in which living conditions are steadily worsened. . . .

The fact that racial restrictive covenants are being enforced by instrumentalities of government has become a source of serious embarrassment to agencies of the Federal Government in the performance of many essential functions.[20]

In its amicus brief in *Shelley,* Truman's Justice Department under Attorney General Clark was at its intellectual best with its uncompromising and legally compelling rejection of restrictive covenants—discriminatory devices that had become an embarrassment at home and abroad for a nation that Truman knew must be the vigilant global role model of a real democracy.

When the oral arguments were over and the final briefs were submitted in *Shelley* and *Hurd,* Chief Justice Fred Vinson obviously recognized and agreed with the president's passionate words to the NAACP in the summer of 1947.

Vinson's agreement with the Justice Department arguments was reflected in his opinions in *Shelley* and *Hurd*—opinions decided on May 3, 1948, by a unanimous Court. In *Shelley*, the Vinson Court, in a 6-to-0 decision, held that, "in granting judicial enforcement of the restrictive agreements in these cases, the States have denied petitioners the equal protection of the laws and that, therefore, the action of the state courts cannot stand. We have noted that freedom from discrimination by the States in the enjoyment of property rights was among the basic objectives sought to be effectuated by the framers of the Fourteenth Amendment. . . . Upon full consideration, we have concluded that in these cases the States have acted to deny petitioners the equal protection of the laws guaranteed by the Fourteenth Amendment."[21]

In *Hurd,* the chief justice, writing again for a unanimous 6-to-0 Court, focused on the Civil Rights Act of 1866 and the joint resolution that was later adopted as the Fourteenth Amendment; in his opinion, Vinson concluded that there was a clear legislative and judicial basis whereby "a colored man is granted the right to acquire property free from interference by discriminatory state legislation." Vinson then cited the companion case of *Shelley v. Kraemer* as the basis for the conclusion that "the Fourteenth Amendment also forbids such discrimination where imposed by state courts in the enforcement of restrictive covenants. That holding is clearly indicative of the construction to be given to the relevant provisions of the Civil Rights Act in their application to the Courts of the District of Columbia." Truman's appointee as chief justice of the Supreme Court then delivered a mortal blow to the widespread reliance on restrictive covenants in the nation's capital by concluding that

> the explicit language employed by Congress to effectuate its purposes, leaves no doubt that judicial [334 U.S. 24, 34] enforcement of the restrictive covenants by the courts of the District of Columbia is prohibited by the Civil Rights Act. That statute, by its terms, requires that all citizens of the United States shall have the same rights "as is enjoyed by white citizens *** to inherit, purchase, lease, sell, hold, and convey real and personal property." That the Negro petitioners have been denied that right by virtue of the action of the federal courts of the District is clear. The Negro petitioners entered into contracts of sale with willing sellers for the purchase of properties upon which they desired to establish homes. Solely because of their race and color they are confronted with orders of court divesting their titles in the properties and ordering that the premises be vacated. White sellers, one of whom is a petitioner here, have been

enjoined from selling the properties to any Negro or colored person. Under such circumstances, to suggest that the Negro petitioners have been accorded the same rights as white citizens to purchase, hold, and convey real property is to reject the plain meaning of language. We hold that the action of the District Court directed against the Negro pur- chasers and the white sellers denies rights intended by Congress to be protected by the Civil Rights Act and that, consequently, the action can- not stand.[22]

While these unanimous holdings by the Vinson Court in 1948 created impor- tant judicial momentum for the civil rights reform called for by President Truman, *Shelley* and *Hurd* only undercut one aspect of *Plessy's* pervasive racist doctrine—namely, state-court enforcement of restrictive covenants.

Even though *Shelley* and *Hurd* were limited to restrictive covenants, public reaction to this landmark ruling was immediate and predictable. The subtitle of one *New York Times* front-page headline on May 4, 1948, heralded the Shelley–Hurd decisions: "Vinson Writes Opinions That Are Hailed as Blow to All Discriminatory Agreements." The *Times* noted, "Chief Justice Fred M. Vinson handed down two opinions advancing the long fight made by Negroes against such covenants and against their enforcement by courts in the states and federal territory."[23]

The *Times* also reported,

Negro and Jewish organizations and church and labor groups hailed last night the ruling of the Supreme Court forbidding use of the courts to enforce racially restrictive real estate covenants. . . . The decision was described by the National Association for the Advancement of Colored People as justification of its thirty-one year fight to outlaw discrimination in housing. Thurgood Marshall, special counsel to the NAACP, said that [the Supreme Court's ruling in *Shelley v. Kraemer*] gave "thousands of prospective home buyers throughout the United States new courage and hope in the American form of government."[24]

The *Washington Post* of Tuesday, May 4, by contrast, headlined, "Race Covenant Rule Disappoints Many." Washington was a city that cherished its Southern traditions, where white and black residents were segregated on every level of life, including housing, schools, playgrounds, and even restrooms and cafeterias in federal buildings. [25]

While noting that *Shelley* and *Hurd* were unanimous decisions, the *Washington Post* also reported that it was only a 6-to-0 decision because three of the Supreme Court justices necessarily recused themselves due to restrictive covenants pertaining to their own housing. That one-third of the Supreme Court's members in 1948 were directly affected by *Shelley* and *Hurd* served to highlight the vast, nationwide impact of this ruling, which applied equally to upscale residential areas of the nation's capital, as well as to modest row-house communities throughout the United States.[26]

Besides immediately eliminating the future use of restrictive covenants throughout the country, *Shelley* and *Hurd* were also significant because they confirmed the new proactive civil rights direction of the Vinson Court. That judicial momentum was advanced by the next Truman administration amicus brief filed before the Court in 1949 in the society-altering case of *Henderson v. United States*. In *Henderson,* the Vinson Court was confronted with a widespread form of segregation in interstate travel sanctioned by the federal government's Interstate Commerce Commission (ICC). Under an ICC-approved practice, railroad corporations allocated ten tables on a train's dining car for white patrons and offered only one table for black travelers. This demeaning form of segregation was aggravated by the routine requirement that black diners be kept out of the sight of white diners by curtains. As incredible and as obnoxious as this apartheid form of segregation seems to travelers today, it was an everyday reality throughout much of the United States in the 1940s.

In its hard-hitting amicus brief filed by Solicitor General Perlman in October 1949, Truman's Justice Department bluntly told the nine members of the Vinson Court,

> The order of the Interstate Commerce Commission approving the dining car regulations involved in this case is invalid on constitutional and statutory grounds. Both the Constitution and the Interstate Commerce Act give all persons traveling on interstate carriers the right to equal treatment, without being subject to governmentally-enforced [*sic*] discriminations based on race or color. . . .
>
> Segregation as enforced by the regulations imports the inferiority of the Negro race. Enforced racial segregation in itself constitutes a denial of the right to equal treatment. Equal treatment means the same treatment. The issues before the Court in this case are not governed by the so-called "separate but equal" doctrine of *Plessy v. Ferguson,* 163 U.S. 537, and related cases. Even assuming, *arguendo,* that that doctrine retains some vitality for constitutional purposes, it does not establish the validity, under

Section 3 of the Interstate Commerce Act, of the railroad's regulations. But if the Court should conclude that the issues here cannot be decided without reference to the "separate but equal" doctrine, the Government submits that the legal and factual assumptions upon which *Plessy v. Ferguson* was decided have been demonstrated to be erroneous, and that the doctrine of that case should now be re-examined and overruled. The notion that separate but equal facilities satisfy constitutional and statutory prohibitions against discrimination is obsolete. The phrase "equal rights" means the same rights.[27]

Here the Truman legal team firmly argued that "'equal rights' means the same rights" and that the factual assumptions that were the basis for the Supreme Court's decision in *Plessy v. Ferguson* fifty-three years earlier were erroneous and should be overturned. This broadside attack by Truman's Justice Department on *Plessy*'s separate-but-equal doctrine was reiterated in oral arguments on April 3, 1950, before a Supreme Court that now included former Attorney General Tom Clark. Arguing before the Court for the administration was Truman's new attorney general, Howard McGrath, and Solicitor General Perlman. Supporting the Truman administration was Thurgood Marshall, who filed an amicus curiae brief on behalf of the NAACP.

In an opinion written by Truman's first appointee to the Supreme Court, Justice Harold Burton, the Court held, by an 8-to-0 vote,

It is clear that appellant has standing to bring these proceedings. He is an aggrieved party, free to travel again on the Southern Railway. Having been subjected to practices of the railroad which the Commission and the court below found to violate the Interstate Commerce Act, he may challenge the railroad's current regulations on the ground that they permit the recurrence of comparable violations. . . .

The right to be free from unreasonable discriminations belongs, under § 3 (1), to each particular person. Where a dining car is available to passengers holding tickets entitling them to use it, each such passenger is equally entitled to its facilities in accordance with reasonable regulations. The denial of dining service to any such passenger by the rules before us subjects him to a prohibited disadvantage. . . .

We need not multiply instances in which these rules sanction unreasonable discriminations. The curtains, partitions and signs emphasize the artificiality of a difference in treatment which serves only to call attention to a racial classification of passengers holding identical tickets and using the same public dining facility.[28]

Importantly, the Court in *Henderson* relied on the Vinson Court's earlier unanimous decision in *Shelley* to broaden its incremental assault on *Plessy's* separate-but-equal doctrine. While the Court's 8-to-0 decision in *Henderson* was unanimous, Justice Clark decided he could not take part in the consideration of this particular case because of his earlier involvement while attorney general in the Justice Department's amicus brief in *Shelley*.

Henderson v. United States was just one of a trio of civil rights decisions handed down by the Vinson Court on June 5, 1950. Along with *Henderson,* the Vinson Court issued its unanimous rulings in *Sweatt v. Painter* and *McLaurin v. Oklahoma State Regents*—cases that were collectively argued with *Henderson* before the Vinson Court over a two-day period on April 3 and 4, 1950. While *Henderson* dealt with segregation in interstate travel, *McLaurin* and *Sweatt* were substantively related cases dealing with long-standing practices of segregation in state-sponsored higher education. In *McLaurin,* the Court detailed the facts triggering the suit by G. W. McLaurin, a black graduate student who sought to augment his Master's degree in education with a Doctorate in education from the University of Oklahoma. The single issue before the Court in this case was whether McLaurin was being denied his constitutional rights of equal protection under the Fourteenth Amendment as a result of Oklahoma's requirement that he sit in seating assigned only for black students while attending classes at the university's graduate school. Thus the issue was not racial discrimination in the availability of education: McLaurin was permitted to sit in the same classroom with white students where he would hear the same lectures and therefore arguably receive the same quality of education; rather, it was the more narrow issue of Oklahoma's demeaning requirement that McLaurin use seating designated for blacks in the university's classrooms, library, and cafeteria.

In authoring the Court's unanimous decision in *McLaurin,* Chief Justice Vinson cut to the heart of the bogus arguments made by the University of Oklahoma that doctoral candidate McLaurin was receiving the exact same quality education as his white colleagues.

> It is said that the separations imposed by the State in this case are in form merely nominal. McLaurin uses the same classroom, library and cafeteria as students of other races; there is no indication that the seats to which he is assigned in these rooms have any disadvantage of location. He may wait

in line in the cafeteria and there stand and talk with his fellow students, but while he eats he must remain apart.

These restrictions were obviously imposed in order to comply, as nearly as could be, with the statutory requirements of Oklahoma. But they signify that the State, in administering the facilities it affords for professional and graduate study, sets McLaurin apart from the other students. The result is that appellant is handicapped in his pursuit of effective graduate instruction. Such restrictions impair and inhibit his ability to study, to engage in discussions and exchange views with other students, and, in general, to learn his profession.

Our society grows increasingly complex, and our need for trained leaders increases correspondingly. Appellant's case represents, perhaps, the epitome of that need, for he is attempting to obtain an advanced degree in education, to become, by definition, a leader and trainer of others. Those who will come under his guidance and influence must be directly affected by the education he receives. Their own education and development will necessarily suffer to the extent that his training is unequal to that of his classmates. State-imposed restrictions which produce such inequalities cannot be sustained.

It may be argued that appellant will be in no better position when these restrictions are removed, for he may still be set apart by his fellow students. This we think irrelevant. There is a vast difference—Constitutional difference—between restrictions imposed by the state which prohibit the intellectual commingling of students, and the refusal of individuals to commingle where the state presents no such bar. Shelley v. Kraemer, *334 U.S. 1,* 13–14 (1948). The removal of the state restrictions will not necessarily abate individual and group predilections, prejudices and choices. But at the very least, the state will not be depriving appellant of the opportunity to secure acceptance by his fellow students on his own merits.[29]

It is noteworthy that the chief justice relied once again on his unanimous *Shelley* decision as the Court in *McLaurin* essentially eliminated discrimination in state-supported graduate schools not only in Oklahoma but throughout the United States.

Chief Justice Vinson's final opinion in the monumental trio of unanimous civil rights rulings handed down on June 5, 1950, dealt with a long-standing pattern of racial discrimination at the University of Texas Law School. In this case, a black man named Heman Sweatt, who had applied for admission to the university's law school, was admitted to a newly established state-funded law school for blacks only. In *Sweatt,* the Vinson Court decided squarely to address the fiction of a separate-but-equal society where, in this case, the state of Texas insisted that it had met the controlling standard of *Plessy* by admitting Sweatt to a comparable—albeit all-black—state-supported law school instead of the all-white University of Texas Law School.

In *Sweatt,* Thurgood Marshall joined Truman's attorney general in arguing forcefully for the petitioner, Sweatt, who adamantly refused to settle for the alternative "blacks only" law school education that the state of Texas frantically tried to assemble. Pointing out that Texas had an integrated bar in 1950, Marshall asked the justices on the Court where he would later sit, "Why can't they study law together?"[30] Marshall asserted that there was no rational relationship between races and public education; education is not a privilege but the foundation for all rights, and those rights belong equally to all Americans under the Fourteenth Amendment. Marshall offered one of his most compelling arguments when he bluntly told the Court that the state of Texas "can build an exact duplicate [of the University of Texas Law School] but if it is segregated, it is unequal."[31]

The Vinson Court obviously paid close attention to Truman's attorney general and to Marshall when rendering its opinion in *Sweatt.* Acknowledging that Sweatt was rejected by the University of Texas solely "because he is a Negro," the chief justice authored a sweeping opinion that reflected his own sensitivity to racism—racism that he had observed firsthand as a young lawyer in the border state of Kentucky:[32]

> The law school, the proving ground for legal learning and practice, cannot be effective in isolation from the individuals and institutions with which the law interacts. Few students and no one who has practiced law would choose to study in an academic vacuum, removed from the interplay of ideas and the exchange of views with which the law is concerned. The law school to which Texas is willing to admit petitioner excludes from its student body members of the racial groups which number 85% of the population of the State and include most of the lawyers, witnesses, jurors, judges and other officials with whom petitioner will inevitably be dealing when he becomes a member of the Texas Bar. With such a substantial and significant segment of society excluded, we cannot conclude that the education offered petitioner is substantially equal to that which he would receive if admitted to the University of Texas Law School. . . .

[Sweatt] may claim his full constitutional right: legal education equivalent to that offered by the State to students of other races. Such education is not available to him in a separate law school as offered by the State. We cannot, therefore, agree with respondents that the doctrine of Plessy v. Ferguson, *163 U.S. 537* (1896), requires affirmance of the judgment below. . . . We hold that the Equal Protection Clause of the Fourteenth Amendment requires that petitioner be admitted to the University of Texas Law School.[33]

Judging by a memorandum that Clark sent to his fellow justices during the Court's October 1949 term, Vinson's direct assault in *Sweatt* on the *Plessy* doctrine of separate but equal had Justice Clark's full support. In this candid assessment by Clark of the significance of the *Sweatt* and *McLaurin* cases, he urged, "The issue of *Plessy v. Ferguson's* application to these cases must be met."[34] Clark, a graduate of the University of Texas Law School, class of 1922, did not hesitate to reject the flawed arguments of Texas officials who claimed that would-be attorney Sweatt would receive an equal law education in the state's alternative "blacks only" law school. In the closing sentence of Clark's memorandum, he confirms a sentiment shared by Chief Justice Vinson and his other colleagues on the Court that ruled unanimously in *Henderson, Sweatt,* and *McLaurin*: "If some say this [series of rulings] undermines *Plessy,* then let it fall, as have many Nineteenth Century oracles."[35]

When evaluating the long-term impact of the Vinson Court's civil rights activism evidenced by the three landmark civil rights rulings of June 5, 1950, it is clear from the language of these cases that the Court was determined to overturn *Plessy* under the judicial leadership of Truman's appointee and dear friend Chief Justice Fred Vinson. That President Truman had named three other justices besides Fred Vinson to the Supreme Court by the time *Henderson, McLaurin,* and *Sweatt* were handed down is also significant since all of Truman's appointees to the Court had a firsthand appreciation of Truman's views on civil rights based on their close professional and personal relationships with the president. By their shared background and experiences, these justices knew how important civil rights reform was to President Truman and to his ability to lead the nation forward, both domestically and globally. And on June 5, 1950, building on its earlier unanimous decisions in *Shelley v. Kraemer* and *Hurd v. Hodge,* the Vinson Court provided for sweeping structural civil rights reform that the Congress refused to embrace. While historians understandably have credited the Warren

Court for finally disposing of *Plessy* in 1954, the important judicial momentum for dismantling *Plessy*'s repugnant separate-but-equal doctrine was in fact generated by the aggressive actions taken by Truman's Justice Department and by the landmark civil rights rulings of the men he appointed to the Supreme Court.

Much of the American public was stunned by the collective and radical impact of *Sweatt, McLaurin,* and *Henderson*—the cases that would immediately change the racial landscape in higher education and interstate travel throughout the United States. The harsh public reaction to the Vinson Court's June 5 rulings was captured by the *Austin American Statesman,* which reported on June 6, 1950, that the south was in turmoil.

> Governor Herman Talmadge of Georgia shouted defiance Monday in first southern reaction to Supreme Court decisions hitting at racial segregation. . . . The Court ruled that a Negro law student must be admitted to the all-white University of Texas because separate facilities for Negroes there are not equal. It said white and Negro students in graduate work at the University of Oklahoma cannot be separated. And it ruled out racial segregation on railroad dining cars. Declared Talmadge: "As long as I am governor, Negroes will not be admitted to white schools. The line is drawn. The threats that have been held over the head of the South for four years are now pointed like a dagger ready to be plunged into the very heart of southern tradition." . . . The decisions found the South with many glaring educational in-equalities. Not a single southern state supports a Negro medical school. A Ph.D. degree is not available at any southern Negro university. . . . Florida Superintendent of Public Instruction Thomas D. Bailey said "the ramifications of those decisions are of such vital nature it's difficult for me to foresee the results." . . . In New York, the National Association for the Advancement of Colored People issued the following statement:
>
> > The NAACP is gratified by the opinion of the Supreme Court in the Henderson, Sweatt and McLaurin cases, particularly since our attorneys argued the latter two cases and filed a brief in the Henderson case. The Supreme Court decisions emphasize once more that the courts of the land are far in advance of the Congress in recognizing the legal and moral obligations of our government to grant civil rights to all citizens regardless of race, creed or color.[36]

While much of the Southern press expressed revulsion at the collective impact of the Vinson Court's rulings in *Henderson, McLaurin,* and *Sweatt,* the *Baltimore Afro-American* celebrated with a banner headline on June 6, 1950: "White Supremacy Takes a Beating: Supreme Court Rules Favorably in All Three Segregation Cases." Praising Baltimore native NAACP attorney Thurgood Marshall for his great victories, the *Afro-American* concluded,

In three sweeping and unanimous decisions handed down on Monday, June 5[, 1950], the United States Supreme Court dealt a serious blow to white supremacy as it affects segregation in schools and on dining cars.

The Court did the following:

1. Reversed the judgment of the special three-judge Federal District Court in the case of G. W. McLaurin, a graduate student at the University of Oklahoma and ordered that the State-supported institution provide the same treatment for him as provided white students.

2. Reversed the decision of the Texas Court of Civil Appeals in the case of Heman Marion Sweatt, who sought admission to the University of Texas Law School and ordered him admitted to it on the grounds that the law school at the "colored" university was in no wise equal to the white.

3. Reversed the ruling of the Federal District Court of Maryland and ordered that court to set aside the order of the Inter-state Commerce Commission which upheld the dining car discrimination of Elmer W. Henderson by the Southern Railroad.

The three decisions represent the greatest victories for the NAACP legal staff, headed by Thurgood Marshall, which had carried them all the way to the highest tribunal.

They also represented a real victory for the Truman Administration, which in briefs filed by the Solicitor General and the U.S. Attorney General, had called for the end of the discrimination involved in the three cases.

Those briefs filed by Philip Perlman, J. Howard McGrath and Tom Clark, who was forced to excuse himself from participation in the Supreme Court because he had taken an active part as Attorney General, declared that the segregation and discrimination were violative of the Constitution and of U.S. principles.[37]

Almost two weeks after the stunning Supreme Court rulings of June 5, Marshall, in a June 17 article in the *Baltimore Afro-American* newspaper, was quoted as praising the rulings, claiming, "The complete destruction of all enforced segregation is now in sight."

> Although the *Plessy v. Ferguson* decision of 1896, which set up the "separate but equal" doctrine, was not specifically overruled Mr. Marshall said, "its effectiveness in graduate and professional education has been destroyed."
>
> "Segregation no longer has the stamp of legality in any public education."
>
> In addition, he said, "There is no question that segregation in all forms and types of segregated transportation is now unlawful." . . .
>
> The opinions in the two successful school cases are expected to bring about a change in the other 15 States and District of Columbia, where jim-crow education is authorized by law. Quick action is expected in the Six States which already have suits pending against them. They are Maryland, 7 suits; North Carolina, 4 suits; Louisiana, 4 suits; Florida, 6 suits; Georgia, 2 suits and South Carolina 1. In Kentucky, a new State law, which became effective June 15, permits boards of trustees for various institutions to vote to allow colored students to take courses not offered at Kentucky State college, the colored land-grant college. Some Kentucky schools already admit all students, as does the University of Arkansas in its Schools of Medicine and Law. In Maryland, a one-man fight is being waged to get around a State Court of Appeals ruling which ordered the University of Maryland to admit Miss Esther McCready to its School of Nursing. Even State officials recognize the futility of trying to fight the case further.[38]

While the NAACP extolled the trio of June 5, 1950, rulings by the Vinson Court mandating nonseparate equality for black Americans, the journey to full academic equality proved challenging for Texas law student Heman Sweatt. On October 18, 1950, just five months after the U.S. Supreme Court ordered the state of Texas to admit Sweatt to a desegregated University of Texas Law School, the *Daily Texan* reported that Austin firemen were called to the law school campus to douse "a 'fiery cross' . . . which stood six feet tall, was sturdily constructed of 4 by 4's and was wrapped in kerosene-soaked rags." The *Daily Texan* also reported that the incident was "near the southern corner of the Law Building. The letters

'KKK' were found painted on the building's steps"—steps that Heman Sweatt would climb each day of class as the first black American in Texas to enjoy "equal" access under the Vinson Court's ruling to the state's law school.[39]

Based on the trio of June 1950 rulings by the U.S. Supreme Court, it was now obvious that the Truman administration's aggressive judicial strategy had helped to trigger significant civil rights reform through utilization of the country's most powerful court, which was now highly sensitized to the constitutional rights of black Americans. It was also clear by midyear 1950 that the Vinson Court had become a pivotal force in the evolving civil rights battle that pitted Truman against states' righters who staunchly opposed Truman's view that full civil rights equality for black Americans was a basic constitutional right. Moreover, while an earlier Supreme Court, in 1944, had set in motion the practice of Supreme Court–generated civil rights reform with a ruling against the Texas "whites only" primary system in *Smith v. Allwright,* it was apparent by June 5, 1950, that judicial activism on civil rights cases had moved into high gear under the Truman-shaped Vinson Court.[40]

Despite the Congress's continued refusal to consider civil rights reform, Truman's legal team at the Justice Department remained vigilant before the Vinson Court. As lame-duck President Truman was preparing to vacate the recently rebuilt White House in December 1952, the Justice Department seized another important opportunity to use the Vinson Court to effectuate civil rights reform. In its December 2, 1952, amicus curiae brief to the Vinson Court in *Brown v. Board of Education,* the Truman administration helped to define both the judicial record and the final outcome of the Supreme Court's 1954 *Brown* decision. Truman's solicitor general argued vigorously in support of the civil rights of five petitioners whose cases had been consolidated before the Supreme Court during the 1952 October term.[41] One of the consolidated cases was brought by Oliver Brown on behalf of his daughter Linda, a black schoolgirl who was refused admission to a white public school in Topeka, Kansas.[42] With the consolidated *Brown* case, Justice Tom Clark and his fellow Supreme Court justices had "representative cases from different parts of the country"; and for the first time, the Vinson Court had before it a set of five geographically diverse cases that could once and for all overturn the separate-but-equal doctrine that the Vinson Court had already substantially attacked and eroded through its holdings in *Shelley, Hurd, Henderson, Sweatt,* and *McLaurin.*[43]

In a hard-hitting thirty-two-page amicus brief in *Brown,* the Department of Justice, arguing for the Truman administration, used excerpts from President Truman's February 2, 1948, Special Message to Congress on Civil Rights. In a conclusion that bluntly reminded the Vinson Court of the new global role of the United States as the beacon of democracy in the Cold War environment, the Truman administration's amicus brief in *Brown* argued,

> The subordinate position occupied by Negroes in this country as a result of governmental discriminations ("second-class citizenship," as it is sometimes called) presents an unsolved problem for American democracy, an inescapable challenge to the sincerity of our espousal of the democratic faith.
>
> In these days, when the free world must conserve and fortify the moral as well as the material sources of its strength, it is especially important to affirm that the Constitution of the United States places no limitation, express or implied, on the principle of the equality of all men before the law. Mr. Justice Harlan said in his dissent in the *Plessy* case (163 U.S. at 562):
>
> > We boast of the freedom enjoyed by our people above all other peoples. But it is difficult to reconcile that boast with a state of the law which, practically, puts the brand of servitude and degradation upon a large class of our fellow-citizens, our equals before the law.
>
> The Government and people of the United States must prove by their actions that the ideals expressed in the Bill of Rights are living realities, not literary abstractions. As the President has stated:
>
> > If we wish to inspire people of the world whose freedom is in jeopardy, if we wish to restore hope to those who have already lost their civil liberties, if we wish to fulfill the promise that is ours, we must correct the remaining imperfections in our practice of democracy.
>
> > We know the way. We need only the will.[44]

By using the Justice Department's amicus brief in *Brown* to reiterate his administration's expansive civil rights vision before the Vinson Court in the final days of his presidency, Truman once again put his remaining, though diminished, political capital squarely behind his radical civil rights program. The December 2, 1952, amicus brief in the consolidated *Brown* case, was also significant because it reinforced and significantly expanded the arguments of the Truman administration against *Plessy*'s still viable separate-but-equal doctrine—a doctrine that had been significantly narrowed but not completely eliminated by the Vinson Court's earlier rulings.

Moreover, by focusing in its *Brown* amicus on current domestic realities, as well as on the negative view of a segregated United States in the fragile global arena, Truman's legal advocates at the Justice Department creatively shaped a host of compelling arguments for the elimination of the separate-but-equal doctrine, charging that it was "a contradiction in terms," "wrong as a matter of constitutional law," and a "source of constant embarrassment to this government in the day-to-day conduct of its foreign relations."[45]

Truman's Department of Justice also used its *Brown* amicus brief to remind Chief Justice Vinson of the president's publicly expressed and privately held views about civil rights—views that Justice Vinson had frequently heard when serving as Truman's secretary of the treasury. Importantly, the Justice Department's December 2 amicus brief provided additional judicial momentum for a Supreme Court that had already been receptive to the Truman administration's earlier admonitions that *Plessy's* separate-but-equal doctrine was an unacceptable anachronism that must be eliminated from the country's judicial landscape if the integrity of the United States as the democratic leader of the world were to be secure.

The positive momentum for judicial reform in the civil rights arena created by the Court's June 5, 1950, rulings was adroitly utilized by Thurgood Marshall who, acting as special counsel to the NAACP, continued to argue his own expansive view of constitutionally protected civil rights before the Vinson Court and later before the Warren Court. Marshall's most famous argument before the Supreme Court would ultimately occur in the *Brown* case. Marshall, like Truman and Truman's Attorneys General Tom Clark, Howard McGrath, and James McGranery, knew that the time was ripe to achieve comprehensive civil rights reform through the Court, and they also fully appreciated the sad fact that even modest civil rights reform would never happen if left in the hands of a Congress in which Southern Democrats, including Senator Lyndon Johnson, routinely aborted any serious civil rights reform legislation, a state of affairs that lasted until long after Truman left the White House.

The hope harbored by Truman that his friend Chief Justice Vinson would finally end *Plessy's* reign of racism was shattered on September 8, 1953, when Vinson died at the age of sixty-three.[46] Vinson's Court, which had been repeatedly sensitized to the plight of black Americans by the Truman administration's amicus briefs, oral arguments, and petitioners' briefs, became the Warren Court. It was this Court that, in 1954, finally and fully destroyed *Plessy's* separate-but-equal doctrine with its decision in *Brown*. While *Brown* was handed down by the Warren Court during the Eisenhower administration, the record of the Vinson Court's civil rights rulings during the late 1940s and early 1950s confirms that the vision for and the accelerated movement toward integrated public education was a presidentially supported concept first articulated to the Supreme Court by Truman's administration. Under Fred Vinson, the Supreme Court mandated, in a way that the Congress refused to do, the integration of residential communities, the integration of the nation's law schools and graduate schools, and equality for travelers in the dining cars of trains that crisscrossed the United States. Thus, well before *Brown,* the structural dismantling of *Plessy v. Ferguson* was being methodically achieved by the Vinson Court; and as Marshall declared after the three Vinson Court rulings of June 5, 1950, "The complete destruction of all enforced segregation is now in sight."[47]

Some court historians have speculated about the fate of *Brown* had Chief Justice Vinson not passed away in 1953, making possible Chief Justice Earl Warren's appointment to the Court. The suggestion that the unanimous outcome in the *Brown* case would have been different if ruled on by the Vinson Court and not by the Warren Court was dismissed as "tommy rot, just pure and simple," by Justice Tom Clark, who served on the Supreme Court with Vinson when *Shelley, Hurd, Henderson, McLaurin,* and *Sweatt* were handed down and who on May 17, 1954, voted with the new chief justice, Earl Warren, when the Warren Court unanimously rendered its *Brown* decision. A historian at the University of Kentucky on May 8, 1973, asked Clark, "What would have happened if Vinson had lived and what was his position with regard to [the *Brown*] decision?" Retired Justice Clark had no doubt about the outcome in *Brown.* "The result would have been the same. . . . The opinion may have been written differently. One can hardly surmise how Chief Justice Vinson would have written it. I don't see how any informed person could conclude to the contrary. Indeed, the result was forecast in *Sweatt* and *Painter. . . .* [Vinson] also had written the *Shelley v. Kraemer* opinion (which had to do with restrictive covenants) and which announced new doctrines in that area. . . . So I don't see how one can support any other conclusion as to *Brown.*"[48]

After the historian conducting the interview persisted in suggesting that Chief Justice Vinson may have stalled the *Brown* decision had he lived on into the mid 1950s, Clark explained that the Supreme Court often deliberately delayed rulings until they felt they were "ripe." Clark explained,

When I came here, the cases [in *Brown*] were here. I came in 1949, and *all* of us thought the climate was not just ripe for change. We often delay adjudication. it's [*sic*] not a question of evading at all. It's just the practicalities of life—common sense. The cases were not really clear cut. The records were cloudy. They came from the South. We wanted to get a national coverage, rather than a sectional one. There were violations, equally repulsive, other than in the South, such as Delaware, Kansas, and the District of Columbia. We delayed, awaiting the filing of additional cases; we hoped to have one based on the Fifth Amendment along with those predicated upon the Fourteenth. And soon we got one here in the District of Columbia. It was deliberate on the part of each of us, just as much so as the term "deliberate speed" was inserted intentionally into the opinion on implementation—a phrase which, of course, was borrowed from Mr. Justice [Oliver Wendell] Holmes. There was no shuffling of feet, no holding back on the legal question. It was simply a question of (1) getting a broad area of coverage; (2) thereby securing the opinions of the various Attorneys General of the states; and (3) getting more light for ourselves. We were successful in this since we were able to consolidate some five cases into one argument, covering a diversified area from this standpoint of geography.[49]

In a separate oral history that Justice Clark provided in 1972 for the Truman Library, he reiterated his view that *Brown* was held for "about three years, because we wanted to try to get a better national coverage."[50]

Justice Vinson's son, Fred Moore Vinson Jr., shed further light on the likely outcome of *Brown* if it had been ruled on by the Vinson Court. In an oral history for the University of Kentucky, Vinson confirmed that his father held liberal views when it came to civil rights cases before the Court. The late chief justice's son also discussed his father's attitude toward black Americans and the impact of that background in shaping Vinson's liberal civil rights rulings during his seven-year tenure as chief justice.

There is another line of cases that Dad participated in that had to do with racial problems. . . . He had a genuine feeling for those problems, which evolved in several opinions which were the forerunners of the landmark decisions of the late '50s and '60s. The case of *Sweatt v. Painter* where, for the first time, the Court held that in higher education "separate is not equal," and that you couldn't have segregation in higher education (to oversimplify the rule of the Court), and Dad wrote that opinion. He wrote the opinion in *Shelley v. Kraemer,* a racial covenant case, saying that you couldn't use the machinery of the courts to enforce racial covenants. In those terms for that time (the late '40s and the early '50s), he would have to be placed on the liberal side of the scale. He's been characterized by many legal writers as a conservative on those scores, but I would suggest to them that what's conservative today may have been quite liberal yesterday.[51]

Despite explicit confirmation from one of Vinson's colleagues on the Court, Justice Tom Clark—that a Vinson-led Supreme Court in 1954 would have handed down the same unanimous ruling that the Warren Court rendered on May 17, 1954—several court historians have speculated that a divided court under Chief Justice Vinson was a probable outcome. In this regard, Supreme Court historian Bernard Schwartz expressed a different opinion from Clark's in *A History of the Supreme Court,* an opinion that Schwartz himself seems to undercut when discussing the earlier behind-the-scenes machinations that preceded the Court's ultimate unanimous ruling in *Brown* in 1954.

Schwartz confirms that in Chief Justice Vinson's last term on the Court before his sudden death on September 8, 1953, Vinson "was distressed over the Court's inability to find a unified position on such an important case."[52] Despite Vinson's leadership role in the Court's earlier unanimous civil rights cases, *Shelley, Hurd, McLaurin,* and *Sweatt,* Schwartz nonetheless concluded that "had Vinson presided over the Court that decided *Brown,* the result would have been a divided decision."[53]

Schwartz's conclusion is curious because he ignores the critical precedent-setting language debunking *Plessy's* separate-but-equal doctrine in Vinson's unanimous opinions in *Shelley, Hurd, McLaurin,* and *Sweatt,* as well as Vinson's support for Justice Burton's unanimous opinion in *Henderson.* In fact, Schwartz never references the Vinson Court's rulings in *Hurd, Henderson, McLaurin,* a puzzling omission for any Court historian who seeks to provide a comprehensive and balanced understanding of the Court's decision against *Plessy v. Ferguson* in *Brown.*

In this regard, Justice Harold Burton's diary entries from the protracted period of the Vinson and Warren Courts' consideration of the consolidated *Brown* segregation cases are illuminating in several areas. Burton, who voted with Chief Justice Vinson in *Shelley, Hurd, Henderson, McLaurin,* and *Sweatt,* noted that "postponement [during Vinson's last term on the Court] was with the hope of a better result later."[54] In this same diary entry just nine days before the Warren Court handed down its unanimous ruling in *Brown,* Justice Burton praised the final unanimous opinion in *Brown*—an outcome achieved in part based on Chief Justice Vinson's earlier support of a delay in the Court's final argument of the consolidated *Brown* cases. As suggested in Justice Burton's diary, a divided decision in *Brown* was possible without adequate time for several justices, including

Vinson, to find a flexible—yet constitutionally sound—basis for the final dismantling of the last bulwark of *Plessy's* separate-but-equal doctrine of segregated public education throughout the United States.

Further confirmation that a Vinson-led Court would ultimately have done essentially the same thing with *Brown* that the Warren Court did is also found in the very words of Chief Justice Vinson's opinions in *Sweatt* and *McLaurin*— opinions that were relied upon as judicial cornerstones in Chief Justice Warren's unanimous opinion in *Brown:*

> We come then to the question presented: Does segregation of children in public schools solely on the basis of race, even though the physical facilities and other "tangible" factors may be equal, deprive the children of the minority group of equal educational opportunities? We believe that it does.
>
> In *Sweatt v. Painter,* supra, in finding that a segregated law school for Negroes could not provide them equal educational opportunities, this Court relied in large part on "those qualities which are incapable of objective measurement but which make for greatness in a law school." In *McLaurin v. Oklahoma State Regents,* supra, the Court, in requiring that a Negro admitted to a white graduate school be treated like all other students, again resorted to intangible considerations: ". . . his ability to study, to engage in discussions and exchange views with other students, and, in general, to learn his profession." [347 U.S. 483, 494] Such considerations apply with added force to children in grade and high schools. To separate them from others of similar age and qualifications solely because of their race generates a feeling of inferiority as to their status in the community and may affect their hearts and minds in a way unlikely ever to be undone.[55]

Clearly, the Warren Court in *Brown* built solidly on the unanimous decisions authored by Chief Justice Vinson in *Sweatt* and *McLaurin*—decisions that only four years earlier incrementally doomed *Plessy v. Ferguson.*

In view of the plain language of the Vinson-authored opinions in *Shelley* and *Hurd* in 1948 and in *McLaurin* and *Sweatt* in 1950, it simply defies logic—and the historical record—to suggest that Fred Vinson was suddenly prepared to reverse himself in 1952 and 1953 and lead his Court in a radically different pro-*Plessy* direction in deciding *Brown.*

Importantly, as noted above, NAACP attorney Thurgood Marshall—who later sat on the U.S. Supreme Court—publicly applauded the Vinson Court's civil rights rulings, calling them his "greatest victories." As reported in the

Baltimore Afro-American on June 6, 1950, Marshall stated, "In three sweeping and unanimous decisions handed down on . . . June 5, 1950, the United States Supreme Court dealt a serious blow to white supremacy as it affects segregation in schools and on dining cars." Marshall went on to predict that, based on the unanimous June 1950 rulings by the Vinson Court, "the complete destruction of all enforced segregation is now in sight."[56]

In analyzing the civil rights record of the Vinson Court from 1946 through the chief justice's untimely death in 1953, Vinson Court historian C. Herman Pritchett wrote, "The liberal record of the Vinson Court in racial discrimination cases stands out in sharp contrast to the generally antilibertarian trend of its decisions in other fields."[57] This liberal trend of the Vinson Court only in the civil rights arena is not surprising. Truman knew what kind of man he was empowering when he vested Vinson with the leadership of the Supreme Court. Truman also knew that he and Vinson were kindred spirits, natives of border states where slaves had once been acceptable "commerce." Both men shared a deep understanding of civil rights inequalities in the United States in the 1940s and 1950s and the dangerous impact that these inequalities could have on America's democratic culture if left unaddressed. And while the Supreme Court is truly a separate-yet-equal part of the federal government under the Constitution, it is obvious that Chief Justice Vinson and President Truman shared a trust and philosophical affinity that helped the president to significantly advance civil rights reform through the Court's rulings. These advances were otherwise impossible to secure given congressional inaction.

Truman's unshakeable trust in his friend is captured in the president's diary entry of June 21, 1951. In this entry, he wrote about the upcoming Fourth of July ceremony to celebrate the nation's 175th birthday. Noting that the chief justice was the national chairman of a special celebration committee, Truman wrote, "It is a Nation Wide Celebration. Ch. Justice Vinson is the National Chairman of a committee made up of the Vice President, the Speaker of the House, and the Floor Leaders of the Senate and the House of Representatives. Looks as if it will be an epoch making affair. Hope it will hook Vinson for the next President!"[58] Here, in June 1951, when the 1952 presidential election was clearly on Truman's mind, he confirms to his diary, as he no doubt confided to Bess, that he felt that Chief Justice Vinson was the ideal person to follow Truman in the White House and to lead the country.

Truman's hope that his friend would succeed him as president is confirmed by the chief justice's son in his 1973 oral history. When Fred Vinson Jr. was asked about Truman's plans to organize a Draft Vinson campaign, the chief justice's son replied, "I think President Truman wanted him to. There wasn't any doubt about that. He wanted him to run for president in '52 and my father declined to do so. . . . He felt very strongly that the judiciary, and particularly the Supreme Court and chief justice, should not be political and shouldn't be thought of as a stepping stone to the presidency."[59]

Truman's love for the presidency was well known to the people who worked around him at the White House, including George Elsey, who served both Presidents Roosevelt and Truman before subsequently becoming president of the Red Cross.

> President Truman had an *enormous* respect for the institution of the Presidency, he loved it, he revered it. He was widely read[,] as we know, [and] he continued, Lord knows how he found the time but he did, all through his White House years to read books on American history. I don't think a biography of a President or other major figure came out during his years in the White House but what [did come out] he acquired . . . and if he didn't have time to read it all he at least absorbed some of it. To him it would have been inconceivable that a man could treat the *Presidency* so casually.[60]

Despite Truman's hope that the presidency he so cherished would fall into the able hands of his dear friend, the chief justice refused to be drafted by Truman as the Democratic Party's standard-bearer in the 1952 presidential race. Nonetheless, Fred Vinson Jr.'s confirmation of Truman's recruitment of the elder Vinson is instructive because it is another reliable indication of Truman's high esteem for his chief justice—a chief justice who by the late 1940s had generated an improved degree of intellectual collegiality on the Court that led to unanimous decisions in *Shelley, Hurd, Henderson, McLaurin,* and *Sweatt.*

Given the similar backgrounds and shared political philosophies of and the deep friendship between Truman and Vinson, it is not surprising that the Vinson Court paid careful attention to the numerous Truman administration amicus briefs and oral arguments urging the country's highest court to take an aggressively expansive and revolutionary approach to the issue of constitutionally protected civil rights for African Americans. And because of Vinson's quiet leadership skills and his sensitivity to Truman's deep concerns about civil rights for all Americans, the Vinson Court effectively assaulted—and significantly weakened—the morally repugnant separate-but-equal doctrine that had shaped a racist American society since 1896.

While most American citizens either were violently opposed to or were simply indifferent to Truman's expansive view of constitutionally guaranteed civil rights for African Americans, Truman knew that Fred Vinson understood the urgent need for nationwide civil rights reform. As a former senator who intimately appreciated the politics of the Congress, Truman also knew that the Congress would not enact the sweeping civil rights legislation that he proposed early in election year 1948.

With this knowledge, and with the certainty that civil rights reform was essential to the interests of the United States, both domestically and globally, Truman creatively and relentlessly used his executive branch prerogatives to shape a Supreme Court and a Justice Department that would be proactive in advancing civil rights reform. Fred Vinson, Harold Burton, Tom Clark, and Sherman Minton were men of proven intellectual integrity, and they all knew that Truman felt strongly about the need for civil rights reform. Moreover, through Truman's effective use of his Justice Department, the president's four appointees to the Vinson Court and the five other members of that Court were reminded again and again of the Truman administration's unequivocal belief that *Plessy v. Ferguson's* separate-but-equal doctrine was "a constitutional anachronism that no longer deserve[d] a place in our law."[61]

The Vinson Court's rulings in *Shelley, Hurd, Henderson, McLaurin,* and *Sweatt* made *Plessy* a terminally ill judicial amputee. Several pervasive elements of *Plessy*—segregated schools of higher education, segregated neighborhoods protected by restrictive covenants, and even curtained-off segregated tables for blacks wishing to eat in dining cars on the nation's trains—died with the unanimous decisions of the Vinson Court. Predictably, *Brown* finally happened on May 17, 1954, a little more than a year after Truman left the White House and just eight months after Truman's kindred spirit and appointee Chief Justice Fred Vinson died. And while Vinson and his colleagues deliberately delayed deciding *Brown* until this consolidated case could result in nationwide coverage, the outcome in *Brown* was predetermined by the Vinson Court's unanimous rulings in *Shelley, Hurd, Henderson, McLaurin,* and *Sweatt.* These five landmark civil rights rulings by the Vinson Court provided the solid legal basis and momentum for the Warren Court's unanimous ruling in *Brown* shortly after Fred Vinson's untimely death. As Justice Clark confirmed, based on his service on both the Vinson and Warren Courts, the result in the *Brown* decision would have been the same had Chief Justice Vinson lived to hand down the Court's decision in 1954.

As history shows, the death of Chief Justice Vinson did not mean the death of Supreme Court–initiated civil rights reform. What started with Truman's appointment of Fred Vinson as chief justice would continue. But it started with Justice Vinson's appointment because Truman was a good judge of character, and he knew that, as chief justice, Fred Vinson would aggressively act on civil rights. And as the judicial record confirms, with his decision to move his friend from the helm of the Treasury Department in 1946 to the leadership of the Supreme Court, Truman was able profoundly to advance his fundamental goal of full equality for African Americans; with *Shelley, Hurd, Henderson, McLaurin,* and *Sweatt,* the energized nationwide civil rights movement of the late 1950s and the 1960s became a reality, and there was no turning back.

While the Vinson Court waited in the early 1950s for the consolidated *Brown* case to attract a more geographically diverse group of petitioners, President Truman had more to say about the need for civil rights reform. What better venues to address the unfinished business of civil rights reform than Howard University and Harlem?

CHAPTER TWELVE

Truman's Howard University Commencement Address: June 13, 1952

Our country is founded on the proposition that all men are created equal.
This means that they should be equal before the law. They should enjoy equal
political rights. And they should have equal opportunities for education,
employment and decent living conditions. This is our belief and we know
it is right. We know it is morally right.
—HST, June 13, 1952

After repeatedly trying throughout most of his seven-year presidency to have his civil rights proposals enacted by the Congress, President Harry Truman resigned himself in 1952 to the reality that his only legacy in the civil rights area would be those actions that required no congressional concurrence. Nonetheless, through his issuance of executive orders, his appointments of men like William Hastie and Fred Vinson to the courts, and his relentless advocacy of full civil rights for all Americans, white and black, Truman knew he had started something significant. But Truman, ever the realist, knew that much more had to be done in June 1952. And it was both his sense of accomplishment and his sense of frustration that the lame-duck president conveyed when he delivered the commencement address on June 13, 1952, to 712 graduates of Howard University's class of 1952 in Washington, D.C.[1]

The sixty-eight-year-old president, who had decided not to seek his party's nomination for reelection at the upcoming Democratic convention, spoke in a reflective yet uncompromising tone to his audience of African American graduates, their relatives, and their friends who gathered in Howard's Quad, an outdoor courtyard in front of Frederick Douglass Hall.[2] Truman's speech was made in response to an eloquent invitation from Howard University's president,

Mordecai W. Johnson—an invitation too compelling for the outgoing president of the United States to decline. In his May 20, 1952, letter of invitation, Johnson wrote, "This invitation is from the heart, Mr. President. It is expressive of the esteem and affection which we and the millions of our people bear toward Harry Truman, because in the high office of President he has remembered the humble and, with greatness of heart and unquenchable boldness of spirit, he has persistently sought to have them possess in fact, every basic freedom and opportunity intended by the Constitution of our country."[3] For Truman, a devoted student of the Constitution, Johnson's words were effective. Just twenty-five days later, he faced the young Howard graduates and provided a frank evaluation of his presidency's achievements in the civil rights area.

After the president decided to speak at Howard's commencement, White House staffer Philleo Nash delighted Howard's president by confirming that Truman would do what no other president had done before at Howard: he would deliver the commencement address and remain for the entire two-and-one-half-hour ceremony. Nash explained in his oral history, "Previous Presidents had made a 'lightning' appearance at Howard University; what the aviation people would call a touch-and-go landing—come [*sic*] in, made an appearance, made a little speech, and left. Even FDR only came in through the back of the building, went out on to the front, made a brief appearance, and left, so that he was not personally present at the moment of pride for the graduates and their parents, when they are actually handed their diplomas."[4] Truman's visit to Howard would be radically different; the class of 1952 and their families would hear a full-blown address from a U.S. president who would then sit through the presentation of diplomas, as well as the singing of the "Battle Hymn of the Republic"—a song that Truman had requested in advance for the commencement ceremony.[5]

For *New York Times* journalist Anthony Leviero, Truman's Howard speech confirmed that the outgoing president had not retreated from his determined civil rights campaign. In a front-page article with a headline declaring "Truman Demands Civil Rights Based on Federal Power," Leviero reported that Truman "reaffirmed his civil rights program without compromise, asserting the rights of individuals could not be left to state protection alone but required the full power of the Federal government."[6]

Leviero had covered Truman's civil rights crusade for the *New York Times* since it commenced with the launching of Truman's Civil Rights Committee in December 1946. As a leading political journalist, Leviero appreciated the bruising political journey that the president had traveled during the previous six years by taking on the volatile issue of civil rights reform and by creating the first Civil

Rights Committee. Leviero also recognized the political heartburn that Truman's stubborn pursuit of civil rights reform was causing presidential candidates in 1952. Truman "had laid down a policy line that, if it were sustained at the forthcoming Democratic National Convention, would repudiate the stand of those leaders in his own party who would mollify Southern Democrats. These leaders recommend a softer civil rights plank than the one that led to the Southern Revolt and the States' Rights defection in 1948."[7]

Truman decided to use the academic environment of Howard University as a forum to give himself and his administration a civil rights report card that detailed the country's progress in the civil rights arena since his presidency had begun just seven years earlier. He also detailed what still needed to be done by federal and state governments to ensure the full enjoyment of civil rights by African Americans.[8]

Howard University's commencement was an ideal venue for the president to deliver his comprehensive civil rights address because Howard is a federally funded university founded in 1867 to provide a center of learning and higher education for former slaves, known as *freedmen*.[9] That Howard provided the president a historically important forum was confirmed by Nash, who was tasked with drafting the president's speech. "The Howard Commencement is one of the major social events for the Washington Negro community. The elite of Washington attended it, of the Negro community. It was a very, very big thing and it goes back into that shadow of history."[10]

Nash also confirmed that President Truman paid special attention to his Howard commencement speech, a speech that Truman "went over in greater detail than almost anyone I had been connected with. On the other hand, as you can see from the previous things I've told you, when he got to a civil rights speech, he wanted to know what was in it in detail personally, more than almost any other kind [of speech]. Oh, yes, we went over that more than once with him."[11] Truman's extra attention to the wording of his commencement address at Howard may have resulted, in part, from Truman's realization that many of the graduates in his audience were themselves the descendants of slaves—slaves like those who had labored on the farms of Truman's grandparents. While Truman was proud of much of his family's heritage, he also knew that slavery had left a horrible legacy for African Americans.

Truman had told friends and associates, including Justice Tom Clark and Jonathan Daniels that he was troubled by the fact that, throughout his life, African Americans had confronted such high hurdles in their path to economic success. Clearly Truman's Howard University graduation address—coming as it did at the end of his presidency—afforded this grandson of slave owners an important and timely opportunity to offer a realistic message of hope to an audience that included grandchildren of American slaves.

Mindful of Howard's proud history as the federally chartered university for freed slaves, the president began his remarks by acknowledging Howard's revered traditions. "The founders of this University had a great vision. They knew that the slaves who had been set free needed a center of learning and higher education. They could foresee that many of the Freedmen, if they were given the chance, would take their places among the most gifted and honored American citizens. And that is what happened."[12]

Truman then spoke of one of Howard's most distinguished alumni, the late Dr. Charles Drew, who pioneered the first blood bank in the world. In referencing Drew, the president revealed his own views about racial equality. Drew, he said, "is a practical illustration of the fact that talent and genius have no boundaries of race, nationality, or creed. The United States needs the imagination, the energy, and the skills, of every one of our citizens."[13] Truman's words here are important; they reflect the president's evolving vision at the end of his seven-year presidency—a presidency repeatedly affected by his controversial commitment to civil rights for all Americans. While Truman spoke with a genuine passion to the Howard graduates about his belief that "talent and genius have no boundaries," Truman was nonetheless a realist, telling the Howard University class of 1952, "I wish I could say to you who are graduating . . . that no opportunity to use your skills and knowledge would ever be denied you. . . . Some of us are denied opportunity for economic reasons. Others are denied opportunity because of racial prejudice and discrimination."[14] With these words, Truman frankly acknowledged the realities of deep-rooted racial discrimination in the early 1950s—an era idealized in such television programs as *Ozzie and Harriet* and *I Remember Momma*—as a nearly perfect, tranquil time in the United States. Despite global concerns, as the frustrating Korean War raged on, and as Soviet expansionism became more threatening, the United States of 1952 was generally prosperous, and the widespread violent civil rights disturbances that would occur in the 1960s were generally unthinkable when Truman delivered his Howard University commencement address.

Truman also used his Howard University address frankly to acknowledge that America remained deeply flawed in the area of civil rights and that this flaw, in the president's mind, represented primarily a moral problem that could not be ignored as many of Truman's political aides had previously advised him. "Back in 1947, a good many people advised me not to raise this whole question of civil rights. They said it would only make things worse. But you can't cure a moral problem, or a social problem, by ignoring it."[15] Truman's words are insightful because the president once again confirmed that he viewed the civil rights failures of the United States government as a moral problem. For Truman, politics obviously remained a secondary consideration when dealing with the civil rights issue. Politics had been irrelevant to him when he created his multiracial Civil Rights Committee in 1946 and when he pushed his ten-point civil rights program on the Eightieth Congress, even as he sought the presidency in 1948. In 1952, the president continued to pursue an aggressive ten-point civil rights legislative program even though a Gallup poll showed that his favorable rating hovered at a miserable 32 percent—almost a threefold decrease from his 87 percent positive rating in June 1945.[16] Politics clearly had also been a secondary consideration when Truman took on the often racist states' rights leaders in the Congress and state houses throughout the country as he publicly advocated a federal civil rights solution in his address before the NAACP on June 29, 1947. And again, the politics of civil rights had been secondary to the moral imperative that guided Truman when he issued Executive Orders 9980 and 9981 on July 26, 1948. So when Truman made his commencement address before the Howard graduates in 1952, it was not surprising that the morality of the civil rights movement was the underlying theme of his remarks.

When closely examined, Truman's words at Howard help to explain why the president consistently acted on his moral conviction that all Americans, regardless of the color of their skin, were equal under the law. This constitutional premise was the consistent basis for his earlier civil rights pronouncements, and it remained the deeply rooted basis for his Howard University commencement address. "This means that . . . [all Americans] should enjoy equal political rights. And they should have equal opportunities for education, employment and decent living conditions. This is our belief and we know it is right. We know it is morally right."[17]

President Truman also used his Howard University address to restate his personal impatience with those Americans who did not want "to rock the boat on civil rights" simply because the country was generally prosperous in 1952. Truman's contempt for the "status quo-ers'" cautious approach to civil rights reform was obvious, as it had been when some of his closest advisers previously urged him to moderate his public views on racial equality. For Truman, it simply was morally unacceptable for the federal government to remain silent as state and local governments—particularly in the South—routinely denied African Americans their civil rights.[18]

In covering the president's Howard University speech, the *Washington Post* of June 14, 1952, reported that "President Truman called anew . . . for a civil rights program backed by 'the full force and power of the federal government,'" a government that Truman had energized since 1946 in the area of civil rights, even though his legislative program was scuttled by the Congress.[19] The article characterized Truman's blunt remarks as "scorning the leave-it-to-the-states approach" when the president told the assembled graduates, "Our Federal Government must live up to the ideals professed in our Declaration of Independence and the duties imposed upon it by our constitution [*sic*]. The full force and power of the Federal Government must stand behind the protection of rights guaranteed by our Federal Constitution."[20]

For Howard graduate Elizabeth Ausbrooks, class of 1952, the president's remarks were inspiring because it was clear that this plainspoken man from Missouri "read the Constitution literally and believed in the spirit of the Constitution. And I think that is what really drove Truman." Ausbrooks, now Dr. Nelson-Ausbrooks, whose grandmother was the daughter of a slave, went on to enjoy a distinguished teaching career at the University of North Carolina in Chapel Hill, the University of Maryland, the University of the District of Columbia, and Howard University.[21]

In reflecting on that sunny graduation day in 1952 in the Quad at Howard University, Nelson-Ausbrooks acknowledged the rather uninspiring delivery style of the president. What was inspiring to her and to so many of her colleagues was the president's obvious, deep-rooted commitment to the civil rights of African Americans—rights fully guaranteed under the Constitution. In her view, Truman

> put his body—and his presidency where his principles were; other presi-
> dents have been kicked into action supporting civil rights reform because
> a steamroller, like events in the 1960s come along, and they can't do any-
> thing else—they are overtaken by events. But President Truman was out
> there in support of federal civil rights reform with his actions, doing
> things that he thought represented the literal interpretation of the
> Constitution for which he was responsible. And I think he was pivotal to
> the civil rights movement; if he had been passive, it would have been a
> totally different story—the sixties would not have happened until the sev-
> enties or the eighties.[22]

To Howard University graduates like Beth Nelson-Ausbrooks, the fact that President Truman had backed up his prior civil rights rhetoric with significant federal actions, made his assessment of the state of civil rights in the United

States in 1952 even more credible. Unlike Presidents Roosevelt, Eisenhower, and Kennedy—all of whom were tentative in their support of federal civil rights reform—President Truman combined his rhetoric on civil rights with action. As many members of Howard's class of 1952 would later confirm, of the four presidents from 1932 through 1963, FDR, Truman, Eisenhower, and JFK, President Truman alone refused to procrastinate or equivocate on civil rights reform, even though he was not subjected to the "steamroller" of public opinion that forced subsequent presidents to act on a comprehensive federal civil rights program similar to the one Truman forwarded in his 1948 civil rights message to Congress.

Though Truman proved to be the only president to act without massive political pressure for federal civil rights reforms, his efforts could not solve all of this country's civil rights problems. Truman was a realist about the country's unfinished civil rights program; nevertheless, he shared his genuine optimism about civil rights progress with the Howard graduates—graduates who soon would be joining the booming U.S. workforce—saying that "our efforts in the field of civil rights have made things better—better in all aspects of our national life, and in all parts of our country. One of my Southern friends said the other day, 'the last five years are the best years in race relations this country has ever had.' And the record proves it."[23]

To emphasize the impressive civil rights progress that had occurred during the Truman administration, the president explicitly detailed for the Howard University graduates the litany of civil rights achievements of which he was most proud. These landmark achievements included the following:

- Poll taxes had been abolished in Tennessee and South Carolina, leaving only five poll-tax states. In discussing this progress in two key Southern states, the president made it clear that any poll tax in any state was unacceptable, promptly adding that "the poll tax and other discriminatory restrictions on voting should be removed in all the States."
- Several important court decisions had been handed down giving blacks the right of equal participation in primary elections.
- In ten states, legislation was enacted that abolished segregation and discrimination in the lower schools and colleges within those states.
- The Supreme Court in 1948, headed by Truman appointee Chief Justice Vinson, opened up the U.S. housing market to black Americans in its *Shelley v. Kraemer* ruling, which outlawed the restrictive covenants that President Truman said "so often make bad housing conditions worse."

- The Court handed down several additional decisions that outlawed discrimination, resulting in more than one thousand African-American graduates and professional students gaining admission to ten state universities that had previously been segregated.
- In 1950, 177 local public housing projects were opened for multiracial, low-income residents.
- Nine states and eight cities passed laws and ordinances outlawing discrimination and segregation in public housing.
- Two additional states enacted antilynching laws, while four states and six cities outlawed the KKK's practice of wearing masks in public.
- Eleven states and twenty municipalities adopted fair employment laws while numerous unions voluntarily eliminated discriminatory employment practices.
- The Civil Rights Division of the Department of Justice and the FBI became more proactive in the use of their powers to reinforce and police the civil rights–related activities of state and local authorities.[24]

To further showcase the new level of federal and state collaboration in civil rights matters, the president also told the Howard University audience about a civil rights success story in which federal authorities helped the governor of Illinois stop racially motivated mob violence in that state. Importantly, federal authorities subsequently prosecuted the local officials who had tacitly supported this racial violence.[25]

In addition to detailing these specific areas of quantifiable civil rights progress since 1945, Truman spoke proudly about his creation in 1948 of the Fair Employment Board in the Civil Service Commission and the 1951 establishment of the Committee on Government Contract Compliance. In the president's view, these two entities contributed significantly to employment opportunities for African Americans who could, by 1952, gain greater access to employment not just in the federal government but from vendors and subcontractors who were doing work for the ever-expanding federal government.[26]

Truman's reference to his administration's successful efforts in promoting employment opportunities for black Americans, both in the federal workforce and in the private sector, prompted Senator Herbert Lehman of New York to applaud Truman's address.

From Senator Lehman, Democrat-Liberal, of New York came high praise for the address. He described it as "a great speech, a statesman-like pronouncement," and he said he would make use of it at the Democratic National Convention.

"I'm on the Platform Committee of the national convention," Senator Lehman added, "and I'm going to cite this speech and fight for strong, specific platform planks for a FEPC law with teeth in it."[27]

While during Truman's presidency he had been unable to convince Republicans and segregationist Southern Democrats in Congress to enact civil rights legislation "with teeth in it," the president did not need congressional approval to issue executive orders, and he reminded the Howard graduates assembled in the Quad that he had unilaterally ordered the integration in 1948 of the entire U.S. armed services by his issuance of Executive Order 9981—an order that had already resulted in substantial progress. "The Navy and the Air Force eliminated all racial distinctions, and the Army has been moving step by step toward this goal. For over two years, every soldier coming into a training unit has been assigned on a basis of individual merit without racial distinction."[28]

By June 1952, many of Howard's graduates knew that the civil rights progress realized in the U.S. armed services, dating from the time Truman had integrated the military, was indeed monumental. It was especially impressive given the deep resentment of the many U.S. military leaders who only four years earlier had been told by this presidential veteran of an earlier world war that their army, navy, and Marine Corps were to be immediately integrated.

For Charles J. Dashiell Jr., another member of the Howard University class of 1952, the president's integration of the U.S. armed forces had set in motion long-overdue reform in a deeply racist institution.[29] Dashiell saw firsthand how the military went from a bastion of segregation to an example of integration, and he served with great distinction in Vietnam, retiring as a decorated major in the air force. For Dashiell, as a Reserve Officers' Training Corps cadet in 1952, it was indeed significant to hear a commencement address delivered by the same commander in chief of the United States who had earlier ignored the public protests of his military chief of staff, General Omar Bradley, after Truman had integrated the country's massive military infrastructure.

For another member of Howard's class of 1952, Inez R. Arrendell, Truman's speech represented a message of optimism and self-worth that empowered the young woman to do her professional best in the decades following her graduation. In recalling graduation day, Arrendell remembered vividly the president urging her classmates to work hard. "Work hard and we could do anything."[30] And that's exactly what Inez Arrendell did: she worked hard and succeeded, enjoying a successful career as an investment counselor in the nation's capital—a city that was replete with the racist trappings of a segregated lifestyle until the mid 1960s.

In assessing the overall impact of his civil rights program for the Howard University graduates and faculty, the normally modest Truman sounded an almost boastful note when he stated, "The prophets of doom have been proved wrong. The civil rights program has not weakened our country—it has made our country stronger. It has not made us less united—it has made us more united."[31]

Truman had good reason to look back with considerable pride on the precedent-setting progress that had been made at the federal, state, and local levels in reducing racial discrimination. While the president told his audience of young graduates of his "deep satisfaction" about the progress to date with the civil rights program that he had launched in 1946, Truman also candidly acknowledged what many in his audience already knew about civil rights reform in 1952: progress "does not mean we have reached the goal or that we can stop working. Much remains to be done. . . . We still need the [comprehensive civil rights] legislation that I recommended to the Congress in 1948. Only two of the recommendations I made in my Civil Rights Program have been adopted so far. I shall continue, in office and out, to urge Congress to adopt the remainder."[32] With these closing remarks, President Truman again evidenced his deeply felt belief that civil rights reform was a moral rather than political matter. And because it was a moral imperative that he took very seriously, it was predictable that he would pledge to the Howard class of 1952 his continued involvement in their ongoing civil rights struggle even after his political chores as president of the United States concluded on inauguration day in January 1953.

While understandably proud of the civil rights progress made during his presidency, Truman knew that in 1952 there was much more to do. That job would not be completed when either Democrat Adlai Stevenson or Republican General Dwight Eisenhower moved into the White House. Mindful that he would return to Missouri in just seven months, Truman viewed his message to the Howard class of 1952 as very possibly the final major civil rights speech of his presidency. Based on that probability, the president wanted his audience at Howard, as well as African Americans around the country, to have a clear understanding of one important point: while he would largely leave politics behind when his train pulled out of Union Station on January 20, 1953, Truman would remain personally committed to forcing a stubborn and, in part, racist Congress to support the sweeping civil rights legislation that he had proposed in 1948. Unfortunately, Truman's comprehensive federal civil rights program would not become a legislative reality until the race riots and civil disobedience of the 1960s rocked much of the country, creating the "steamroller" of public opinion about which graduate Nelson-Ausbrooks spoke.[33] That steamroller finally forced a reluctant Congress in 1964 and 1965 to enact comprehensive civil rights legislation that was similar to the ten-point civil rights package that Truman had proposed more than one and one-half decades earlier.

When reflecting on Truman's Howard University commencement address, Philleo Nash—who had drafted both the Harlem speech of 1948 and the Howard speech—suggested that the president "was approaching the end of the career, and here was a chance to make, as in 1948 in Harlem, a philosophical utterance that would be definitive for its time."[34] In Nash's opinion, Truman's place in history would be tied forever to his presidential civil rights activism, which triggered "the whole revolution of the minorities in this country, a peaceful revolution, but no less revolutionary because . . . [blacks] were moving towards more nearly full participation. . . . When Mr. Truman became President they were on the defensive and when he ended his Presidency, they were not on the defensive, and this was the great contribution to civil rights."[35]

The significance of President Truman's commencement address to the Howard University graduates, class of 1952, was captured in the words of Mordecai Johnson in his letter of December 17, 1952, to President Truman. As Howard's legendary president, Mordecai Johnson intimately knew the university's history, which included visits to the campus by Presidents William Howard Taft, Calvin Coolidge, Herbert Hoover, and Franklin Roosevelt. However, when he wrote the president just a month before Truman's departure from the White House, Johnson put President Truman in a special category—a category that Mordecai Johnson reserved for Abraham Lincoln and for this pioneering civil rights president, Harry Truman.[36]

Dear Mr. President,

. . . Your visit to Howard University on Commencement Day, was inspiring beyond measure to all our graduates, alumni and friends. . . .

We are grateful that in your address on that day you centered upon the theme of civil rights. Hesitancy and equivocation were in the air during those days; and we needed the reaffirmation of your great convictions and purposes in this field. Under your leadership, Mr. President, the civil rights of the Negro people have moved forward to a greater extent than at any time since the Emancipation Proclamation; and the relationship of the principles underlying these rights to the nature of democracy and to the world purposes of the United States have received a more thorough discussion and a deeper confirmation in the hearts and minds of the people than we have ever known. It was inevitable that the clear and forthright course of your action in this field should have aroused resistance among fearful hearts, with resulting cleavages in allegiance. Your course of action was, nevertheless, inspired by God, we believe, as a necessary stimulus toward the maturation of a responsible social will in this nation that could be trusted around the world.

When the smoke of battle is cleared away and the years have allowed the people to see these times in perspective, they all will reverently link your name with that of Abraham Lincoln, and they will speak of you with esteem and affection as one who waded through much misunderstanding and suffering to bring a major blessing to this nation. . . .

Sincerely yours,
Mordecai W. Johnson
President
Howard University[37]

Nearly a half century later, graduates of Howard University's class of 1952 echoed Mordecai Johnson's words as they discussed the impact on their lives of President Truman's commencement address. When they reflected back on President Truman's words and his actions, many proud Howard alumni of the class of 1952 spoke about their improved lives during the intervening years—lives that had been made different as a result of President Truman's words on June 13, 1952, and importantly, his actions as president of the United States.

CHAPTER THIRTEEN

Truman's Final Civil Rights Address in Harlem: October 11, 1952

*I am here to say to you now that the [civil rights] fight will never
cease with me as long as I live.*
—HST, October 11, 1952

At sixty-eight, after seven years' service as the nation's first Cold War president, Truman decided to pack it in; but even as a lame-duck president, he was still a fierce partisan. Although Truman had unsuccessfully tried to persuade his dear friend Chief Justice Fred Vinson to run for president in 1952, he was stuck with Governor Adlai Stevenson. Truman felt that the Illinois governor lacked the quiet decisiveness and the wisdom that he saw in Fred Vinson. Nonetheless, as a committed partisan, Truman believed that he had a job to do in the 1952 presidential campaign: keep the GOP presidential candidate, General Dwight Eisenhower, out of the White House on January 20, 1953.[1] To achieve that goal, a vigorous and combative Truman traveled eighty-five hundred miles across the country in the fall of 1952 on a whistle-stop campaign tour reminiscent of his victorious come-from-behind presidential campaign four years earlier.[2]

One of the last stops on Truman's rigorous campaign schedule was "speech #90"—a major civil rights address delivered at one in the afternoon on Saturday, October 11, 1952, before sixty-five thousand Harlem residents who gathered in Dorrance Brooks Park.[3] This was the same square in Harlem where candidate Truman had delivered his landmark civil rights speech on October 29, 1948, just four days before he won the most spectacular surprise presidential victory of the twentieth century. Unlike the deeply spiritual tone of Truman's 1948 campaign visit to Harlem, his swan song civil rights speech in Harlem in 1952 was a lively campaign event. Philleo Nash, who accompanied the president on both of his visits to Harlem, recalled that the 1952 Harlem speech "was not as much like a religious revival as 1948, after all, that only happens once, but it was subdued, and kind of a little bit more like a going away party."[4]

Unbowed by age or by the prolonged frustrations of the deadlocked Korean War, a pugnacious President Truman greeted the huge crowd of New York voters by reflecting on his 1948 campaign visit to Harlem. "That meeting was the high point of the 1948 Campaign. I knew then that you had placed your trust in me. We pledged ourselves that day to a great enterprise—the end of racial injustice and unfair discrimination. I am here to say to you now that fight will never cease with me as long as I live."[5]

African American voters in his Harlem audience had ample reason by October 11, 1952, to know that President Harry Truman was one politician who kept his word. But just in case anyone in his audience had forgotten the details of civil rights reform under his presidency, Truman used his campaign address on Adlai Stevenson's behalf to remind black voters of his administration's significant achievements in the civil rights arena since the end of World War II.

> Right after World War II, religious and racial intolerance began to show
> up just as it did in 1919. There were a good many incidents of violence
> and friction, but two of them in particular made a very deep impression
> on me. One was when a Negro veteran, still wearing this country's uni-
> form, was arrested, and beaten and blinded. Not long after that, two
> Negro veterans with their wives lost their lives at the hands of a mob. . . .
> As President of the United States, I felt I ought to do everything in my
> power to find what caused such crimes and to root out the causes. It was
> for that reason that I created the President's Committee on Civil Rights.[6]

For Harlem voters, the blinding of Sergeant Isaac Woodard by a racist Batesburg, South Carolina, police sheriff on February 12, 1946, was a well-known horror story—a story subsequently made all the more horrific when an all-white jury on November 5, 1946, acquitted the infamous Sheriff Shull after the sheriff admitted in federal court to using the blinding force.[7]

All-white juries were still common throughout the South in 1952 and would remain the norm until congressional legislation was enacted more than a decade later.[8] Nonetheless, under the Truman administration, considerable civil rights progress had been made in a variety of other areas. Moreover, by the time Truman delivered his farewell presidential civil rights address, African American voters knew with certainty that Truman really cared. When he spoke personally about Isaac Woodard and other black victims of often deadly racial violence, African American voters knew that it was more than political rhetoric; this president from Missouri had proven again and again that he cared about basic fairness as guaranteed under the Constitution. And by October 11, 1952, Harlem voters also knew that President Truman had done much more than merely talk about civil rights equality; he had acted to promote full equality of opportunity.

Because Truman had addressed hundreds of political rallies since he first ran for Jackson County judge in 1922, the president knew that some voters had short memories. Accordingly, the president reminded his Harlem audience of how he had reacted to the increase in racial violence following World War II. "First I acted to stop racial discrimination in the armed services. The Navy and the Air Force have now eliminated all racial distinctions. And for over 2 years, every soldier coming into an Army training unit in this country has been assigned on the basis of his individual merit—regardless of race or color. All the troops in Korea are now integrated."[9]

For black voters in 1952, the fact that all the U.S. forces serving in Korea were integrated was a spectacular reversal of the pervasive segregationist policy that had governed the twelve million American men fighting just seven years earlier.[10] In terms of promoting social change, Dr. Dorothy Height suggested fifty years later that no single act by President Truman was more provocative and far-reaching than his July 26, 1948, issuance of Executive Order 9981, which began the process of integrating the workplaces and living facilities wherever U.S. soldiers, sailors, and airmen were assigned, whether at military bases in the Deep South or on navy ships on the high seas.[11]

Based on his own experiences in World War I, Truman knew how important his integration of the vast U.S. military infrastructure was in terms of promoting financial and social equality in the decades after he left the White House. And while the journey to equality of opportunity would prove elusive throughout much of the United States, Truman, as well as many black voters in his Harlem audience, knew on October 11, 1952, that the journey to equality of opportunity was well under way in one vital part of American life: the U.S. military.

When speaking about his integration of the U.S. military establishment—an elite establishment in which Republican presidential candidate Eisenhower was a living legend, Truman took off his rhetorical gloves and played political hardball. The *Washington Post* reported in a front-page story on October 12, 1952, that a partisan Truman adroitly used his Harlem speech to remind black voters across the country that the GOP presidential nominee, when he was General Dwight D. Eisenhower, had been a proponent of the army's traditional segregationist policy.

President Truman said, too, that Eisenhower while still in Uniform told the Senate Armed Services Committee that a certain amount of segregation is necessary in the Army.

"You and I know that this is morally wrong," said Mr. Truman. "What's more, it's even militarily wrong. Our troops in Korea are demonstrating every day that Americans can stand side by side, regardless of color—and fight better because of it."

Mr. Truman said "all troops in Korea are now integrated and integration is going forward elsewhere overseas."[12]

Eisenhower's ambivalence about integrating the U.S. military was not the only partisan jab that Truman verbally landed on Ike during the president's campaign speech in Harlem. In a valiant effort to help his Democratic Party retain the leadership in both houses of the new Congress, which also would be elected on November 4, 1952, Truman also warned his Harlem audience that

the Republican candidate, and his party, and his party's platform have refused to pledge effective action for assuring equal rights for all our citizens. You could not even depend on them to save what we have now— and goodness knows that isn't enough.

And now, while the Republican candidate is whispering promises to you, he has been touring the South to woo the Dixiecrats into the Republican fold. What do you think the Republican candidate and a Dixiecrat Governor talk about when they sit down together for lunch? Do you think they talk about civil rights?[13]

According to *Washington Post* reporter Edward F. Ryan, the sixty-five-thousand-person crowd roared "no" in response to Truman's rhetorical question.[14]

The Harlem audience's lively interaction with Truman served to enliven the president. Despite fatigue from intensive campaigning for Governor Stevenson, the president went on to talk about the judicial progress made under his administration. A large portion of Truman's speech focused on the series of important rulings by the Vinson Court that were inspired in part by President Truman's aggressive use of his Department of Justice to file amicus curiae briefs in civil rights cases that had often begun in Southern federal courts and had progressed to the Supreme Court. In view of the Justice Department's early success in a number of the Court's civil rights rulings, he had ample justification to remind the Harlem voters about his efforts, efforts that had not been rewarded in the Congress.

At my request the Solicitor General of the United States went before the Supreme Court to argue that Negro citizens have the right to enter State colleges and universities on exactly the same basis as any other citizens. And we won that fight. And more than a thousand Negro graduate and professional students have been accepted by 10 State universities that had barred their doors to Negroes before. . . .

At my request, the Solicitor General again went before the Supreme Court and argued against the vicious, restrictive covenants that had prevented houses in many places from being sold to Negroes and to Jews. It was a great day in the history of civil rights when we won that case, also, before the Supreme Court.

As one result of that decision, more Negroes are homeowners today than ever before in American history. . . .

Progress has been made in assuring Negroes the opportunity to exercise their right to vote as citizens. The courts have made the infamous "white primary" a thing of the past. Thank God for that. And there are only five poll tax States left in this Union.[15]

Voters in Truman's Harlem audience shared the president's pleasure when he exclaimed "Thank God for that" in reference to the elimination of the white primary throughout much of the South. Many of those gathered in Dorrance Brooks Square knew firsthand about the white primary, the poll tax, and other discriminatory states' rights devices that had driven thousands upon thousands of African Americans from the South to northern urban communities like Harlem, where they were finally able to cast their votes.[16] Truman, the consummate politician, wanted to remind recently enfranchised black voters that it was the Democratic Party of Harry Truman and Adlai Stevenson, not the GOP of General Eisenhower, that was making their participation in the elective process a reality.

Mindful of the fact that voter apathy was a chronic problem—even in 1952—President Truman admonished the people gathered in Harlem, "It's not enough to nod your heads in agreement when we talk about this fight we have been making together. You must go to the polls in such numbers that you can defeat the forces of reaction. You have until 10:30 tonight to register. And you are not worth a hoot to the Democratic Party unless you are registered. Make sure your name is on the books—and that your friends' and neighbors' names are on the books—by the time those books close tonight. And on November 4, let's roll up a great majority for Adlai Stevenson and a Democratic Congress and we will support him in his battle for civil rights."[17] Nash, standing near Truman, realized that when the tireless campaigner reached the end of his prepared speech, "he obviously felt as though it needed a little more of an arouser than it had, which it did need, it wasn't in there, and he kind of threw the script away and he said—and it had all been quite holy, so to speak, quote and unquote at this point[—]and he said, 'Now the question comes, what are you going to do about it, and I tell you if you don't get out there and get registered,' you see this was October 11th, and there was still time to register, 'get out there and register and make your influence felt, and make your vote felt, you're bigger damn fools than I think you are.'"[18]

With these stern fatherly words urging his Harlem audience to register to vote before the 10:30 P.M. cutoff, Truman made his final effort to energize black voters, just as he had successfully done four years earlier, on October 29, 1948, when he had first spoken to a Harlem audience. The president wanted this audience to do on November 4, 1952, what black American voters throughout the industrial North and Midwest had done on November 2, 1948, when they had turned out in record numbers to help keep a Democrat in the White House for the next four years.[19]

Truman's campaign efforts on behalf of Adlai Stevenson proved to be in vain; voters overwhelmingly elected General Eisenhower president by a 55 percent popular vote margin.[20] Nevertheless, the president's final speech in Harlem was significant because it provided yet another public and final presidential forum for Harry Truman to assure black Americans that he would never stop fighting for civil rights reform.

Harlem was a fitting final venue for Truman's promise of continued support for full civil rights for African Americans, and it was a promise that his audience knew—based on his remarkable record of real civil rights progress—to be genuine. The Harlem audience that cheered Truman on again and again on October 11, 1952, fully appreciated that this little man from Missouri really cared about their well-being; and because he really cared, President Truman had repeatedly taken politically high risk actions throughout his presidency to make life better for blacks in an America that was just awakening to its pervasive racial malaise.

CHAPTER FOURTEEN

The Truman Civil Rights Legacy

On January 7, 1953, just thirteen days before he would become a former president of the United States, Harry Truman submitted his eighth and final state of the union address to the Congress. The president's words appropriately focused only on the record of the prior eight years and not on the legislative proposals for the new Congress that were now the prerogative of President-Elect General Dwight D. Eisenhower. Consistent with his previous state of the union addresses, Truman once again made the goal of full civil rights and equality of opportunity for all Americans a top priority for the United States in 1953.

In recalling the fundamental questions confronting the country when he suddenly became president on April 12, 1945, Truman asked,

> Would we continue, in peace as well as war, to promote equality of opportunity for all our citizens, seeking ways and means to guarantee for all of them the full enjoyment of their civil rights?
>
> During the war we achieved great economic and social gains for millions of our fellow citizens who had been held back by prejudice. Were we prepared, in peacetime, to keep on moving toward full realization of the democratic promise? Or would we let it be submerged, wiped out, in post-war riots and reaction, as after World War I?
>
> We answered these questions in a series of forward steps at every level of government and in many spheres of private life. In our armed forces, our civil service, our universities, our railway trains, the residential districts of our cities—in stores and factories all across the Nation—in the polling booths as well—the barriers are coming down. This is happening, in part, at the mandate of the courts; in part, at the insistence of the Federal, State and local governments; in part, through the enlightened action of private groups and persons in every region and every walk of life.

There has been a great awakening of the American conscience on the issues of civil rights. And all this progress—still far from complete but still continuing—has been our answer, up to now, to those who questioned our intention to live up to the promises of equal freedom for us all.[1]

While proud of his civil rights achievements, Truman—ever the political realist—reminded the reluctant members of Congress who had repeatedly blocked his comprehensive civil rights proposals that the civil rights fight was "still far from complete."[2]

Though Truman's civil rights crusade was not yet over, incoming President Eisenhower was happy to leave it that way. For states' rights advocates in both houses of the Eighty-third Congress, as well as for some of the senior racist Southern Democrats in the Senate, it was comforting to realize that the man coming into the White House in just two weeks had a much more cautious view on civil rights than the outgoing president. While Truman acknowledged the remaining civil rights work to be done—particularly during the Eisenhower administration—he would not overlook the progress that had been made. "The [civil rights] barriers are coming down," he said. And as was clear from this last message to the Congress, Truman took public pride in the fact that he, his administration, and his appointees, such as the chief justice of the Supreme Court, had collectively started to tear down these barriers to full civil rights protections for all Americans.[3]

Just eight days later at 10:30 P.M. on January 15, 1953, President Truman personally delivered his final—and in some ways most poignant—address to the nation during a live television and radio broadcast from the Oval Office. In a front-page *New York Times* story the next morning, journalist Paul Kennedy characterized the president's speech as "a nostalgic farewell, but not a sad one. He offered his best wishes to his successor, General Dwight D. Eisenhower. He held out high hopes for a better and more peaceful world in the future. He saw an inevitable change in the Soviet regime. The President asserted a restrained pride in the record of his stewardship. He said he would leave the White House with no regrets."[4]

When Truman told his nationwide audience, "I have tried to give it everything that was in me," he was speaking generally of his multifaceted role as the thirty-third president of the United States but also as the country's first Cold War president.[5] Regarding the global arena, the president spoke with firmness about the ongoing Korean conflict, which he viewed as a limited war necessary to avoiding a third world war. He was prescient, yet optimistic in his view of the

Soviet menace. Truman predicted the ultimate collapse of communism, stating, "I have never once doubted that you, the people of our Country, have the will to do what is necessary to win this terrible fight against communism."[6] Citing the creation of the United Nations, the enactment of the Truman Doctrine and the Marshall Plan, the creation of NATO—all bulwarks against the flawed communist system—the moralist Truman spoke with certainty about the demise of the communist world because "Theirs is a godless system, a system of slavery."[7]

Truman's use of the word *slavery* in his final presidential address to the nation is significant because servitude based on race had been an acceptable way of life for his grandparents. Despite this fact, and despite the racism in the president's immediate family, Truman at sixty-eight remained repulsed by the concept of slavery. Slavery for Truman was a real-life tangible evil—so evil that it would, in his confident view, result in internal decay and cause the ultimate collapse of communism. This event did in fact occur forty years later for the very reasons that Truman predicted on January 15, 1953. And as his presidential record confirmed, Truman believed that slavery's decaying impact had to be eliminated in both the domestic and the global arena.

As the first U.S. president to confront a growing system of communism that had, under Joseph Stalin and his political heirs, effectively enslaved millions of people in Central and Eastern Europe, Truman viewed slavery as the enemy of democratic governments. Regardless of whether it was the slavery of a godless communist system aggressively seeking to dominate the globe in 1953 or the sad heritage of slavery in the United States, which had caused the rampant racism documented by Truman's Civil Rights Committee, slavery in any form was simply unacceptable to Truman.

In 1947, the first Presidential Civil Rights Committee confirmed for Truman in its exhaustive report what the president already knew: while slavery might have legally ended with Lincoln's Emancipation Proclamation and the ratification of the Thirteenth Amendment, the toxic racist by-products of slavery were still a pervasive force in post–World War II America.[8] Truman also knew that, unless the federal government mounted a massive domestic effort to provide constitutionally guaranteed equality to all Americans, the United States, because of its lingering racism, was just as vulnerable to the decaying corruption of slavery as the godless and growing Soviet empire. As Truman fully realized, for the United States, slavery was dead—but its debilitating heritage, racism—was still pervasive in American society.

When his Civil Rights Committee delivered their report—a report that a national journalist characterized as social dynamite—President Truman did not downplay it. He ignored Gallup polls that indicated that 82 percent of the American public opposed his civil rights program and dismissed the counsel of cautious political advisers. He publicly embraced the thirty-five recommendations of his multiracial Civil Rights Committee and he went to work for the balance of his presidency to remedy the politically challenging problems of racism at every level of American society.[9] From "whites only" restrooms in federal buildings to segregated schools of higher learning in the South to the all-white federal bench and all-white juries throughout the South, Truman and his administration went on the offensive.[10] When the Southern-dominated Congress repeatedly refused to enact President Truman's revolutionary ten-point civil rights program, Truman went around the Congress and advanced his federal civil rights agenda in numerous creative and lawful ways. Using his executive order authority, which required no congressional concurrence, Truman did the unthinkable in 1948 and integrated the massive U.S. armed services while also prohibiting race-based employment discrimination in the federal government, a practice that had been deeply entrenched in the federal bureaucracy since the early days of the Wilson presidency.[11]

Incredibly, Truman the politician took these revolutionary and politically high risk actions knowing with certainty that his unequivocal stand would seriously jeopardize his chances of being elected to the White House in 1948. Despite the certain adverse political impact of his civil rights program, and despite the fact that he was free of the nationwide race riots and resulting public pressure for civil rights reform that developed in the 1960s, he repeatedly did what he felt was morally right.

Even when Southern Democratic states' rights leaders threatened an election-year revolt unless the president tempered his proactive federal civil rights program, Truman was unmoved. Instead, candidate Truman embraced a tough civil rights plank that ruptured the Democratic Party, causing the creation of the splinter Dixiecrat Party, which under racist Governor Strom Thurmond of South Carolina threatened to attract enough Southern voter support to cost Truman the White House in November 1948.[12]

Regardless of political risk, Truman embraced civil rights reform with a temerity that was in sharp contrast to the timidity of future presidents, who acted only in response to massive racial upheaval throughout the country. Richard Kluger, in his history of African American jurisprudence titled *Simple Justice,* put President Truman's pioneering civil rights role in concise perspective: "No president before or since Lincoln had put his political neck on the chopping block to help the colored people of the nation [as Truman had]."[13] And he did it when the vast majority of the American public were either hostile or indifferent to the civil rights of thirteen million black citizens.[14]

When Congress continued to balk at his ten-point civil rights program, Truman used his executive branch powers to integrate the federal appellate bench—a first-time occurrence in the long, 170-year judicial history of the United States.[15] In addition, the president used the economic leverage of the FHA to force integrated housing on a reluctant public—a first-time presidential incursion into the nation's vast mortgage marketplace.[16] Through the Department of Justice, Truman aggressively pursued a strategy of filing hard-hitting amicus curiae briefs before his close friend and appointee Chief Justice Fred Vinson of the Supreme Court. The Vinson Court showed repeated deference to Truman's admonitions that *Plessy's* separate-but-equal doctrine was an anachronism that must be repealed if the integrity of this country's democratic traditions were to survive. The Vinson Court's rulings in *Shelley v. Kraemer, Hurd v. Hodge, Sweatt v. Painter, McLaurin v. Oklahoma State Regents,* and *Henderson v. United States* were landmark civil rights rulings that altered America's segregated racial landscape in housing, higher education, and interstate transportation—large chunks of American life that would never again be separate but equal.

Vinson, who joined Truman on the steps of the Lincoln Memorial on June 29, 1947, for the first presidential address before the NAACP, knew intimately how deeply the president felt about the constitutionally based civil rights of all Americans. The chief justice also had repeatedly heard the president explain the important nexus between the integrity of this country's domestic civil rights program and its credibility in the Cold War global arena, where the United States had become the preeminent advocate for democratic governments.[17]

Even in the last month of his presidency, Truman's Justice Department made one final compelling attack on the corrupting, but still viable separate-but-equal doctrine in its amicus brief filed in the case of *Brown v. Board of Education.* And despite the fact that Truman's dear friend Chief Justice Vinson would die in 1953, the record of the Vinson Court confirms that the judicial momentum for the repeal of *Plessy* was already well in place by January 20, 1953.[18] The Vinson Court's record was in fact the necessary legal predicate for the Warren Court's 1954 holding in *Brown,* which finally freed the country of the decaying, but still widespread impact of *Plessy's* institutionalized segregation.

While Truman obviously could not know with certainty that *Brown* would replace *Plessy* as the law of the land, he had ample reason to be upbeat about civil rights progress in his farewell address to the nation on January 15, 1953. As he had done again and again during his presidency, Truman focused one final time on his fundamental theme that all Americans were entitled to equality under the Constitution. Speaking with some pride about his civil rights record, the president said, "We have made progress in spreading the blessings of American life to all of our people. There has been a tremendous awakening of the American conscience on the great issues of civil rights—equal economic opportunities, equal rights of citizenship, and equal educational opportunities for all our people, whatever their race or religion or status of birth."[19]

The same sense of restrained pride that President Truman evinced in his farewell address on January 15 was also apparent in a brief thank-you note that President Truman sent on January 14, to Roy Wilkins, who was then serving as the NAACP's administrator. "It was good of you to write as you did. The progress in equal rights that has been made in the past seven years is a source of pride and satisfaction to me and I am very glad to have your confirmation of what I feel is a substantial change. It is most gratifying to me to have you say that there is a new climate of opinion on civil rights. Respect for human rights is fundamentally a thing of the mind and heart. As a government we must take the steps that improve human rights; as a people we must feel deeply about them."[20]

When he wrote to Roy Wilkins six days before leaving the White House, the president had a miserably low popularity rating with the American public that hovered just above 30 percent.[21] The Korean War raged on with no end in sight. The NATO commander whom Truman once admired, General Dwight Eisenhower, would soon be sworn in as president after a bitter campaign in which Eisenhower had publicly castigated his onetime commander in chief, claiming that Truman's "crooks and cronies" were an embarrassment to the country.[22]

Given these grim circumstances, most politicians would have been despondent. But not President Truman. Less than a week before again becoming citizen Truman, he was noting with considerable pride his accomplishments in launching the federal civil rights movement—a movement that was only just emerging into the important political force that would dominate domestic politics for the next two decades.

It is a curious fact that most Americans have failed to take note of President Truman's pioneering civil rights role. The general failure of the public to appreciate his moral leadership in this arena may be due in large part to the fact that Truman was a modest man who recoiled at self-promotion and rejected the relentless legacy-building public relations campaigns of subsequent presidents and their apologists. Moreover, since the public often thinks of the civil rights movement in terms of the violent protests of the late 1950s and the 1960s, many scholars fail to realize that the frustrations evident in those protests had their roots in the liberating words and actions taken by President Truman from 1946 through the last days of his presidency. Regardless of the reasons for his under-appreciated role in the civil rights movement, the ample record of the Truman presidency confirms that he was in fact this country's twentieth-century pioneering civil rights president.

For Supreme Court Justice Tom Clark—who together with his colleagues voted to destroy *Plessy's* separate-but-equal doctrine with their unanimous votes in *Shelley, Hurd, Henderson, McLaurin, Sweatt,* and *Brown,* there was no doubt about the pioneering role played by President Harry Truman as he tenaciously and creatively used his presidential prerogatives to bring constitutionally guaranteed equality and civil rights protection to African Americans. When asked in 1972 to name President Truman's greatest domestic achievement, Clark replied, "I think [it] was in the domestic field, and that is in the area of civil rights. I think for one who came in under the circumstances in which he did, to be able to have accomplished as much as he did, and to lay the framework for the great advancements that have been made by Democratic administrations since is really phenomenal, really phenomenal. . . . Mr. Truman's [civil rights] program inspired much that has been accomplished—it was largely inspired by him. It was the beginning of the civil rights crusade that eventually got us where we are today."[23]

Justice Clark's conclusion was shared by the NAACP's Roy Wilkins, who was himself one of the pioneers of the nationwide civil rights movement that would dominate the 1960s. In Wilkins's letter of January 12, 1953, to President Truman, the respected leader and early architect of the civil rights movement wrote,

Dear Mr. President:

You must be receiving many letters and your hours in these last days of office must be filled with many duties, but I felt that I could not see you leave Washington without telling you how I feel about one phase of your administration.

I want to thank you and to convey to you my admiration for your efforts in the civil rights field, for your pronouncements and definitions of policy on racial and religions discrimination and segregation.

You have many accomplishments on record during your tenure of the White House (many more by far than is admitted publicly by the Republicans or the majority of the nation's press) but none more valuable to our nation and its ideals than your outspoken championing of equality of opportunity for all Americans without regard to race, color or national origin.

Mr. President, no Chief Executive in our history has spoken so plainly on this matter as yourself, or acted so forthrightly. We have had in the White House great men—great diplomats, great politicians, great scholars, great humanitarians, great administrators. Some of these have recognized inequality as undesirable, as being at variance with the democratic principles of our country; but none has had the courage, either personal or political, to speak out or act in the Truman manner.

You spoke, Sir, when you knew that many powerful influences in your own party (and in the party of the opposition) would not heed you. You reiterated your beliefs and restated your demands for legislation when political expediency dictated a compromise course. This is sheer personal courage, so foreign to the usual conduct in political office—high or low—as to be unique in the annals of our government. . . .

In urging that America erase inequality between its citizens, as citizens, you were outlining a component of the complex mosaic for peace in the world: the hope, dignity and freedom that democracies offer mankind in contrast to the offering of totalitarianism. Your sure realization of the truism that preachment without practice would be powerless as a force for peace is a measure of the quiet greatness you brought to your high office.

As you leave the White House you carry with you the gratitude and affectionate regard of millions of your Negro fellow citizens who in less than a decade of your leadership, inspiration and determination, have seen the old order change right before their eyes.

Their sons are serving their country's armed forces in pride and honor, instead of humiliation and despair.

A whole new world of opportunity in education is opening to their children and young people.

The barriers to employment and promotion on the basis of merit have been breached and will be destroyed.

Some of the obstacles in the way of enjoyment of decent housing have been removed and others are under attack.

Restrictions upon the precious citizenship right of casting a ballot have been reduced and soon this right will be unfettered.

Some of the cruel humiliations and discriminations in travel and accommodation in public places have been eliminated and others are on the way out. . . .

You have said often that the people will act when they have understanding. The people who have had their faith fanned fresh by you will not fail to press toward the goals you have indicated. No change of personnel or party labels will stay them.

May God's blessing and guidance be with you in your new endeavors.

Respectfully yours,
Roy Wilkins
(Administrator, National Association for the Advancement of
Colored People)[24]

Wilkins would continue to work in the evolving civil rights struggle with Martin Luther King Jr., John Lewis, and other African Americans during the tumultuous years following Truman's departure from the White House. But long after the president returned to Independence as citizen Harry Truman, Wilkins's words on January 12, 1953, would remain an informed expression of gratitude and validation for Truman's moral leadership in the nascent federal civil rights movement. As Roy Wilkins, Walter White, Dorothy Height, Percy Sutton, William Hastie, and other black American leaders knew so well, the federal civil rights movement had been launched when Truman, and the reluctant nation he led, crossed one civil rights frontier after another.

After January 20, 1953, it was a movement that could no longer be ignored. Nor could it be stopped.

Epilogue

When Harry Truman returned to Independence, Missouri, on January 21, 1953, the sixty-eight-year-old former president seemed unconcerned that his popularity rating was a miserable 31 percent. Since 1922, Truman had reveled in politics—at the local, state, and national levels. In retirement, the thirty-third president—while always a fierce partisan—gracefully accepted the fact that his days in mainstream American politics were over.

Unlike some restless, often depressed former modern American presidents, Lyndon Johnson and Richard Nixon in particular, Truman thoroughly enjoyed his retirement years—years filled with daily walks around Independence, visits in Kansas City with some of the Battery D boys, and hours of reading with Bess in the snug den of Bess's family home at 219 N. Delaware Street.

When national events of note occurred, reporters would sometimes catch the always frank president on a walk; as these dogged reporters hoped, Truman occasionally would make a spontaneous remark that added spice to their stories. And sometimes, in his letters—which Truman still wrote prolifically even in retirement—the former president would offer a controversial view that found its way into the national press. One such event involved Truman's comments about sit-ins, the protests that became a popular—and necessary—part of the energized civil rights movement of the late 1950s and the 1960s. In response to the sit-ins of the late 1950s, citizen Truman, aged seventy-five, bluntly suggested in April 1960 that protesters should respect the property rights of store owners. When the former president went so far as to suggest that the Communist Party might be inspiring the lawless conduct of civil rights activists, Truman's respected Secretary of State Dean Acheson, wrote his former boss to ask him to restrain himself on the subject.

Dear Boss:

As the Convention approaches we partisans are likely to become, shall we say, emphatic in our statements to the press. Could we make a treaty on what we shall *not* say?

On the positive side we can, and doubtless will, say that our candidate—

yours and mine—has all the virtues of the Greats from Pericles through
Churchill. . . .

About the Negro sit-in Strikes:

(a) Do not say that they are communist inspired. The evidence is all
the other way, despite alleged views of J. Edgar Hoover, whom
you should trust as much as you would a rattlesnake with the
silencer on its rattle.

(b) Do not say that you disapprove of them. Whatever you think you
are under no compulsion to broadcast it. Free speech is a restraint
on government; not an incitement to the citizen.

The reason: Your views, as reported, are wholly out of keeping with
your public record. The discussion does not convince anyone of anything.
If you want to discuss the sociological, moral and legal interests involved,
you should give much more time and thought to them.[1]

While Truman subsequently modified his comments about the sit-ins being
communist inspired, it was predictable that he spoke out against civil disobedience. Based on his longstanding belief in the basic property rights of farmers and
shopkeepers—occupations he once pursued—Truman, at seventy-five, was obviously concerned about any breakdown in basic law and order. Ironically, however,
it was Truman and his administration that had been the catalyst for energizing
the federal civil rights movement. That movement would now be taken by John
Lewis, Martin Luther King Jr., and other younger black activists in new and often
confrontational directions during the years following the Truman presidency.

As Dr. Dorothy Height noted, Truman's actions in integrating the military
and the federal workforce brought about "a structural change" in the segregated
lifestyle of Americans.[2] And based on the president's tenacious efforts with other
executive branch actions, as well as through the landmark rulings of his
appointees to the Vinson Court, a volatile environment was created wherein the
federal civil rights movement necessarily moved into high gear with a more confrontational tone following Truman's exit from the White House.

Because of Truman's actions as president, America's racism was assaulted
and altered by the structural changes that Dr. Height applauded. With those
structural changes also came the legitimate expectations for full civil rights equality for African Americans—citizens who no longer would suffer the unconstitutional civil rights abuses, including routine lynchings, that had haunted blacks
since Abraham Lincoln's Emancipation Proclamation.

With the diverse and life-altering civil rights reforms mandated by the Vinson
Court in *Shelley, Hurd, Henderson, Sweatt,* and *McLaurin,* with the resulting pre-

destined ruling of the Warren Court in *Brown,* and with the desegregation of the vast armed services after 1948, the explosive nature of the civil rights movement of the late 1950s and 1960s was inevitable.

Truman had ignited the civil rights movement from a federal perspective, and many of the more cautious leaders of America's civil rights movement were now joined in the 1950s and 1960s by younger, more impatient women and men who were emboldened by Truman's vision of full civil rights equality—a vision that he had first publicly articulated in his remarks in the summer of 1947 to NAACP members gathered at the steps of Lincoln's memorial. Thus while Truman in retirement stayed largely on the sidelines of the energized civil rights movement as it ripened into a nationwide confrontation during the 1960s, this president from a racist rural background in Missouri could take comfort in knowing that he had awakened the nation—including Southern segregationists in the Congress—to the fact that federally enforced civil rights reform was morally and politically necessary under the Constitution of the United States. With that Truman-forced awakening, the Civil Rights Act of 1964 and the Voting Rights Act of 1965 became the law of the land in Truman's lifetime—albeit more than fifteen tumultuous years after he had proposed his comprehensive ten-point civil rights legislation to the Eightieth Congress in 1948.

In private life, the former president never wavered from his view of full equality on civil rights. In a 1959 *Ebony* magazine interview, when asked by journalist Carl Rowan about his views on civil rights, Truman replied, "My views in the White House were exactly the same as when I was back in Jackson County, Missouri. I grew up with Negroes. I was always friendly with them, and they were just like part of my family. I learned a long time ago that the composition of the human animal is about the same no matter what color the skin is."[3]

Truman's continued empathy with and concern for black citizens in his retirement years was evident in a little-noted event in the early 1960s involving a black janitor named Bob Brown who worked at the Kansas City barber shop owned by one of Truman's favorite Battery D boys, Frank Spina. During one of the former president's trips to his barber, Bob Brown mentioned a pending trip to the South, where he planned to visit his sister in Mississippi. Due to the civil rights violence that was prevalent in much of the South at this time, Brown expressed concern for his safety because black outsiders could be viewed as a threat by racist sheriffs in some Southern communities. When Truman heard Brown's concerns, the former president responded without hesitation, offering his assistance and backing up that offer by giving janitor Brown his home phone number. Truman knew that Brown was scared, and Truman also knew from his own dealings with the Klan four decades earlier that Brown had reason to be afraid, so if this former president of the United States could help address those fears, he would gladly do so.

At the very end of his long life—a life that spanned eighty-eight years and concluded peacefully on December 26, 1972—Truman was honored in absentia at a civil rights ceremonial dinner on October 4, 1972, in Kansas City. Truman's former attorney general, retired Supreme Court Justice Tom Clark, accepted for Truman the award presented by the National Association of Human Rights Workers, a group of distinguished civil rights leaders who celebrated Truman's pioneering role in making the civil rights of African Americans a federal priority—and a reality—throughout America. The award that Justice Clark accepted on behalf of the former president was inscribed as follows: "In tribute to President Harry S Truman who turned the nation's conscience to the task of making equality a reality. Nothing he did aroused more controversy or did him greater honor."[4] In reflecting on this final tribute to Truman, Justice Clark recalled that the Human Rights Association "regarded Harry Truman as the greatest president since Abraham Lincoln that this country has ever had."[5] In his 1972 oral history, Justice Clark noted that the energized spirit of the nationwide civil rights movement in America was captured by an articulate young black man named Julian Bond, who was serving as a legislator in Georgia; in Clark's opinion, "Julian Bond made a rip-roaring speech, praising Mr. Truman."[6]

It was particularly fitting for Bond, a firebrand leader of a new generation of civil rights activists, to honor Truman as he lay ill in Independence. Bond, a tireless proponent of the more aggressive civil rights movement of the 1960s, was representative of the first generation of America's black citizens who enjoyed the new freedoms that Truman secured. It was fitting for Bond and his generation of civil rights activists to join together with older, more patient civil rights leaders on October 4, 1972, to collectively and publicly honor this courageous former president who had left the White House twenty years earlier.

From janitor Bob Brown to legislator Julian Bond, from entrepreneur Percy Sutton to civil rights pioneers Dr. Dorothy Height and Roy Wilkins, from White House butler Alonzo Fields to Judge William Hastie and White House reporter Alice Allison Dunnigan, black Americans knew with certainty that their full civil rights under the Constitution had been an absolute goal for the morally courageous and politically reckless Truman. And as the thirty-third president of the United States lay near death after his long and full life, it was indeed appropriate that African Americans once more honored him for his pioneering role in making their civil rights equality a reality in America—an America that even today is fighting to free itself of the racism that Harry Truman rejected in his own lifetime.

NOTES
BIBLIOGRAPHY
INDEX

NOTES

INTRODUCTION

1. President's Committee on Civil Rights, *To Secure These Rights*, 44.
2. "Klan at Convention Hall," *Jackson Examiner*, 1; "Klan Puts Out Ticket," *Independence Examiner*, 1.
3. Ferrell, *Harry S. Truman*, 3; McCullough, *Truman*, 18.
4. McCullough, *Truman*, 385.
5. President's Committee on Civil Rights, *To Secure These Rights*, 79, 86, and 87.
6. Clay, *Just Permanent Interests*, 125–26.
7. President's Committee on Civil Rights, *To Secure These Rights*, 35–40.
8. Ibid., 20.
9. Bethune, letter to President Harry S. Truman, Feb. 13, 1948.
10. White, *Man Called White*, 348.

I. THE HISTORICAL BACKGROUND FOR TRUMAN'S CIVIL RIGHTS CRUSADE

1. Ferrell, *Harry S. Truman*, 3–4.
2. McCullough, *Truman*, 31–32.
3. Ibid., 385.
4. Clifford, *Counsel to the President*, 73.
5. Fields, *My 21 Years in the White House*, 126–27.
6. Ferrell, *Harry S. Truman*, 3–4.
7. McCullough, *Truman*, 43, 75–77, and 116.
8. "KKK in Big Meet," *Jackson Examiner*, 1.
9. "Klan Puts Out Ticket," *Independence Examiner*, 1.
10. McCullough, *Truman*, 349–50.
11. Ibid., 381, 401, 450–52, and 455–58.
12. *Plessy v. Ferguson*, 544.
13. Ibid.
14. National Committee on Segregation in the Nation's Capital, *Segregation in Washington*, 16.
15. Ibid.
16. McCoy and Ruetten, *Quest and Response*, 68.

17. Ibid., 347.

18. "Armies Mobilized and Casualties."

2. TRUMAN'S COMMITTEE ON CIVIL RIGHTS: DECEMBER 5, 1946

1. Gallup Organization, "Presidential Popularity—Harry S. Truman," Sept. 1946.

2. McCoy and Ruetten, *Quest and Response,* 52.

3. Truman, Executive Order 9808, vii.

4. Nash, by Jerry N. Hess, 626–27.

5. Gallup Organization, "Presidential Popularity—Harry S. Truman," Dec. 1946.

6. Ferrell, *Off the Record,* 310.

7. Dawson, personal interview.

8. White, *Man Called White,* 331.

9. Truman, letter to Attorney General Tom C. Clark.

10. Morehead, "Negro Vet Tells How Dixie Cops Gouged Out Both Eyes with Club"; "Blinded Veteran Tells Court of Beating by Policeman," *Washington Evening Star.*

11. Clark, by Jerry N. Hess, 76–77.

12. Ibid., 147–49.

13. Department of Justice, press release.

14. "Police Chief Freed in Negro Beating," *New York Times;* "Federal vs. State Issue at S.C. Trial."

15. "Police Chief Freed in Negro Beating," *New York Times.*

16. White, *Man Called White,* 331.

17. Ibid.

18. Elsey, personal interview, 1997.

19. Truman, Executive Order 9808.

20. Clay, *Just Permanent Interests,* 53.

21. Kennedy, televised speech to the American public.

22. Truman, Executive Order 9808, vii.

23. Ibid.

24. Ferrell, *Dear Bess,* 265.

25. Ibid., 265–66.

26. Ibid., 272.

27. National Committee on Segregation in the Nation's Capital, *Segregation in Washington,* 15.

28. Nash, by Jerry N. Hess, 629.

29. President's Committee on Civil Rights, press release.

30. White, *Man Called White,* 332.

31. Alexander-Minter, personal interview, 1998.

32. Nash, by Jerry N. Hess, 631.

33. Alexander, letter to President Harry S. Truman, Dec. 9, 1946.

34. Alexander-Minter, personal interview, 1998.

35. Truman, "Executive Order 9808," Dec. 5, 1946.

36. Truman, Remarks to Members of the President's Committee on Civil Rights, 98.

37. Truman, "Executive Order 9808," Dec. 5, 1946.

3. TRUMAN'S SPEECH TO THE NAACP AT THE LINCOLN MEMORIAL: JUNE 29, 1947

1. Hamby, *Man of the People*, 433.

2. "612 Delegates from 34 States Attend 38th Annual Conference of Civic Body," *Baltimore Afro-American*, 10.

3. Gross, "Truman Holds Civil Rights a Key to Peace," 1 and 4; Streator, "Truman Demands We Fight Harder to Spur Equality," 1 and 3.

4. Truman, Address Before the National Association for the Advancement of Colored People, 200.

5. Sutton, telephone interview.

6. Hamby, *Man of the People*, 475.

7. Truman, letter to Sister Mary Jane.

8. Truman, Address Before the National Association for the Advancement of Colored People.

9. White, *Man Called White*, 35.

10. Clay, *Just Permanent Interests*, 125–26.

11. White, *Man Called White*, 348.

12. Truman, Address Before the National Association for the Advancement of Colored People, 200.

13. White, *Man Called White*, 349.

14. Ibid.

15. McCullough, *Truman*, 569–70.

16. "Dangerous World," Lancer Productions.

17. Hastie, by Jerry N. Hess, 54.

18. White, *Man Called White*, 347–48.

19. Truman, Address Before the National Association for the Advancement of Colored People.

20. Ibid.

21. McCullough, *Truman*, 547–48.

22. McCoy and Ruetten, *Quest and Response*, 73.

23. Holeman, "U.S. Must End Racial Bias, Says Truman," 1 and 2.

24. Streator, "Truman Demands We Fight Harder to Spur Equality," 1 and 3.

25. Truman, Address Before the National Association for the Advancement of Colored People, 200.

26. Berman, *Politics of Civil Rights*, 65–66.

27. Ibid., 62.

28. National Committee on Segregation in the Nation's Capital, *Segregation in Washington*, 6.

29. Ibid.

30. Truman, Address Before the National Association for the Advancement of Colored People, 200.

31. McCullough, *Truman*, 53–54.

32. Truman, Address Before the National Association for the Advancement of Colored People, 200.

33. Gross, "Truman Holds Civil Rights a Key to Peace," 1 and 4.

34. "Floor Leaders of the House of Representatives."

35. Truman, Address Before the National Association for the Advancement of Colored People, 200.

36. President's Committee on Civil Rights, *To Secure These Rights*, 20.

37. White, *Man Called White*, 348.

38. McCullough, *Truman*, 247.

39. Streator, "Truman Demands We Fight Harder to Spur Equality," 1 and 3.

40. Gallup Organization, "How do you feel about Truman's Civil Rights Program?" Apr. 5, 1948.

41. "Civil Rights, Human Freedom," *Baltimore Afro-American*, 4.

42. Truman, Address Before the National Association for the Advancement of Colored People, 200.

43. White, *Man Called White*, 348–49.

44. Ibid., 348.

45. Truman, letter to Sister Mary Jane.

4. THE REPORT OF TRUMAN'S COMMITTEE ON CIVIL RIGHTS: OCTOBER 29, 1947

1. President's Committee on Civil Rights, *To Secure These Rights*.

2. White, *Man Called White*, 348.

3. Truman, "Statement by the President Making Public a Report by the Civil Rights Committee," 479–80.

4. Truman, Remarks to Members of the President's Committee on Civil Rights, 98–99.

5. McCoy and Ruetten, *Quest and Response*, 45.

6. Ibid., 45–46.

7. McCoy and Ruetten, *Quest and Response*, 46.

8. Truman, Executive Order 9808, viii.

9. Ibid.

10. Ibid.

11. Rowan, *Breaking Barriers*, 66.

12. President's Committee on Civil Rights, *To Secure These Rights*, ix.

13. President's Committee on Civil Rights, press release.

14. President's Committee on Civil Rights, *To Secure These Rights*, x.

15. Truman, letter to Chairman of the American Veterans Committee Charles G. Bolte.

16. President's Committee on Civil Rights, *To Secure These Rights*, 77.

17. *Revised Statutes of the State of Missouri*, 1949, vol. 1.

18. Ibid.

19. Missouri Commission on Human Rights, "Missouri Statutes on Fair Housing, Fair Employment Practices, and Public Accommodations."

20. President's Committee on Civil Rights, *To Secure These Rights*, 74–78.

21. Ibid., 42.

22. Truman, "Executive Order 9808," Dec. 5, 1946.

23. President's Committee on Civil Rights, *To Secure These Rights,* 20–24.

24. Rowan, *Breaking Barriers,* 66.

25. President's Committee on Civil Rights, *To Secure These Rights,* 20–24.

26. "23 Confessions Signed in S.C. Lynching Case," *Washington Times-Herald.*

27. President's Committee on Civil Rights, *To Secure These Rights,* 20.

28. Ibid., 20–24.

29. Ibid., xi.

30. Ibid.

31. Stavisky, "Need for Guarantee of Equal Rights to All Emphasized in Report to Truman," 1.

32. President's Committee on Civil Rights, *To Secure These Rights,* 99.

33. Ibid., 151–73.

34. Ibid., 23–25.

35. Ibid., 24.

36. Ibid., 23.

37. Ibid., 20, 32, 47, and 53.

38. Ibid., 24.

39. Ibid., 26.

40. Ibid., 119.

41. Clark, by Jerry N. Hess, 124.

42. Ibid.

43. Clifford, *Counsel to the President,* 176.

44. Daniel, by Ron Cockrell, 32.

45. President's Committee on Civil Rights, *To Secure These Rights,* 29.

46. Ibid., 35.

47. Ibid., 37.

48. Ibid., 38.

49. Ibid., 39.

50. Sutton, telephone interview.

51. President's Committee on Civil Rights, *To Secure These Rights,* 41.

52. Ibid.

53. Ibid., 42.

54. Ibid., 46.

55. Ibid., 47.

56. Ibid., 49.

57. Ibid., 52.

58. Ibid., 53.

59. Ibid.

60. Ibid.

61. Ibid., 59.

62. Ibid., 62–63.

63. Ibid., 66–67.

64. Ibid., 68–69.

65. Ibid., 71.

66. Ibid., 77.

67. Ibid., 87.

68. Stavisky, "Need for Guarantee of Equal Rights to All Emphasized in Report to Truman," 1 and 10.

69. President's Committee on Civil Rights, *To Secure These Rights*, 99.

70. Morgan, *FDR*, 595.

71. Ibid.

72. Clark, by Jerry N. Hess, 97–98.

73. McCoy and Ruetten, *Quest and Response*, 49.

74. White, "President Means It."

75. President's Committee on Civil Rights, *To Secure These Rights*, 151–73.

76. Ibid., 151.

77. Ibid., 154.

78. Ibid., 157–58.

79. Ibid., 160.

80. Ibid., 160–61.

81. Ibid., 162.

82. Ibid., 164.

83. Ibid., 166.

84. Ibid., 167.

85. Ibid., 168.

86. Ibid., 169.

87. "Truman Sees Rights Report as 'Human Freedom Charter,'" *Washington Post*, 11.

88. Rowan, "Harry Truman and the Negro," 47.

89. Quoted in "Southern Newspapers Hit Civil Rights Report," *Washington Post*, 11.

90. Howell, "You Can't Legislate Tolerance," 1.

91. M. R. Baker, letter to President Harry S. Truman, Nov. 4, 1947.

92. Morgan, *FDR*, 569.

93. White, *Man Called White*, 333.

94. Clark, by Jerry N. Hess, 97.

95. Height, personal interview.

96. Rowan, "Harry Truman and the Negro," 45.

97. Ibid.

98. President's Committee on Civil Rights, *To Secure These Rights*, ix.

5. TRUMAN'S STATE OF THE UNION ADDRESS: JANUARY 7, 1948

1. McCullough, *Truman*, 523.

2. Truman, Personal Diary, Jan. 6, 1948.

3. Elsey, by Charles T. Morrissey and Jerry N. Hess, 137–38.

4. Truman, Annual Message to the Congress on the State of the Union, Jan. 7, 1948, 2.

5. Ibid.

6. Truman, Address Before the National Association for the Advancement of Colored People.

7. Truman, Annual Message to the Congress on the State of the Union, Jan. 7, 1948, 2.

8. Ibid., 2–3.

9. Ibid., 3.

10. See Truman, Annual Message to the Congress on the State of the Union, Jan. 7, 1948, 1–7.

11. Ibid., 10.

12. Trussell, "Congress Is Cool to Truman Pleas."

13. Ibid., 1–2.

14. Clark, by Jerry N. Hess, 153.

6. TRUMAN'S SPECIAL MESSAGE TO CONGRESS ON CIVIL RIGHTS: FEBRUARY 2, 1948

1. Truman, Annual Message to the Congress on the State of the Union, Jan. 7, 1948, 3.

2. Truman, Personal Diary, Feb. 2, 1948.

3. McCullough, *Truman*, 582–83.

4. Rowan, "Harry Truman and the Negro," 46.

5. Truman, Special Message to the Congress on Civil Rights, 121.

6. Lewis, *Walking with the Wind*, 12.

7. Ambrose, *Eisenhower*, 445.

8. See, for example, Brief for the Petitioner, *Smith v. Allwright;* Brief for the United States as Amicus Curiae, *Shelley v. Kraemer.*

9. Ambrose, *Eisenhower*, 445.

10. Rowan, "Harry Truman and the Negro," 50.

11. Branch, *Parting the Waters,* 670.

12. Ibid., 670–71.

13. Ibid., 672.

14. Kennedy, Executive Order 11063, 11527–30.

15. Popham, "Negro in South Still Lags in Political Power," E9.

16. Truman, Special Message to the Congress on Civil Rights, 122.

17. Ibid.

18. Krock, "Democrats Try Hard for a Show of Unity," 4B.

19. Trussell, "Southerners in House Plan New 'Revolt' on Civil Rights," 1 and 3.

20. Bell, "President's Civil Rights Program Angers South."

21. McCullough, *Truman*, 645.

22. Clifford, *Counsel to the President,* 207 and 208.

23. Leviero, "President Renews Civil Rights Plea," 1 and 6.

24. Elsey, by William D. Stilley and Jerald L. Hill, 49.

25. Truman, Special Message to the Congress on Civil Rights, 122.

26. Ibid., 123.

27. Ibid., 123–24.

28. Clark, by Jerry N. Hess, 99.

29. "Floor Leaders of the House of Representatives."

30. See Johnson, "Challenge of a New Day."

31. Ibid.

32. Ibid.

33. Clark, by Jerry N. Hess, 98.

34. Gallup Organization, "How do you feel about Truman's Civil Rights Program?" Apr. 5, 1948.

35. White, "President Means It."

36. Elsey, by Charles T. Morrissey and Jerry N. Hess, 450.

37. Ibid., 203.

38. Ibid., 449–50.

39. Truman, Special Message to the Congress on Civil Rights, 125.

40. Ibid., 126.

41. Ibid.

42. Clark, by Jerry N. Hess, 160.

43. Ibid., 163.

44. See McCullough, *Truman*, 449–50.

45. Gallup Organization, "How do you feel about Truman's Civil Rights Program?" Apr. 5, 1948.

7. THE 1948 DEMOCRATIC PARTY CONVENTION AND THE CIVIL RIGHTS PLANK: JULY 14–15, 1948

1. Clark, by Jerry N. Hess, 155.

2. McCullough, *Truman*, 632.

3. Ibid., 642–43.

4. Daniels, *Man of Independence*, 336–38.

5. Ibid., 339.

6. Ibid.

7. White, "President Means It."

8. Berman, *Politics of Civil Rights*, 44.

9. Daniels, *Man of Independence*, 339.

10. Clifford, memorandum for the president, 1.

11. Elsey, personal interview, 1997.

12. McCullough, *Truman*, 639 and 645.

13. Ibid., 632; Clifford, *Counsel to the President*, 196.

14. Clifford, *Counsel to the President*, 196.

15. Berman, *Politics of Civil Rights*, 128.

16. Ibid., 103–4.

17. Wright, "Negro Migration from South Will Follow War, Survey Finds."

18. McCoy and Ruetten, *Quest and Response*, 11.

19. "USAFE Humanitarian Operations," *Berlin Airlift Facts and Figures*.

20. See Truman, Address Before the National Association for the Advancement of Colored People.

21. Berman, *Politics of Civil Rights*, 109.

22. Quoted in Berman, *Politics of Civil Rights*, 109–10.

23. Ibid., 110.

24. Clark, by Jerry N. Hess, 185.

25. Berman, *Politics of Civil Rights,* 110–11; Clark, by Jerry N. Hess, 185.
26. Quoted in Berman, *Politics of Civil Rights,* 111.
27. Dunnigan, *Black Woman's Experience,* 244.
28. Quoted in Berman, *Politics of Civil Rights,* 111.
29. Truman, *Memoirs by Harry S. Truman, Volume 2,* 182.
30. Quoted in Berman, *Politics of Civil Rights,* 112.
31. Truman, Personal Diary, July 14, 1948.
32. Truman, *Memoirs by Harry S. Truman, Volume 2,* 182.
33. See Truman, Address in Philadelphia upon Accepting the Nomination of the Democratic National Convention.
34. White, "Truman Is Shunned in Votes of South," 1.
35. Lawrence, "Nominees Go Before Convention to Make Acceptance Talks," 1.
36. Quoted in Berman, *Politics of Civil Rights,* 114.
37. Truman, Address in Philadelphia upon Accepting the Nomination of the Democratic National Convention, 409–10.
38. Ibid., 407.
39. Berman, *Politics of Civil Rights,* 114.
40. J. Strom Thurmond, telegram to President Harry S. Truman.
41. Berman, *Politics of Civil Rights,* 114.
42. Ibid., 115–16.
43. McCoy and Ruetten, *Quest and Response,* 98.
44. Daniels, *Man of Independence,* 339.
45. Berman, *Politics of Civil Rights,* 111.
46. "Negro Leader Hails Action," *New York Times,* 2.

8. THE TURNIP DAY CONGRESSIONAL SESSION AND EXECUTIVE ORDERS 9980 AND 9981: JULY 26, 1948

1. Truman, Address in Philadelphia upon Accepting the Nomination of the Democratic National Convention.
2. Berman, *Politics of Civil Rights,* 116.
3. "President Truman Wipes Out Segregation in Armed Forces," *Chicago Defender,* 1.
4. Gallup Organization, "How do you feel about Truman's Civil Rights Program?" Apr. 5, 1948.
5. Gallup Organization, "Presidential Popularity—Harry S. Truman," May–June 1948.
6. Truman, Message to the Special Session of the 80th Congress, see 116–22.
7. Trussell, "Republican Chiefs Cautious, Awaiting President's Word," 1.
8. Truman, Executive Order 9980.
9. Trussell, "Republican Chiefs Cautious, Awaiting President's Word," 1.
10. Truman, Executive Order 9980, 720–21.
11. Ibid.
12. Link, *Wilson,* 243–48; Salzman, et al., *Encyclopedia of African-American Culture and History,* 2789.
13. Villard, letters to Woodrow Wilson, Aug. 18, 1913, and Aug. 27, 1913.

14. Cashman, *African-Americans and the Quest for Civil Rights,* 25.

15. Fields, *My 21 Years in the White House,* 41–42.

16. McCullough, *Truman,* 483–84.

17. Truman, Executive Order 9980, 720–21.

18. Leviero, "Truman Orders End of Bias in Forces and Federal Jobs; Addresses Congress Today," *New York Times,* 1.

19. Truman, Executive Order 9980, 720–21.

20. Ibid.

21. Ibid., 721.

22. Dunnigan, *Black Woman's Experience,* 283.

23. McCoy and Ruetten, *Quest and Response,* 129.

24. Truman, Executive Order 9981.

25. Height, personal interview.

26. Truman, Executive Order 9981, 2673.

27. President's Committee on Civil Rights, *To Secure These Rights,* 40–42.

28. "Army to Keep Segregation Bradley Says," *Washington Post,* 1.

29. "NAACP Hits Bradley," *Washington Post,* 3.

30. See Attendance at the Ceremony for the Promotion of Omar N. Bradley to the Rank of General of the Army, Sept. 22, 1950.

31. Leviero, "Truman Orders End of Bias in Forces and Federal Jobs," *New York Times,* 1.

32. Truman, Executive Order 9981, 2673.

33. President's Appointments, Wednesday, May 25, 1949.

34. Clifford, *Counsel to the President,* 208–9.

35. President's Committee on Equality Treatment and Opportunity in the Armed Services, minutes of meeting with President Truman and the four service secretaries.

36. Symington, telephone interview.

37. Ibid.

38. Williams, *Thurgood Marshall,* 171.

39. Symington, telephone interview.

40. President's Committee on Equality of Treatment and Opportunity in the Armed Services, *Freedom to Serve.*

41. Truman, press release, May 22, 1950.

42. Clifford, *Counsel to the President,* 212.

43. Height, personal interview.

44. "Federation Backs Race Separation," *Washington Post,* 14M.

45. Omohundro, telegram to President Harry S. Truman.

46. Alexander, telegram released through Associated Negro Press, July 30, 1948.

47. Sutton, telephone interview.

9. THE GREAT "COMEBACK" CAMPAIGN AND TRUMAN'S HARLEM SPEECH: OCTOBER 29, 1948

1. McCullough, *Truman,* 678–79.

2. "Election Forecast," *Newsweek,* 20.

3. Symington, by James R. Fuchs, 59.

4. Clifford, *Counsel to the President,* 234–35.

5. McCullough, *Truman,* 629 and 654.

6. Ibid., 654.

7. Elsey, by Charles T. Morrissey and Jerry N. Hess, 195–96.

8. Ibid., 197.

9. Ferrell, *Harry S. Truman,* 275.

10. Truman, Rear Platform and Other Informal Remarks in Texas, 580–81.

11. Ibid., 581–83.

12. Ibid., 582.

13. Evans and Novak, *Lyndon B. Johnson,* 5.

14. Truman, Rear Platform and Other Informal Remarks in Texas, 588–90.

15. Pace, "Live up to Talk of Unity," 1.

16. Dawson, by William D. Stilley and Jerald L. Hill, 3.

17. Dawson, personal interview.

18. Berman, *Politics of Civil Rights,* 114.

19. Truman, Rear Platform and Other Informal Remarks in Texas.

20. Turner, "Dr. Harry S. Truman, LL.D. Visits Waco for Second Time," 1.

21. Dunnigan, *Black Woman's Experience,* 242–43.

22. Roberts, letter to President Harry S. Truman, Aug. 1948.

23. Truman, letter to Ernest W. Roberts, Aug. 18, 1948 (also quoted in Ferrell, *Off the Record,* 146–47).

24. "1946 Killing of 4 Blacks Is Recalled," *New York Times,* A16.

25. Truman, letter to Ernest W. Roberts, Aug. 18, 1948.

26. Berman, *Politics of Civil Rights,* 114; Truman, letter to Ernest W. Roberts, Aug. 18, 1948.

27. Truman, letter to Ernest W. Roberts, Aug. 18, 1948.

28. Ibid.

29. President's Committee on Civil Rights, *To Secure These Rights,* 66–67.

30. Fields, *My 21 Years in the White House,* 125–26.

31. Ibid., 186.

32. Ibid., 185.

33. Ibid., 8.

34. Hastie, by Jerry N. Hess, 47–48.

35. Ibid., 51–52.

36. For example, Brief for the Petitioner, *Smith v. Allwright;* Brief for the United States as Amicus Curiae, *Brown v. Board of Education;* Brief for the United States as Amicus Curiae, *Shelley v. Kraemer.*

37. Truman, Address in Harlem, New York, upon Receiving the Franklin Roosevelt Award, Oct. 29, 1948.

38. Ibid.

39. Nash, by Jerry N. Hess, 299–300.

40. Ibid., 393–94.

41. Ibid., 399–400.

42. Truman, Address in Harlem, New York, upon Receiving the Franklin Roosevelt Award, Oct. 29, 1948, 923.

43. President's Committee on Civil Rights, *To Secure These Rights,* 21–27.

44. Nash, by Jerry N. Hess, 401.

45. Truman, Address in Harlem, New York, upon Receiving the Franklin Roosevelt Award, Oct. 29, 1948, 923.

46. Ibid., 923–24.

47. See Truman, Address in Harlem, New York, upon Receiving the Franklin Roosevelt Award, Oct. 29, 1948, 924.

48. Height, personal interview.

49. Truman, Address in Harlem, New York, upon Receiving the Franklin Roosevelt Award, Oct. 29, 1948, 924–25.

50. Sutton, telephone interview.

51. Hastie, by Jerry N. Hess, 76.

52. Leviero, "President Renews Civil Rights Plea," 6.

53. Ibid., 1.

54. Kent, "Truman Campaign Highlight," 45.

55. Nash, by Jerry N. Hess, 401.

56. Ibid., 401–2.

57. Ibid., 404.

58. Sutton, telephone interview.

59. Leviero, "President Renews Civil Rights Plea," 1.

60. Ibid.

61. Berman, *Politics of Civil Rights,* 132.

62. Graf, *Statistics,* 49.

63. "Negro Prefers Truman," *New Republic.*

64. Nash, by Jerry N. Hess, 335–36.

10. CIVIL RIGHTS PROGRESS DESPITE A RECALCITRANT CONGRESS: 1949–1952

1. McCullough, *Truman,* 711.

2. Clifford, *Counsel to the President,* 229.

3. Humphrey, transcript of oral history interview, 4–7.

4. Evans and Novak, *Lyndon B. Johnson,* 32.

5. Truman, Annual Message to the Congress on the State of the Union, Jan. 5, 1949, 6–8.

6. Clark, by Jerry N. Hess, 142.

7. Ibid., 141–42.

8. M. Truman, *Harry S. Truman,* 403.

9. Dunnigan, *Black Woman's Experience,* 259.

10. Truman, Inaugural Address, 112.

11. Quoted in "Mrs. Bethune Visits Truman," *Sun-Reporter.*

12. Berman, *Politics of Civil Rights,* 146.

13. "Standing Rules of the Senate."

14. White, "Drive on Filibuster Opened in Senate on Truman Order," 1 and 3.

15. Berman, *Politics of Civil Rights,* 146.

16. See Amendment of Cloture Rule, 2227–75.

17. White, "Drive on Filibuster Opened in Senate on Truman Order," 1.

18. "Not the Last Word," *New York Times,* 24.

19. Berman, *Politics of Civil Rights,* 157.

20. Davis, "Truman Nominates Hastie for Federal Circuit Bench," 1 and 14.

21. Wynn, "William Henry Hastie."

22. Truman, press release, Nov. 19, 1949.

23. "News and Views," *Journal of Blacks in Higher Education.*

24. Truman, press release, Nov. 19, 1949.

25. Berman, *Politics of Civil Rights,* 165.

26. Hastie, by Jerry N. Hess, 77.

27. Ibid., 78.

28. Morris, "2 U.S. Agencies Bar Aid to Housing with Bias Pacts Filed after Feb. 15," 1 and 15.

29. "CAA Orders End of Racial Segregation at Washington National Airport in Virginia," *New York Times,* 1.

30. Truman, Address Before the National Council of Negro Women, 10–11.

31. Truman, Annual Message to the Congress on the State of the Union, Jan. 4, 1950, 4 and 9.

32. Sigal, "A.D.A. on Swimming Pools."

33. Spingarn, memorandum to Clark Clifford, June 15, 1949.

34. Quoted in National Committee on Segregation in the Nation's Capital, *Segregation in Washington,* 14.

35. "Swimming Pools," *Washington Post,* 12M.

36. McCullough, *Truman,* 790–91.

37. Berman, *Politics of Civil Rights,* 179–80.

38. Truman, Annual Message to the Congress on the State of the Union, Jan. 8, 1951; McCullough, *Truman,* 815.

39. Truman, Annual Message to the Congress on the State of the Union, Jan. 8, 1951.

40. Ibid., 12.

41. Ibid.

42. Truman, Executive Order 10210, 391.

43. Berman, *Politics of Civil Rights,* 191.

44. "Proceedings in Washington," *New York Times,* 8.

45. Truman, memorandum, Nov. 2, 1951.

46. Rowan, "Harry Truman and the Negro," 47.

47. Truman, Executive Order 10308, 838.

48. Ibid., 837–38.

49. Gallup Organization, Presidential Popularity—Harry S. Truman, Jan. 1952.

50. McCullough, *Truman,* 843–44.

51. Truman, Annual Message to the Congress on the State of the Union, Jan. 9, 1952, 9–17.

52. "President Urged to Run," *New York Times,* 58.

II. TRUMAN AND THE VINSON COURT

1. Clark, by Jerry N. Hess, 50.
2. "1860 State Level Census Data—Sorted by State/County Name."
3. Dawson, personal interview.
4. Clifford, *Counsel to the President*, 70–71.
5. Quoted in Ferrell, *Off the Record*, 46.
6. Clark, by Jerry N. Hess, 140.
7. "New Justice," *Washington Post*, 10.
8. Vinson Jr., by Charles L. Archer, 17–18.
9. Swinford, by Elizabeth B. Corman, 20.
10. Rehnquist, *Supreme Court*, 172.
11. Ibid.
12. Ibid., 173.
13. Hamby, *Man of the People*, 279.
14. Clark, by Jerry N. Hess, 76–77.
15. Ibid., 128–30.
16. Ibid., 51.
17. Ferrell, *Harry S. Truman*, 103–4.
18. Clark, by Jerry N. Hess, 122–26.
19. Ibid., 129–30.
20. Brief for the United States as Amicus Curiae, *Shelley v. Kraemer*, 1–5.
21. *Shelley v. Kraemer*, 8 and 10.
22. *Hurd v. Hodge*, 4.
23. "Anti-Negro Pacts on Realty Ruled Not Enforceable," *New York Times*, 1 and 2.
24. Ibid.
25. Wilder, "Race Covenant Rule Disappoints Many," 3.
26. Ibid., 1 and 3.
27. Brief for the United States as Amicus Curiae, *Henderson v. United States*, 9–11.
28. *Henderson v. United States*, 816–26.
29. *McLaurin v. Oklahoma State Regents*, 640–42.
30. "Racial 'Segregation' Attacked," *United States Law Week*, 10.
31. Ibid.
32. *Sweatt v. Painter*, 629.
33. Ibid., 634–36.
34. Clark, memorandum to Supreme Court justices.
35. Ibid.
36. "South in Turmoil over Sweatt Rule," *Austin American Statesman*, 1–2.
37. Lautier, "White Supremacy Takes a Beating," 1–2.
38. "Made Illegal by 3 Rulings," *Baltimore Afro-American*, 1.
39. Lewis, "Cross Is Burned Near Law School," 1.
40. Pritchett, *Civil Liberties and the Vinson Court*, 145.
41. Brief for the United States as Amicus Curiae, *Brown v. Board of Education*.
42. *Brown v. Board of Education*.
43. Kluger, *Simple Justice*, 540.

44. Brief for the United States as Amicus Curiae, *Brown v. Board of Education*, 31–32.
45. Ibid.
46. McCullough, *Truman*, 969.
47. "Made Illegal by 3 Rulings," *Baltimore Afro-American*, 1.
48. Clark, by Robert Ireland, 1–2.
49. Ibid., 5–6.
50. Clark, by Jerry N. Hess, 126.
51. Vinson Jr., by Charles L. Archer, 20–21.
52. Schwartz, *History of the Supreme Court*, 287.
53. Ibid., 286.
54. Burton, Burton Diary.
55. *Brown v. Board of Education*, 5.
56. Quoted in "Made Illegal by 3 Rulings," *Baltimore Afro-American*, 1.
57. Pritchett, *Civil Liberties and the Vinson Court*, 145.
58. Quoted in Ferrell, *Off the Record*, 213.
59. Vinson Jr., by Charles L. Archer, 16.
60. Elsey, by Charles T. Morrissey and Jerry N. Hess, 190–91.
61. Brief for the United States as Amicus Curiae, *Henderson v. United States*, 65.

12. TRUMAN'S HOWARD UNIVERSITY COMMENCEMENT ADDRESS: JUNE 13, 1952

1. Truman, Commencement Speech at Howard University.
2. Cannon, notes from conversation with Howard University archivist Clifford Muse.
3. M. Johnson, letter to President Harry S. Truman, May 20, 1952.
4. Nash, by Jerry N. Hess, 440.
5. Ibid., 442–44.
6. Leviero, "Truman Demands Civil Rights Based on Federal Power," 1.
7. Ibid.
8. Truman, Commencement Speech at Howard University.
9. Cannon, notes from conversation with Howard University archivist Clifford Muse.
10. Nash, by Jerry N. Hess, 452.
11. Ibid., 445.
12. Truman, Commencement Speech at Howard University, 1.
13. Ibid., 2.
14. Ibid.
15. Ibid., 3.
16. Gallup Organization, Presidential Popularity—Harry S. Truman, June 1952.
17. Truman, Commencement Speech at Howard University, 3.
18. Ibid., 1–15.
19. "Truman Asks Speedup on Civil Rights," *Washington Post*, 1 and 7.
20. Ibid.
21. Nelson-Ausbrooks, telephone interview.

22. Ibid.

23. Truman, Commencement Speech at Howard University, 4.

24. See Truman, Commencement Speech at Howard University, 6–10.

25. Ibid., 9.

26. Ibid., 9–10.

27. Quoted in "Reaction Mixed on Truman Plea for Civil Rights," *Washington Evening Star,* 1.

28. Truman, Commencement Speech at Howard University, 11.

29. Dashiell, telephone interview.

30. Arrendell, telephone interview.

31. Truman, Commencement Speech at Howard University, 12.

32. Ibid.

33. Nelson-Ausbrooks, telephone interview.

34. Nash, by Jerry N. Hess, 449.

35. Ibid.

36. Cannon, notes from conversation with Howard University archivist Clifford Muse.

37. M. Johnson, letter to President Harry S. Truman, Dec. 17, 1952.

13. TRUMAN'S FINAL CIVIL RIGHTS ADDRESS IN HARLEM: OCTOBER 11, 1952

1. McCullough, *Truman,* 959.

2. "Fists Fly, N.Y. Crowds Hail Truman," *Washington Post,* 1.

3. Ryan, "Truman Accuses Eisenhower of Being 'New Isolationist,'" 1.

4. Nash, by Jerry N. Hess, 480.

5. Truman, Final Address in Harlem, New York, upon Receiving the Franklin Roosevelt Award, Oct. 11, 1952, 797.

6. Ibid., 798.

7. "Police Chief Freed in Negro Beating," *New York Times.*

8. President's Committee on Civil Rights, *To Secure These Rights,* 28.

9. Truman, Final Address in Harlem, New York, upon Receiving the Franklin Roosevelt Award, Oct. 11, 1952, 798.

10. President's Committee on Civil Rights, *To Secure These Rights,* 40–47.

11. Height, personal interview.

12. Ryan, "Truman Accuses Eisenhower of Being 'New Isolationist,'" 2.

13. Truman, Final Address in Harlem, New York, upon Receiving the Franklin Roosevelt Award, Oct. 11, 1952, 800.

14. Ryan, "Truman Accuses Eisenhower of Being 'New Isolationist,'" 2.

15. Truman, Final Address in Harlem, New York, upon Receiving the Franklin Roosevelt Award, Oct. 11, 1952, 799.

16. Wright, "Negro Migration from South Will Follow War, Survey Finds."

17. Truman, Final Address in Harlem, New York, upon Receiving the Franklin Roosevelt Award, Oct. 11, 1952, 801.

18. Nash, by Jerry N. Hess, 481.

19. Berman, *Politics of Civil Rights*, 129–30.
20. Miller, *Atlas of United States Presidential Elections.*

14. THE TRUMAN CIVIL RIGHTS LEGACY

1. Truman, Annual Message to the Congress on the State of the Union, Jan. 7, 1953, 1117.
2. Ibid.
3. Ibid.
4. P. Kennedy, "Truman, in Adieu, Hopeful of Peace and Soviet Change," 1.
5. Truman, President's Farewell Address to the American People, 1197.
6. Ibid., 1202.
7. Ibid., 1201.
8. President's Committee on Civil Rights, *To Secure These Rights.*
9. Gallup Organization, "How do you feel about Truman's Civil Rights Program?" Apr. 5, 1948.
10. Truman, Executive Order 9980; Truman, memorandum, Nov. 2, 1951; Waggoner, "McGohey Is Named Federal Judge," 1 and 44.
11. Truman, Executive Order 9980; Truman, Executive Order 9981.
12. White, "Truman Is Shunned in Votes of South," 1; Berman, *Politics of Civil Rights*, 114.
13. Kluger, *Simple Justice*, 249–50.
14. President's Committee on Civil Rights, *To Secure These Rights*, 15.
15. Waggoner, "McGohey Is Named Federal Judge," 1 and 44.
16. Berman, *Politics of Civil Rights*, 166–67.
17. Berman, *Politics of Civil Rights*, 60–61.
18. Brief for the United States as Amicus Curiae, *Brown v. Board of Education;* Pritchett, *Civil Liberties and the Vinson Court*, 136–38.
19. Truman, President's Farewell Address to the American People, 1202.
20. Truman, letter to Roy Wilkins.
21. Gallup Organization, Presidential Popularity—Harry S. Truman, Dec. 1952.
22. McCullough, *Truman*, 909.
23. Clark, by Jerry N. Hess, 225.
24. Wilkins, letter to Harry S. Truman.

EPILOGUE

1. Quoted in McCullough, *Truman*, 971–73.
2. Height, personal interview.
3. Rowan, "Harry Truman and the Negro," 50.
4. Quoted in "Former Justice Honors HST for Rights Work," *Independence Examiner*, 1.
5. Ibid.
6. Clark, by Jerry N. Hess, 228.

BIBLIOGRAPHY

PUBLISHED SOURCES

Albright, Robert C. "Civil Rights Report Draws Broad Backing." *Washington Post,* Oct. 30, 1947.

———. "Senate Votes Civil Rights, Foreign Aid, FBI Files and 'Hardship' Alien Bills." *Washington Post,* Aug. 30, 1957.

"Along the N.A.A.C.P. Battlefront," editorial. *Crisis,* Aug. 1947, 247–50.

Ambrose, Stephen. *Eisenhower: Soldier and President.* New York: Simon and Schuster, 1990.

Amendment of Cloture Rule, 81st Congress, 1st Session (1949). *Congressional Record* 95, pt. 2: 2227–75.

"Anti-Negro Pacts on Realty Ruled Not Enforceable." *New York Times,* May 4, 1948.

"Army to Keep Segregation Bradley Says." *Washington Post,* July 28, 1948.

Ball, Howard. *A Defiant Life: Thurgood Marshall and the Persistence of Racism in America.* New York: Crown, 1998.

Ball, John W. "Some Republicans Approve President's Plan While an Occasional Democrat Opposes It." *Washington Post,* Jan. 21, 1949.

Belair, Felix, Jr. "Truman Asks Move to Check Bigotry." *New York Times,* Jan. 16, 1947.

Bell, Jack. "President's Civil Rights Program Angers South." *Canton (Ohio) Repository,* Feb. 3, 1948.

Berman, William C. *The Politics of Civil Rights in the Truman Administration.* Columbus: Ohio State University Press, 1970.

Biskupic, Joan, and Elder Witt. *The Supreme Court and Individual Rights.* Washington, D.C.: Congressional Quarterly, 1997.

"Black Newspaper Finds Backer." *Las Vegas Sun,* May 21, 1999.

Blank, Gerald. "Vets Back Cop Victim." *PM,* July 25, 1946.

"Blinded Veteran Tells Court of Beating by Policeman." *Washington Evening Star,* Nov. 5, 1946.

Branch, Taylor. *Parting the Waters: America in the King Years, 1954–1963.* New York: Simon and Schuster, 1988.

Brief for the Petitioner. *Smith v. Allwright.* 321 U.S. 649 (1944).

Brief for the United States as Amicus Curiae. *Brown v. Board of Education.* 247 U.S. 483 (1954).

Brief for the United States as Amicus Curiae. *Henderson v. United States.* 339 U.S. 816 (1950).

Brief for the United States as Amicus Curiae. *Shelley v. Kraemer.* 334 U.S. 1 (1948).

Brown-Scott, Wendy. "Race Consciousness in Higher Education: Does 'Sound Educational Policy' Support the Continued Existence of Historically Black Colleges?" *Emory Law Journal* 43, no. 1 (winter 1994): 3–13.

Brown v. Board of Education. 347 U.S. 483 (1954).

"Byrd Says 'Rights' Mean Dictatorship." *New York Times,* Feb. 20, 1948.

"CAA Orders End of Racial Segregation at Washington National Airport in Virginia." *New York Times,* Dec. 28, 1948.

"Capital Termed Graphic Example of Non-Democracy; Segregation Hit." *Washington Post,* Oct. 30, 1947.

Caro, Robert A. *Years of Lyndon Johnson, Volume II: Means of Ascent.* New York: Vintage Books–Random House, 1990.

Cashman, Sean Dennis. *African-Americans and the Quest for Civil Rights, 1900–1990.* New York: New York University Press, 1991.

Chachkin, Norman. *History of Constitutional Litigation for Human Rights in U.S. Especially Race Issues.* Litigation and Administrative Practice Course Handbook Series. New York: Practicing Law Institute, Dec. 1994.

"Civic Group to Continue Non-Partisan Political Activity, Conference Rules." *Baltimore Afro-American,* July 5, 1947.

"Civil Rights, Human Freedom," opinion. *Baltimore Afro-American,* July 5, 1947.

Clark, Tom, by Jerry N. Hess. Transcript of oral history. Oct. 17, 1972. Harry S. Truman Library, Independence, Mo.

Clark, Tom, by Robert Ireland. Transcript of oral history. May 8, 1973. Fred M. Vinson Oral History Project, University of Kentucky Library. University of Kentucky, Lexington.

Clay, William L. *Just Permanent Interests: Black Americans in Congress 1870–1992.* New York: Amistad, 1993.

Clements, Kendrick A. *The Presidency of Woodrow Wilson.* Lawrence: University Press of Kansas, 1992.

Clifford, Clark. *Counsel to the President: A Memoir.* New York: Random House, 1991.

Coleman, James E., Jr., and Todd D. Peterson. "Report of the Special Committee on Race and Ethnicity to the D.C. Circuit Task Force on Gender, Race, and Ethnic Bias." *George Washington Law Review* 64 (Jan. 1996): 1–405.

"The Country's Gain," editorial. *Washington Post,* Aug. 31, 1957.

"Cross Is Burned at Negro's Home." *Washington Post,* June 13, 1948.

"Dangerous World: The Kennedy Years." Produced by Lancer Productions. ABC Network Television. Aired Dec. 4, 1997.

Daniel, Margaret Truman, by Ron Cockrel. Transcript of oral history. Nov. 17, 1983. Harry S. Truman Library, Independence, Mo.

Daniels, Jonathan. *The Man of Independence.* Philadelphia: Lippincott, 1950.

Davenport, Walter. "Race Riots Coming." *Collier's,* Sept. 18, 1943, 11 and 79.

Davis, Charles E. "Truman Nominates Hastie for Federal Circuit Bench." *Washington Post,* Oct. 16, 1949.

Dawson, Donald S., by James R. Fuchs. Transcript of oral history. Aug. 8, 1977. Harry S. Truman Library, Independence, Mo.

Dawson, Donald S., by William D. Stilley and Jerald L. Hill. Transcript of oral history. Mar. 16, 1976. Harry S. Truman Library, Independence, Mo.

Donnelly, Eugene, and Edward Meisburger, by William D. Stilley and Jerald L. Hill. Transcript of oral history. Dec. 27, 1975. Harry S. Truman Library, Independence, Mo.

Duckworth, Allen. "South Texas Multitudes Hail President Truman." *Dallas Morning News*, Sept. 27, 1948.

Dunnigan, Alice Allison. *A Black Woman's Experience: From School House to White House*. Philadelphia: Dorrance, 1974.

"Election Forecast: 50 Political Experts Predict a GOP Sweep." *Newsweek*, Oct. 11, 1948, 20.

Elsey, George M., by Charles T. Morrissey and Jerry N. Hess. Transcript of oral history. Feb. 10 and 17, 1964; Mar. 9, 1964; July 10 and 17, 1969; Apr. 9 and July 7 and 10, 1970. Harry S. Truman Library, Independence, Mo.

Elsey, George M., by William D. Stilley and Jerald L. Hill. Transcript of oral history. Mar. 17, 1976. Harry S. Truman Library, Independence, Mo.

Evans, Rowland, and Robert Novak. *Lyndon B. Johnson: The Exercise of Power*. New York: New American Library, 1966.

"Federal Help Sought for Blinded Veteran." *New York Times*, July 25, 1946.

"Federal vs. State Issue at S.C. Trial." No publication information available.

"Federation Backs Race Separation." *Washington Post*, Jan. 5, 1947.

Ferrell, Robert H. *Harry S. Truman: A Life*. Columbia: University of Missouri Press, 1996.

———, ed. *Dear Bess: The Letters from Harry to Bess Truman, 1910–1959*. Columbia: University of Missouri Press, 1998.

———, ed. *Off the Record: The Private Papers of Harry S. Truman*. Columbia: University of Missouri Press, 1997.

Fields, Alonzo. *My 21 Years in the White House*. New York: Coward-McCann, 1960.

Finch, Minnie. *The NAACP: Its Fight for Justice*. Metuchen, N.J.: Scarecrow, 1981.

"Fists Fly, N.Y. Crowds Hail Truman." *Washington Post*, Oct. 11, 1952.

Foliard, Edward T. "Dazzling Sun Glorifies Day as Chief Executive Rides in Triumph." *Washington Post*, Jan. 21, 1949.

"Former Justice Honors HST for Rights Work." *Independence Examiner*, Oct. 5, 1972.

"40% of Public School Pupils in U.S. Are in Areas Where Laws Require Segregation." *New York Times*, May 18, 1954.

Fox, J. A. "Burton Is Confirmed for Supreme Court by Unanimous Vote." *Washington Evening Star*, Sept. 19, 1945.

Furman, Mark. "Schools in Capital Prepared for Segregation Ban; Superintendent Foresees Fast, Smooth Transition." *New York Times*, May 18, 1954.

Gallup Organization. "How do you feel about Truman's civil rights program? Do you think Congress should or should not pass the program as a whole?" Apr. 5, 1948. Princeton, N.J.

———. "How do you feel about Truman's civil rights program? Do you think Congress should or should not pass the program as a whole?" Dec. 3, 1948. Princeton, N.J.

————. "One of President Truman's (civil rights) proposals concerns employment practices. How far do you yourself think the federal government should go in requiring employers to hire people without regard to their race, religion, color, or nationality?" Jan. 17, 1949. Princeton, N.J.

————. "Presidential Popularity—Harry S. Truman." Various dates, May–June 1945–Dec. 1952. Princeton, N.J.

"Gen. Davis Urges No Bias in Army." *New York Times,* June 7, 1947.

Gibson, Truman K., Jr. "Gillem Report Aims to End Segregation in the U.S. Army." *Pittsburgh Courier,* Mar. 23, 1946.

Goodwin, Doris Kearns. *No Ordinary Time: Franklin & Eleanor Roosevelt: The Homefront in World War II.* New York: Simon and Schuster, 1995.

"GOP Can Pass Antilynching Law, NAACP Delegates Told." *Baltimore Afro-American,* July 5, 1947.

Graf, William. *Statistics of the Presidential and Congressional Election of November 2, 1948.* Washington, D.C.: Government Printing Office, 1949.

Gross, Gerald G. "Truman Holds Civil Rights a Key to Peace." *Washington Post,* June 30, 1947.

Hamby, Alonzo L. *Man of the People: A Life of Harry S. Truman.* New York: Oxford University Press, 1995.

Harrison, Maureen, and Steve Gilbert, eds. *Civil Rights Decisions of the United States Supreme Court: The 19th Century.* San Diego, Calif.: Excellent Books, 1994.

Hastie, William H., by Jerry N. Hess. Transcript of oral history. Jan. 5, 1972. Harry S. Truman Library, Independence, Mo.

Henderson v. United States. 339 U.S. 816 (1950).

Higginbothom, A. Leon, Jr. "Black Judges Vanishing from the Federal Bench." *New York Times,* Aug. 1, 1992.

Hixon, Fred. "The Klan, on the March, Seeks to Sway Georgia Election." *New York Times,* Feb. 15, 1948.

Holden-Smith, Barbara. "Lynching, Federalism, and the Intersection of Race and Gender in the Progressive Era." *Yale Journal of Law and Feminism* 8, no. 31 (1996): 1, 23, 79, and 99.

Holeman, Frank. "U.S. Must End Racial Bias, Says TrumanCalls Action Vital to Foreign Policy." *Washington Times-Herald,* June 30, 1947.

Howell, Clark. "You Can't Legislate Tolerance," editorial. *Atlanta Constitution,* Oct. 31, 1947.

Hurd v. Hodge. 334 U.S. 24 (1948).

Juhnke, William E. "President Truman's Committee on Civil Rights: The Interaction of Politics, Protest, and Presidential Advisory Commission." *Presidential Studies Quarterly* 19 (summer 1989): 593–610.

Kennedy, John F. Executive Order 11063. "Equal Opportunity in Housing." *Federal Register* 27, no. 228 (Nov. 20, 1962): 11527–30.

————. Televised Speech to the American Public. June 11, 1963. John F. Kennedy Library, Boston.

Kennedy, Paul. "Truman, in Adieu, Hopeful of Peace and Soviet Change." *New York Times,* June 16, 1953.

Kent, Carleton. "Truman Campaign Highlight." *Chicago Sun-Times,* Nov. 17, 1948.

Kirkendall, Richard S. *History of Missouri, 1919–1953.* Columbia: University of Missouri Press, 1986.

———, ed. *The Harry S. Truman Encyclopedia.* Boston: G. K. Hall, 1990.

"KKK in Big Meet." *Jackson Examiner,* July 14, 1922.

"Klan at Convention Hall." *Jackson Examiner,* Oct. 13, 1922.

"Klan Puts Out Ticket." *Independence Examiner,* Nov. 6, 1922.

Kluger, Richard. *Simple Justice: The History of Brown v. Board of Education and Black America's Struggle for Equality.* New York: Alfred A. Knopf, 1975.

Knowles, Clayton. "South in Congress Backs Rights Test." *New York Times,* Feb. 9, 1948.

———. "Truman Conciliation of South in Civil Rights Is Denied." *New York Times,* Feb. 10, 1948.

Krock, Arthur. "Democrats Try Hard for a Show of Unity," editorial. *New York Times,* Feb. 15, 1948.

"The Ku Klux Klan." *Jackson Examiner,* Mar. 3, 1922.

Lash, Joseph P. *Eleanor & Franklin.* New York: W. W. Norton, 1971.

"Last-Ditch Southerner." *New York Times,* Aug. 30, 1957.

Lautier, Louis. "White Supremacy Takes a Beating: Supreme Court Rules Favorably in All Three Segregation Cases." *Baltimore Afro-American,* June 6, 1950.

Lawrence, W. H. "Nominees Go Before Convention to Make Acceptance Talks." *New York Times,* July 15, 1948.

Lee, Harper. *To Kill a Mockingbird.* Philadelphia: Lippincott, 1960.

Leviero, Anthony. "Anti-Lynching Law, Civil Liberties Sought by Truman." *New York Times,* Feb. 3, 1948.

———. "Guardians for Civil Rights Proposed by Truman Board; Report Asks End of Biases." *New York Times,* Oct. 30, 1947.

———. "President Renews Civil Rights Plea." *New York Times,* Oct. 30, 1948.

———. "President Speaks." *New York Times,* Jan. 8, 1948.

———. "Truman Demands Civil Rights Based on Federal Power." *New York Times,* June 14, 1952.

———. "Truman Orders End of Bias in Forces and Federal Jobs; Addresses Congress Today." *New York Times,* July 27, 1948.

Lewis, Charlie. "Cross Is Burned Near Law School." *Daily Texan,* Oct. 18, 1950.

Lewis, John. *Walking with the WindA Memoir of a Movement.* New York: Simon and Schuster, 1998.

Link, Arthur S. *Wilson: The New Freedom.* Princeton, N.J.: Princeton University Press, 1956.

"The Long Shot Who Won't Give Up." *Newsweek,* Oct. 11, 1948, 25–26.

"Made Illegal by 3 Rulings, Marshall Says Time Will Change Picture." *Baltimore Afro-American,* June 17, 1950.

Mann, Robert. *The Walls of Jericho.* New York: Harcourt Brace, 1996.

Matthews, Ralph. "Behind Convention Stage with Ralph Matthews." *Baltimore Afro-American,* July 5, 1947.

———. "15,000 Hear HST's Civil Rights Appeal." *Baltimore Afro-American,* July 5, 1947.

McCoy, Donald, and Richard T. Ruetten. *Quest and Response: Minority Rights and the Truman Administration.* Lawrence: University Press of Kansas, 1973.

McCullough, David. *Truman.* New York: Simon and Schuster, 1992.

McLaurin v. Oklahoma State Regents. 339 U.S. 637 (1950).

Meisburger, Edward. "Bob Brown, Barber Shop Porter, Enjoys Chat with President Truman." *Kansas City Call,* Nov. 4, 1966.

Miller, Merle. *Plain Speaking: An Oral Biography of Harry S. Truman.* New York: Berkley, 1973.

Minor, Robert. "Ala. Bias and Ruin Policy Set in N.Y. by Steel Trust." *Daily Worker,* Feb. 13, 1946.

"Mississippi Governor Calls Protest Rally." *New York Times,* Feb. 6, 1948.

Missouri Commission on Human Rights. "Missouri Statutes on Fair Housing, Fair Employment Practices, and Public Accommodations." *Vernon's Annotated Missouri Statutes Under Arrangement of the Official Missouri Revised Statutes,* vol. 16A, secs. 311–24. Jefferson City, Mo., 1965.

Mitchell v. United States. 313 U.S. 80 (1941).

Morehead, Eleanor. "Negro Vet Tells How Dixie Cops Gouged Out Both Eyes with Club." *PM,* July 17, 1946.

Morgan, Ted. *FDR: A Biography.* New York: Simon and Schuster, 1985.

Morgan v. Commonwealth of Virginia. 328 U.S. 373 (1946).

Morris, John D. "2 U.S. Agencies Bar Aid to Housing with Bias Pacts Filed after Feb. 15." *New York Times,* Dec. 16, 1949.

"Mrs. Bethune Visits Truman." *Sun-Reporter,* Feb. 11, 1949.

"Mr. Truman: An Appraisal," editorial. *New York Times,* Jan. 16, 1953.

"Mr. Truman on Civil Liberty," editorial. *New York Times,* Feb. 4, 1948.

"NAACP Hits Bradley." *Washington Post,* July 29, 1948.

Nash, Philleo, by Jerry N. Hess. Transcript of oral history. June 24, Aug. 17–19, Oct. 13, 17–18, 24, and 31, Nov. 9 and 29, 1966; Feb. 21, June 5 and 8, 1967; May 15, 1969. Harry S. Truman Library, Independence, Mo.

National Committee on Segregation in the Nation's Capital. *Segregation in Washington.* Washington, D.C.: Government Printing Office, Nov. 1948.

"Negro Has Trod a Century-Long Road in His Legislative and Legal Battles for Equality." *New York Times,* May 18, 1954.

"Negro Leader Hails Action." *New York Times,* July 16, 1948.

"Negro Paper Puts 17 on Honor Roll." *New York Times,* Jan. 2, 1949.

"The Negro Prefers Truman." *New Republic,* Nov. 22, 1948.

"New Justice," editorial. *Washington Post,* Sept. 19, 1945.

"News and Views: New Judicial Opportunities and the Surge in Black Law School Enrollment." *Journal of Blacks in Higher Education* 3/31/94, no. 26 (1994): 1–2.

"New Tactics in U.S. Election." *New York Times,* Oct. 13, 1952.

"1946 Killing of 4 Blacks Is Recalled." *New York Times,* June 1, 1999.

"Not the Last Word," editorial. *New York Times,* Mar. 18, 1949.

Pace, Clint. "Live up to Talk of Unity; Truman Dares GOP Here." *Dallas Morning News,* Sept. 28, 1948.

Phillips, Cabel. *The Truman Presidency*. New York: Macmillan, 1966.

Plessy v. Ferguson. 163 U.S. 537 (1896).

"Police Chief Freed in Negro Beating." *New York Times*, Nov. 6, 1946.

Popham, John N. "4,000 in Mississippi Want Truman Out." *New York Times*, Feb. 13, 1948.

————. "High Court Bans School Segregation; 9-to-0 Decision Grants Time to Comply." *New York Times*, May 18, 1954.

————. "Negro in South Still Lags in Political Power." *New York Times*, Feb. 15, 1948.

————. "Southern Governors Delay Civil Rights Action 40 Days." *New York Times*, Feb. 8, 1948.

President's Committee on Civil Rights. *To Secure These Rights*. Washington, D.C.: Government Printing Office, 1947.

President's Committee on Equality of Treatment and Opportunity in the Armed Services. *Freedom to Serve*. Washington, D.C.: Government Printing Office, May 22, 1950.

"President Truman Wipes Out Segregation in Armed Forces." *Chicago Defender*, July 31, 1948.

"President Urged to Run." *New York Times*, Mar. 9, 1952.

Pritchett, C. Herman. *Civil Liberties and the Vinson Court*. Chicago: Chicago University Press, 1954.

"The Proceedings in Washington: Yesterday [Nov. 2, 1951]." *New York Times*, Nov. 3, 1951.

The Public Papers of the Presidents of the United States: Harry S. Truman, 1945. Washington, D.C.: Government Printing Office, 1961.

The Public Papers of the Presidents of the United States: Harry S. Truman, 1946. Washington, D.C.: Government Printing Office, 1962.

The Public Papers of the Presidents of the United States: Harry S. Truman, 1947. Washington, D.C.: Government Printing Office, 1963.

The Public Papers of the Presidents of the United States: Harry S. Truman, 1948. Washington, D.C.: Government Printing Office, 1964.

The Public Papers of the Presidents of the United States: Harry S. Truman, 1949. Washington, D.C.: Government Printing Office, 1964.

The Public Papers of the Presidents of the United States: Harry S. Truman, 1950. Washington, D.C.: Government Printing Office, 1965.

The Public Papers of the Presidents of the United States: Harry S. Truman, 1951. Washington, D.C.: Government Printing Office, 1965.

The Public Papers of the Presidents of the United States: Harry S. Truman, 1952–1953. Washington, D.C.: Government Printing Office, 1966.

The Public Papers of the Presidents of the United States: John F. Kennedy, 1961. Washington, D.C.: Government Printing Office, 1962.

The Public Papers of the Presidents of the United States: John F. Kennedy, 1962. Washington, D.C.: Government Printing Office, 1963.

The Public Papers of the Presidents of the United States: John F. Kennedy, 1963. Washington, D.C.: Government Printing Office, 1964.

"Push Probe, Talmadge Orders." *Atlanta Constitution,* Nov. 25, 1948.

"Reaction Mixed on Truman Plea for Civil Rights." *Washington Evening Star,* June 14, 1952.

Reeves, Richard. *President Kennedy: Profile of Power.* New York: Simon and Schuster, 1994.

Rehnquist, William H. *The Supreme Court.* New York: Alfred A. Knopf, 2001.

"Republicans Assail 'Left Wing' Program Offered by President." *Washington Evening Star,* Jan. 8, 1948.

Reston, James. "Speech Seen as Aid to Western World." *New York Times,* Jan. 21, 1949.

Revised Statutes of the State of Missouri, 1929, 1939, 1949. Vol. 1, compiled, arranged, classified, and indexed by the Committee on Legislative Research. Vol. 16A, secs. 311–24. Jefferson City: Committee on Legislative Research, 1949.

Robinson, Major. "Woodard Tells Bitter Story." *Chicago Defender,* July 27, 1946.

Rowan, Carl T. *Breaking Barriers.* Boston: Little Brown, 1991.

———. "Harry Truman and the Negro." *Ebony,* Nov. 1959, 44–54.

"Roy Wilkins Reports to Truman Group." *Memphis World,* May 3, 1949.

Ryan, Edward F. "Truman Accuses Eisenhower of Being 'New Isolationist.'" *Washington Post,* Oct. 12, 1952.

Salser, Mark R., ed. *Black Americans in Congress.* Portland, Oreg.: National Book, 1991.

Salzman, Jack, David Lionel Smith, and Cornel West, eds. *Encyclopedia of African-American Culture and History.* New York: Simon and Schuster, 1996.

"Schools to Obey Supreme Court Action." *Houston Informer,* June 17, 1950.

Schwartz, Bernard. *A History of the Supreme Court.* New York: Oxford University Press, 1993.

Shelley v. Kraemer. 334 U.S. 1 (1948).

Shesol, Jeff. *Mutual Contempt: Lyndon Johnson, Robert Kennedy, and the Feud That Defined a Decade.* New York: W. W. Norton, 1997.

Sigal, Benjamin C. "A.D.A. on Swimming Pools," editorial. *Washington Evening Star,* Apr. 21, 1950.

Sipuel v. Board of Regents of University of Oklahoma. 332 U.S. 631 (1948).

"612 Delegates from 34 States Attend 38th Annual Conference of Civic Body." *Baltimore Afro-American,* July 5, 1947.

Smith v. Allwright. 321 U.S. 649 (1944).

S. 1725, 81st Congress, 1st Session (1949). *Congressional Record* 95, pt. 17: 752.

S. 1726, 81st Congress, 1st Session (1949). *Congressional Record* 95, pt. 17: 752.

S. 1727, 81st Congress, 1st Session (1949). *Congressional Record* 95, pt. 17: 752.

S. 1728, 81st Congress, 1st Session (1949). *Congressional Record* 95, pt. 17: 752.

"Southern Democrats May Desert Truman." *New Haven Evening Register,* Feb. 3, 1948.

"Southerners to Skip Fetes with Negroes." *New York Times,* Feb. 19, 1948.

"Southern Newspapers Hit Civil Rights Report." *Washington Post,* Oct. 30, 1947.

"Southern Threats to Democrats Rise." *New York Times,* Feb. 5, 1948.

"South Has Made Big Gains in Improving Educational Facilities for Negroes Since '45." *New York Times,* May 18, 1954.

"South in Turmoil over Sweatt Rule." *Austin American Statesman,* June 6, 1950.

Spore, John B., and Robert F. Cocklin. "Our Negro Soldiers." Harry S. Truman Library, Independence, Mo.

Staples, Brent. "Citizen Sengstacke." *New York Times Magazine*, Jan. 4, 1998. p. 27–28.

"State of the Union," editorial. *New York Times*, Jan. 8, 1948.

Stavisky, Sam. "Need for Guarantee of Equal Rights to All Emphasized in Report to Truman." *Washington Post*, Oct. 30, 1947.

Stewart, Ollie. "Skies Smile on Crowd at Truman Talk." *Baltimore Afro-American*, July 5, 1947.

Stokes, Dillard. "California and Ohio Courts Are Overruled on Covenants." *Washington Post*, May 11, 1948.

————. "High Court Voids Racial Ban in Realty Transactions." *Washington Post*, May 4, 1948.

Streator, George. "Truman Demands We Fight Harder to Spur Equality." *New York Times*, June 30, 1947.

"Sweatt UT Appeal Upheld." *Austin American Statesman*, June 6, 1950.

Sweatt v. Painter. 339 U.S. 629 (1950).

"Swimming Pools." *Washington Post*, Sept. 10, 1950.

Swinford, Mac, by Elizabeth B. Corman. Transcript of oral history. July 22, 1974. Fred M. Vinson Oral History Project, University of Kentucky Library. University of Kentucky, Lexington.

Symington, Stuart, by James R. Fuchs. Transcript of oral history. May 29, 1981. Harry S. Truman Library, Independence, Mo.

Thompson, Perry. "Pastor Fight, Pray: Many Head up Militant Units of Civic Group." *Baltimore Afro-American*, July 5, 1947.

"Thurmond's Talkathon," editorial. *Washington Post*, Aug. 30, 1957.

"Thurmond Talks Hours on Rights." *New York Times*, Aug. 29, 1957.

Truman, Harry S. Address at the Convention of the National Colored Democratic Association. United States Senate, Washington, D.C. Aug. 30, 1940. *Congressional Record* 86, pt. 19: 596.

————. Address Before the National Association for the Advancement of Colored People. Washington, D.C. June 29, 1947. *The Public Papers of the Presidents of the United States: Harry S. Truman, 1947.* Washington, D.C.: Government Printing Office, 1963, 311–13.

————. Address Before the National Council of Negro Women, Inc. Washington, D.C. Nov. 15, 1949. *The Public Papers of the Presidents of the United States: Harry S. Truman, 1949.* Washington, D.C.: Government Printing Office, 1964, 564–66.

————. Address in Harlem, New York, upon Receiving the Franklin Roosevelt Award. New York, N.Y. Oct. 29, 1948. *The Public Papers of the Presidents of the United States: Harry S. Truman, 1948.* Washington, D.C.: Government Printing Office, 1964, 923–25.

————. Address in Philadelphia upon Accepting the Nomination of the Democratic National Convention. Philadelphia, Penn. July 15, 1948. *The Public Papers of the Presidents of the United States: Harry S. Truman, 1948.* Washington, D.C.: Government Printing Office, 1964, 406–10.

————. Address of the President at Monticello, the Home of Thomas Jefferson.

Charlottesville, Va. July 4, 1947. *The Public Papers of the Presidents of the United States: Harry S. Truman, 1947.* Washington, D.C.: Government Printing Office, 1963, 323–26.

———. Annual Message to the Congress on the State of the Union. Washington, D.C. Jan. 6, 1947. *The Public Papers of the Presidents of the United States: Harry S. Truman, 1947.* Washington, D.C.: Government Printing Office, 1963, 1–12.

———. Annual Message to the Congress on the State of the Union. Washington, D.C. Jan. 7, 1948. *The Public Papers of the Presidents of the United States: Harry S. Truman, 1948.* Washington, D.C.: Government Printing Office, 1964, 1–10.

———. Annual Message to the Congress on the State of the Union. Washington, D.C. Jan. 5, 1949. *The Public Papers of the Presidents of the United States: Harry S. Truman, 1949.* Washington, D.C.: Government Printing Office, 1964, 1–7.

———. Annual Message to the Congress on the State of the Union. Washington, D.C. Jan. 4, 1950. *The Public Papers of the Presidents of the United States: Harry S. Truman, 1950.* Washington, D.C.: Government Printing Office, 1965, 2–11.

———. Annual Message to the Congress on the State of the Union. Washington, D.C. Jan. 8, 1951. *The Public Papers of the Presidents of the United States: Harry S. Truman, 1951.* Washington, D.C.: Government Printing Office, 1965, 6–13.

———. Annual Message to the Congress on the State of the Union. Washington, D.C. Jan. 9, 1952. *The Public Papers of the Presidents of the United States: Harry S. Truman, 1952–1953.* Washington, D.C.: Government Printing Office, 1966, 9–17.

———. Annual Message to the Congress on the State of the Union. Washington, D.C. Jan. 7, 1953. *The Public Papers of the Presidents of the United States: Harry S. Truman, 1952–1953.* Washington, D.C.: Government Printing Office, 1966, 1114–28.

———. Commencement Speech at Howard University. Washington, D.C. June 13, 1952. *The Public Papers of the Presidents of the United States: Harry S. Truman, 1952–1953.* Washington, D.C.: Government Printing Office, 1966, 420–24.

———. Executive Order 9808. "Establishing the President's Committee on Civil Rights." *United States Code Congressional Service.* Laws of the 79th Congress, 2nd Session (Dec. 5, 1946): sec. 11 F.R. 74153.

———. Executive Order 9980. "Regulations Governing Fair Employment Practices Within the Federal Establishment." *United States Code Congressional Service.* Laws of the 80th Congress, 2nd Session, vol. 2 (July 26, 1948): sec. 13 F.R. 4311.

———. Executive Order 9981. "Establishing the President's Committee on Equality of Treatment and Opportunity in the Armed Services." *United States Code Congressional Service.* Laws of the 80th Congress, 2nd Session, vol. 2 (July 26, 1948): sec. 13 F.R. 4313.

———. Executive Order 10210. "Authorizing the Department of Defense and the Department of Commerce to Exercise the Functions and Powers Set Forth in Title II of the First War Powers Act, 1941, as Amended by the Act of January 12, 1951, and Prescribing Regulations for the Exercise of Such Functions and Powers." *United States Code Congressional and Administrative Service.* Laws of the 82nd Congress, 1st Session (Feb. 2, 1951): sec. 16 F.R. 1049.

———. Executive Order 10308. "Improving the Means for Obtaining Compliance with the Nondiscrimination Provisions of Federal Contracts." *United States Code*

Congressional and Administrative Service. Laws of the 82nd Congress, 1st Session (Dec. 3, 1951): sec. 16 F.R. 12303.

———. Final Address in Harlem, New York, upon Receiving the Franklin Roosevelt Award. New York, N.Y. Oct. 11, 1952. *The Public Papers of the Presidents of the United States: Harry S. Truman, 1952–1953*. Washington, D.C.: Government Printing Office, 1966, 797–802.

———. Inaugural Address. Washington, D.C. Jan. 20, 1949. *The Public Papers of the Presidents of the United States: Harry S. Truman, 1949*. Washington, D.C.: Government Printing Office, 1964, 112–16.

———. Letter to Chairman of the American Veterans Committee Charles G. Bolte. Aug. 28, 1946. *The Public Papers of the Presidents of the United States: Harry S. Truman, 1946*. Washington, D.C.: Government Printing Office, 1962, 215.

———. *Memoirs by Harry S. Truman, Volume 1: Year of Decisions*. Garden City, N.Y.: Doubleday, 1955.

———. *Memoirs by Harry S. Truman, Volume 2: Years of Trial and Hope*. Garden City, N.Y.: Doubleday, 1956.

———. Message to the Special Session of the 80th Congress. July 27, 1948. *The Public Papers of the Presidents of the United States: Harry S. Truman, 1948*. Washington, D.C.: Government Printing Office, 1964, 416–22.

———. The President's Farewell Address to the American People. The White House, Washington, D.C. Jan. 15, 1953. *The Public Papers of the Presidents of the United States: Harry S. Truman, 1952–1953*. Washington, D.C.: Government Printing Office, 1966, 1197–202.

———. Rear Platform and Other Informal Remarks in Texas. Cities include San Marcos, Austin, Georgetown, Temple, Waco, Hillsboro, Fort Worth, Grand Prairie, Dallas, Greenville, and Bells. Sept. 27, 1948. *The Public Papers of the Presidents of the United States: Harry S. Truman, 1948*. Washington, D.C.: Government Printing Office, 1964, 580–92.

———. Remarks to Members of the President's Committee on Civil Rights. Washington, D.C. Jan. 15, 1947. *The Public Papers of the Presidents of the United States: Harry S. Truman, 1947*. Washington, D.C.: Government Printing Office, 1963, 98–99.

———. Special Message to the Congress on Civil Rights. Washington, D.C. Feb. 2, 1948. *The Public Papers of the Presidents of the United States: Harry S. Truman, 1948*. Washington, D.C.: Government Printing Office, 1964, 121–26.

———. Statement by the President Making Public a Report by the Civil Rights Committee. Washington, D.C. Oct. 29, 1947. *The Public Papers of the Presidents of the United States: Harry S. Truman, 1947*. Washington, D.C.: Government Printing Office, 1963, 479–80.

———. "Tribute to the Negro." United States Senate, Washington, D.C. July 25, 1940. *Congressional Record* 86, pt. 19: 596.

Truman, Margaret. *Harry S. Truman*. New York: William Morrow, 1972.

Truman, Mary Jane, by Jerald L. Hill and William D. Stilley. Transcript of oral history. Jan. 2, 1976. Harry S. Truman Library, Independence, Mo.

Truman, Mary Jane, by Stephen and Cathy Doyal and Fred and Audrey Truman. Transcript of oral history. 1975. Harry S. Truman Library, Independence, Mo.

"Truman Arrives; Continues Attacks on General Here." *New York Times,* Oct. 11, 1952.

"Truman Asks Speedup on Civil Rights." *Washington Post,* June 14, 1952.

"Truman, Mrs. F.D.R. Are Speakers." *Washington Post,* June 29, 1947.

"Truman Sees Rights Report as 'Human Freedom Charter.'" *Washington Post,* Oct. 30, 1947.

"Truman's Popularity Highest in Three Years, Survey Shows." Gallup Poll. *Washington Post,* Jan. 21, 1949.

"Truman to the NAACP," editorial. *Crisis,* Aug. 1947, 233.

Trussell, C. P. "Congress Is Cool to Truman Pleas." *New York Times,* Jan. 8, 1948.

———. "Praise in Congress." *New York Times,* Jan. 21, 1949.

———. "Republican Chiefs Cautious, Awaiting President's Word." *New York Times,* July 27, 1948.

———. "Southerners in House Plan New 'Revolt' on Civil Rights." *New York Times,* Feb. 20, 1948.

———. "Truman Asks Increased Taxes, Debt Cut, Taft Labor Act Repeal, Authority to Build Steel Mills." *New York Times,* Jan. 6, 1949.

———. "Truman Calls on Public to Spur Congress to Act in Labor Crisis." *New York Times,* Jan. 4, 1946.

Turner, Thomas E. "Dr. Harry S. Truman, LL.D. Visits Waco for Second Time." *Dallas Morning News,* Sept. 28, 1948.

"23 Confessions Signed in S.C. Lynching Case." *Washington Times-Herald,* Feb. 21, 1947.

Van Doren, Charles, and Robert McHenry, eds. "Hastie, William Henry (1904–1976)." *Webster's American Biographies.* Springfield, Mass.: Merriam-Webster.

Vinson, Fred M., Jr., by Charles L. Archer. Transcript of oral history. May 22, 1973. Fred M. Vinson Oral History Project, University of Kentucky Library. University of Kentucky, Lexington.

Waggoner, Walter H. "McGohey Is Named Federal Judge; Hastie First Negro in Appeals Court." *New York Times,* Oct. 16, 1949.

Walz, Jay. "Carolinian Sets Talking Record." *New York Times,* Aug. 30, 1957.

———. "Supreme Court Rulings Bar Segregation in 2 Colleges, Also Void Bias in Rail Diners." *New York Times,* June 6, 1950.

White, Walter. *A Man Called White.* New York: Viking, 1948.

———. "The President Means It." *Graphic Syndicate,* Feb. 12, 1948.

———. "Virgin Islands' Regime Praised as Race-Relations Experiment." *New York Herald Tribune,* Mar. 30, 1947.

White, William S. "Drive on Filibuster Opened in Senate on Truman Order." *New York Times,* Mar. 1, 1949.

———. "More Than a Million Roar in Approval of Inauguration." *New York Times,* Jan. 21, 1949.

———. "Senate Bloc Plans Rigid 'Rights' Fight." *New York Times,* July 27, 1948.

———. "Senate Votes Rights Bill and Sends It to President; Thurmond Talks 24 Hours." *New York Times,* Aug. 30, 1957.

———. "Truman Is Shunned in Votes of South." *New York Times,* July 15, 1948.

Wilder, Frank. "Race Covenant Rule Disappoints Many." *Washington Post,* May 4, 1948.

Williams, Juan. *Thurgood Marshall: American Revolutionary.* New York: Times Books, 1998.

"Women Praise Pres. Truman's Equality Stand." *Indianapolis Recorder,* Oct. 23, 1948.

Wood, Lewis. "Supreme Court Rulings Bar Segregation in 2 Colleges, Also Void Bias in Rail Diners; Bench Unanimous, but It Stops Short of Saying If Separation of Races Is Illegal." *New York Times,* June 6, 1950.

Wright, Wellington. "Negro Migration from South Will Follow War, Survey Finds." *Atlanta Constitution,* Apr. 8, 1945.

UNPUBLISHED SOURCES

Alexander, Sadie T. M. Letter to Philleo Nash. June 7, 1950. Harry S. Truman Library, Independence, Mo.

———. Letter to President Harry S. Truman. Dec. 9, 1946. Harry S. Truman Library, Independence, Mo.

———. Letter to President Harry S. Truman. July 30, 1948. Harry S. Truman Library, Independence, Mo.

———. Telegram released through Associated Negro Press. July 30, 1948. Harry S. Truman Library, Independence, Mo.

Alexander-Minter, Rae. Daughter of presidential committee member Sadie Alexander, professor at Rutgers University. Personal interviews. Washington, D.C., 1996 and 1997.

Arrendell, Inez R. Howard University class of 1952. Telephone interview. Nov. 1997.

Attendance at the Ceremony for the Promotion of Omar N. Bradley to the Rank of General of the Army. The White House, Sept. 22, 1950. Document 1285-F. Harry S. Truman Library, Independence, Mo.

Baker, M. R. Letter to President Harry S. Truman. Nov. 4, 1947.

Berle, Adolf A., Jr. Letter to President Harry S. Truman. Aug. 9, 1948. Harry S. Truman Library, Independence, Mo.

Bethune, Mary McLeod. Letter to President Harry S. Truman. Feb. 13, 1948. Mary McLeod Bethune Council House, National Historic Site, Washington, D.C.

———. Letter to President Harry S. Truman. Mar. 9, 1948. Mary McLeod Bethune Council House, National Historic Site, Washington, D.C.

———. Telegram to President Harry S. Truman. Apr. 14, 1948. Mary McLeod Bethune Council House, National Historic Site, Washington, D.C.

Blackwell, Mel. Treasurer of the Congressional Black Caucus. Telephone interview. Aug. 12, 1999.

Brown, Jeanetta W. National Council of Negro Women. Press Release. Oct. 14, 1948. Mary McLeod Bethune Council House, National Historic Site, Washington, D.C.

Burton, Harold Hitz. Burton Diary. May 8, 1954. Burton Papers, Library of Congress.

Byrd, Harry F. Letter to President Harry S. Truman. Nov. 5, 1947. Harry S. Truman Library, Independence, Mo.

Cannon, Corinne. Notes from conversation with Howard University archivist Clifford Muse. Dec. 15, 1997. Author's collection.

Clark, Thomas. Letter to President Harry S. Truman. Oct. 11, 1946. Harry S. Truman Library, Independence, Mo.

Clark, Tom C. Address at the Twenty-Fifth Anniversary Conference of the National Association of Human Rights Workers. Kansas City, Mo. Oct. 4, 1972. Harry S. Truman Library, Independence, Mo.

———, Associate Justice. Memorandum to Supreme Court Justices. Apr. 1950. Tom C. Clark Papers, U.S. Supreme Court Case Files. Box A2, Folder 3. Rare Books and Special Collections, Tarlton Law Library, University of Texas at Austin.

Clifford, Clark M. Letter to Adolf A. Berle Jr. Aug. 18, 1948. Harry S. Truman Library, Independence, Mo.

———. Memorandum for the President. Nov. 19, 1947. Papers of Harry S. Truman. Files of Clark M. Clifford. Harry S. Truman Library, Independence, Mo.

Crook, Dr. Jere L. Letter to President Harry S. Truman. July 4, 1949. Harry S. Truman Library, Independence, Mo.

Dashiell, Major Charles J., Jr. Howard University class of 1952. Telephone interview. Dec. 4, 1997.

Dawson, Donald S. Letter to Mary McLeod Bethune. Apr. 1, 1948. Mary McLeod Bethune Council House, National Historic Site, Washington, D.C.

———. Memorandum for President Harry S. Truman. Sept. 9, 1948. Records of Philleo Nash. Harry S. Truman Library, Independence, Mo.

———. U.S. Air Force general and Truman personal aide. Personal interview. Washington, D.C., July 23, 1999.

Department of Justice. Press Release. "Statement Regarding the Filing of Charges Against Lynwood Lanier Shull." Sept. 26, 1946. Papers of Philleo Nash. Harry S. Truman Library, Independence, Mo.

Document 43. Papers of David K. Niles. Harry S. Truman Library, Independence, Mo.

Document 44. Papers of Philleo Nash. Harry S. Truman Library, Independence, Mo.

Document 89. Papers of Harry S. Truman, White House Central Files-Official File. Harry S. Truman Library, Independence, Mo.

Document 91. Papers of Harry S. Truman, Files of Clark M. Clifford. Harry S. Truman Library, Independence, Mo.

Document 116. Papers of Harry S. Truman, White House Central Files-Official File. Harry S. Truman Library, Independence, Mo.

Elsey, George. Senior aide to President Truman. Personal interviews. Washington, D.C., 1997, 1998, 1999.

Elsey, George, and Clark Clifford. Sixth draft of Special Message from President Harry S. Truman to the Congress of the United States in regards to the president's state of the union address on Jan. 7, 1948, and the discussion of human rights of U.S. citizens. Harry S. Truman Library, Independence, Mo.

Ferris, Joseph A. Letter to President Harry S. Truman. Nov. 23, 1948. Harry S. Truman Library, Independence, Mo.

Gardner, Michael R. Letter to James Murray. Feb. 27, 1998. Author's collection.

Height, Dorothy I. President and CEO of the National Council of Negro Women. Personal interview. Washington, D.C., June 24, 1998.

Henderson, Leon. Letter to President Harry S. Truman. July 22, 1948. Harry S. Truman Library, Independence, Mo.

Highlights of NAACP History, 1909–1979. New York [now Baltimore]: National Association for the Advancement of Colored People, Sept. 1979.

Hillman, Sidney. Telegram to President Harry S. Truman. June 21, 1946. Harry S. Truman Library, Independence, Mo.

Howard University Graduate List from Class of 1952. Howard University Alumni Development and Research System, Department of Alumni Affairs. Howard University, Washington, D.C., Nov. 19, 1997.

Indritz, Phineas. Memorandum to Oscar Chapman. Apr. 5, 1950. Harry S. Truman Library, Independence, Mo.

Javits, Representative Jacob K. Press Release. Jan. 12, 1950, P.M.; Jan. 13, 1950, A.M. papers. President's Committee on Equality of Treatment and Opportunity in the Armed Service. Harry S. Truman Library, Independence, Mo.

Johnson, Dr. Mordecai W. Letter to President Harry S. Truman. May 28, 1952. Harry S. Truman Library, Independence, Mo.

———. Letter to President Harry S. Truman (inviting him to speak at the 1952 Commencement Exercises). May 20, 1952. Harry S. Truman Library, Independence, Mo.

———. Letter to President Harry S. Truman (thanking him for speaking at the 1952 Commencement Exercises). Dec. 17, 1952. Harry S. Truman Library, Independence, Mo.

Johnson, Lyndon B. "The Challenge of a New Day." Speech by Congressman Johnson at Kick-Off Rally for the 1948 Senate Campaign. Wooldridge Park, Austin, Tex. May 22, 1948. Statement of Lyndon B. Johnson, Box 6. Lyndon B. Johnson Presidential Library, Austin, Tex.

Memorandum for the Honorable David K. Niles. "Memorandum Regarding the Agenda for the First Day's Session of the Civil Rights Committee." Jan. 13, 1947. Harry S. Truman Library, Independence, Mo.

Nash, Philleo. Memorandum for the President. "Regarding the Commencement at Howard University." May 5, 1952. Harry S. Truman Library, Independence, Mo.

National Citizens' Council on Civil Rights. Letter to President Harry S. Truman. Jan. 12, 1949. Harry S. Truman Library, Independence, Mo.

Nelson-Ausbrooks, Elizabeth. Howard University class of 1952. Telephone interview. Dec. 15, 1997.

Niles, David K. Memorandum to Matthew J. Connelly. "Proposed Speech by the President to the NAACP." June 16, 1947. Harry S. Truman Library, Independence, Mo.

———. Memorandum to President Harry S. Truman. Oct. 5, 1949. Papers of David Niles. Harry S. Truman Library, Independence, Mo.

———. Memorandum to President Harry S. Truman. Feb. 7, 1950. Papers of David Niles. Harry S. Truman Library, Independence, Mo.

Omohundro, Howard Uriah. Telegram to President Harry S. Truman. Oct. 5, 1948. Harry S. Truman Library, Independence, Mo.

Palmer, Dwight R. G. "Treatment of Civil Rights in the Platform of the Democratic Party." Papers of Harry S. Truman. Harry S. Truman Library, Independence, Mo.

Perlman, Philip B., Chairman of the President's Committee on Immigration and Naturalization. Cross-reference sheet. Commending the president on his Harlem speech on civil rights and expressing appreciation of his mentioning some cases Perlman handled in the Supreme Court. Oct. 14, 1952. Harry S. Truman Library, Independence, Mo.

Planck, E. H. Letter to President Harry S. Truman. July 28, 1948. Harry S. Truman Library, Independence, Mo.

The President's Appointments. Wednesday, May 25, 1949. Harry S. Truman Library, Independence, Mo.

President's Committee on Civil Rights. Press Release. Feb. 6, 1947. Harry S. Truman Library, Independence, Mo.

President's Committee on Equality Treatment and Opportunity in the Armed Services. Memorandum to President Harry S. Truman. Oct. 11, 1949. Harry S. Truman Library, Independence, Mo.

President's Committee on Equality Treatment and Opportunity in the Armed Services. Memorandum to President Harry S. Truman. "A Progress Report for the President." June 7, 1949. Harry S. Truman Library, Independence, Mo.

President's Committee on Equality Treatment and Opportunity in the Armed Services. Minutes of meeting with President Truman and the four service secretaries. Cabinet Room, the White House. Jan. 12, 1949. Harry S. Truman Library, Independence, Mo.

Revised Draft of Omnibus Civil Rights Bill, *Civil Rights Act of 1948*. Feb. 3, 1948. Harry S. Truman Library, Independence, Mo.

Roberts, Ernest W. Letter to President Harry S. Truman. Aug. 1948. Harry S. Truman Library, Independence, Mo.

———. Letter to President Harry S. Truman. Sept. 2, 1948. Harry S. Truman Library, Independence, Mo.

Scouten, Rex. Former secret service agent at Truman White House and former curator of the White House. Personal interviews. Washington, D.C., 1995, 1996, and 1997.

Sengstacke, John H. Letter to Charles Fahy. July 14, 1949. Harry S. Truman Library, Independence, Mo.

———. Telegram to President Harry S. Truman. Aug. 13, 1949. Harry S. Truman Library, Independence, Mo.

Spingarn, Stephen J. Memorandum to Clark Clifford. Mar. 25, 1949. Harry S. Truman Library, Independence, Mo.

———. Memorandum to Clark Clifford. "FEPC and Other Civil Rights Bills." Mar. 24, 1949. Harry S. Truman Library, Independence, Mo.

———. Memorandum to Clark Clifford. "Interior Department Request for Presidential Pressure to End the Segregation Policy in District Recreation." June 15, 1949. Harry S. Truman Library, Independence, Mo.

———. Memorandum to Clark Clifford. "Progress Report on Civil Rights Legislation." Mar. 21, 1949. Harry S. Truman Library, Independence, Mo.

————. Memorandum [unidentified recipient]. Jan. 22, 1948. Harry S. Truman Library, Independence, Mo.

Spore, John B., and Robert F. Cocklin. "Our Negro Soldiers." Harry S. Truman Library, Independence, Mo.

Sutton, Percy. Attorney, politician, and media businessman. Telephone interview. July 9, 1999.

Symington, James. Son of the late Stuart Symington. Telephone interview. Jan. 30, 1998.

Thurmond, J. Strom. Telegram to President Harry S. Truman. Oct. 10, 1948. Harry S. Truman Library, Independence, Mo.

Tobias, Channing H., and Walter White. Telegram to Mary McLeod Bethune. Feb. 13, 1948. Mary McLeod Bethune Council House, National Historic Site, Washington, D.C.

Truman, Bess W. Telegram to Congressman Adam Clayton Powell Jr. Oct. 12, 1945. Harry S. Truman Library, Independence, Mo.

Truman, Harry S. Letter to Attorney General Tom C. Clark. Sept. 20, 1946. Harry S. Truman Library, Independence, Mo.

————. Letter to Congressman Adam Clayton Powell Jr. Oct. 12, 1945. Harry S. Truman Library, Independence, Mo.

————. Letter to Dr. Dorothy Ferebee. Nov. 15, 1950. Harry S. Truman Library, Independence, Mo.

————. Letter to Dr. Mordecai W. Johnson. May 23, 1952. Harry S. Truman Library, Independence, Mo.

————. Letter to Dr. Mordecai W. Johnson. May 24, 1952. Harry S. Truman Library, Independence, Mo.

————. Letter to Ernest W. Roberts. Aug. 18, 1948. Harry S. Truman Library, Independence, Mo.

————. Letter to Ernest W. Roberts. Sept. 8, 1948. Harry S. Truman Library, Independence, Mo.

————. Letter to Mary McLeod Bethune. Mar. 19, 1948. Harry S. Truman Library, Independence, Mo.

————. Letter to Mary McLeod Bethune. Feb. 3, 1949. Harry S. Truman Library, Independence, Mo.

————. Letter to Roy Wilkins. Jan. 14, 1953. Harry S. Truman Library, Independence, Mo.

————. Letter to Sister Mary Jane. June 28, 1947. Harry S. Truman Library, Independence, Mo.

————. Memorandum. "Memorandum of Disapproval of Bill Requiring Segregation in Certain Schools on Federal Property." Nov. 2, 1951.

————. Personal Diary. June 29, 1947. Harry S. Truman Library, Independence, Mo.

————. Personal Diary. Jan. 6, 1948. Harry S. Truman Library, Independence, Mo.

————. Personal Diary. Feb. 2, 1948. Harry S. Truman Library, Independence, Mo.

————. Personal Diary. Feb. 8, 1948. Harry S. Truman Library, Independence, Mo.

————. Personal Diary. July 14, 1948. Harry S. Truman Library, Independence, Mo.

————. Press Release. President Truman's response to William Hastie's resignation. Nov. 19, 1949. Harry S. Truman Library, Independence, Mo.

————. Press Release. President Truman's statement regarding the report of the President's Committee on Equality of Treatment and Opportunity in the Armed Services. May 22, 1950. Harry S. Truman Library, Independence, Mo.

Turner, Edward M., and Arthur L. Johnson. Telegram to Harry S. Truman. Mar. 22, 1960. Harry S. Truman Library, Independence, Mo.

————. Telegram to Harry S. Truman. Mar. 24, 1960. Harry S. Truman Library, Independence, Mo.

University of Chicago. *Round Table: Should We Adopt President Truman's Civil Rights Program?* Transcript of NBC Radio discussion by Allen J. Ellender, Hubert Humphrey, and Louis Wirth. Number 568. Feb. 6, 1949. Papers of Philleo Nash. Harry S. Truman Library, Independence, Mo.

Villard, Oswald Garrison. Letter to Woodrow Wilson. Aug. 18, 1913. Manuscript Division. Library of Congress, Washington, D.C.

————. Letter to Woodrow Wilson. Aug. 27, 1913. Manuscript Division. Library of Congress, Washington, D.C.

Washington Committee of the Southern Conference for Human Welfare. Flyer. Invitation to a funeral march to the Lincoln Memorial on Aug. 5, 1946, in memory of the victims of mob violence. Aug. 3, 1946. Harry S. Truman Library, Independence, Mo.

White, Walter. Letter to David K. Niles. June 11, 1951. Harry S. Truman Library, Independence, Mo.

————. Letter to Oscar Chapman. Dec. 15, 1948. Harry S. Truman Library, Independence, Mo.

Wilkins, Roy. Letter to President Harry S. Truman. Jan. 12, 1953. Harry S. Truman Library, Independence, Mo.

ELECTRONIC SOURCES

"African Missouri." Thomas Jefferson Library, Reference Department. University of Missouri–St. Louis. http://www.umsl.edu/~libweb/blackstudies/afmoindx.htm (Mar. 20, 2000).

"Armies Mobilized and Casualties: 1914–18." Spartacus Educational. http://www.spartacus.schoolnet.co.uk/FWWdeaths.htm (Dec. 23, 2000).

Civil Rights Act of 1866. The Environmental Justice Home Page. New York University School of Law. http://www.nyu.edu/law/environmental-center/landuse/ej/civrts.htm (May 21, 1997).

Civil Rights Act of 1866. U.S. House of Representatives Internet Law Library. U.S. House of Representatives. http://law2.house.gov (Feb. 9, 1997).

"The Congressional Black Caucus Foundation." Congressional Black Caucus Foundation. http://www.cbcfonline.org/people/mission.html (Sept. 14, 1999).

"Dates of the Sessions of the U.S. Congress, 1789–1988." National Archives and Records Administration. http://www.nara.gov/nara/legislative/house_guide/hgapf.html (Sept. 15, 1997).

"The Documentary History of the Truman Presidency, Volume 11." University Publications of America. http://www.us.net/upa/books/tru11.html (Sept. 1997).

"The Documentary History of the Truman Presidency, Volume 12." University Publications of America. http://www.us.net/upa/books/tru12.html (Jan. 1997).

"Dwight D. Eisenhower (1890–1969)." University of Maryland, Baltimore County. http://www.gl.umbc.edu/~cgehrm1/de.html (Oct. 1, 1997).

"1860 State Level Census DataSorted by State/County Name." Inter-University Consortium for Political and Social Research. Study 00003: *Historical Demographic, Economic, and Social Data: U.S., 1790–1970.* Ann Arbor: ICPSR. http://fisher.lib.virginia.edu/cgi-local/censusbin/census/cen.pl (Mar. 24, 1999).

"Floor Leaders of the House of Representatives." National Archives and Records Administration. http://www.nara.gov/nara/legislative/house_guide/hgapf.html (Feb. 1998).

"Frederick Moore Vinson Biography." *The Frederick Moore Vinson Collection, University of Kentucky Libraries.* University of Kentucky. http://www.uky.edu/Libraries/Special/mpa/vinson-biography.html (Oct. 1, 1996).

Greene, Lorenzo J., Antonio F. Holland, and Gary Kremer. "The Role of the Negro in Missouri History, 1719–1970." University of Missouri, St. Louis. http://www.umsl.edu/~libweb/blackstudies/manual.htm (July 1, 1996).

"Historical National Population Estimates." U.S. Bureau of the Census. http://www.census.gov/population/estimates/nation/popclockest.txt (July 28, 2000).

Historical United States Census Data Browser. Inter-university Consortium for Political and Social Research. http://fisher.lib.virginia.edu/census (Mar. 24, 1998).

Hollaway, Kevin. "The War Ends, the Violence Begins." *Civil Rights: A Status Report.* GHG Corporation. http://www.ghgcorp.com/hollaway/civil/civil28.htm (Dec. 1, 1997).

Humphrey, Hubert H. Transcript of Oral History Interview, I, by Joe B. Frantz. Internet copy. Lyndon B. Johnson Presidential Library, Austin, Tex. National Archives and Records Administration. http://www.nara.gov (Aug. 17, 1971).

Miller, Alan William. *Atlas of United States Presidential Elections, 1932–1996.* Klipsan Press. http://www.klipsan.com/usp32-96.htm (Sept. 27, 2000).

Murphy, Gerald, preparer. "The Emancipation Proclamation." National Public Telecomputing Network. National Park Service, United States Government. http://www.nps.gov/ncro/anti/emancipation.html (Dec. 14, 2000).

———, preparer. "The Gettysburg Address." National Public Telecomputing Network. http://jefferson.village.virginia.edu/readings/gettysburg.txt (Mar. 29, 1994).

"National Weather Service Summary of the Day." NCDC Home Page. National Climatic Data Center. http://www.ncdc.noaa.gov/onlineprod/tfsod/climvis/main.html (Nov. 3, 2000).

"Officially Designated Majority Leaders." National Archives and Records Administration. gopher://gopher.nara.gov/11/inform/dc/legislat/senguide (Sept. 15, 1997).

"Percy Sutton Blast [sic] His Critics over the Apollo Finances Flap." *World African*

News. http://www.worldafrican.com/entertain/entertain2088.html (May 12, 1998).

"Racial 'Segregation' Attacked." *United States Law Week.* http://www.law.du.edu/-russell/lh/sweatt/uslw/uslw41150.html (reprinted with permission from *United States Law Week* 18, no. 39 [Apr. 11, 1950]: 3277).

Schwarz, Frederic D. "1948: Fifty Years Ago." *American Heritage: The Time Machine.* http://www.americanheritage.com/98/feb/timemachine/1948.htm (July 14, 1999).

"Speakers of the House of Representatives." National Archives and Records Administration. http://www.nara.gov/nara/legislative/house_guide/hgapa.html (Feb. 1998).

"Standing Rules of the Senate." U.S. Senate Committee on Rules and Administration Web Site. U.S. Senate. http://www.senate.gov/~rules/srules.htm (Aug. 16, 1999).

"*Sweatt v. Painter:* Archival and Textual Sources." University of Texas. http://ccwf.cc.utexas.edu/~russell/seminar/sweatt/sweattindex.html (Apr. 16, 2001).

Truman, Elizabeth Virginia Wallace. "Harry S. Truman, Thirty-Third President, 1945–1953." The White House Web Site. http://www.whitehouse.gov/WH/glimpse/presidents/html.ht33.html (June 22, 2000).

"USAFE Humanitarian Operations." *Berlin Airlift Facts and Figures.* United States Air Force. http://www.usafe.af.mil/berlin/humanops.htm (Jan. 5, 2000).

"What You Should Know about the NAACP." NAACP Home Page. National Association for the Advancement of Colored People. http://www.naacp.org/about/factsheet.html (June 29, 1999).

Wynn, Linda T. "William Henry Hastie (1904–1976)." Tennessee State University. http://www.tnstate.edu/library/digital/hastie.htm (Nov. 29, 2000).

INDEX

MICHAEL R. GARDNER is a communications policy attorney in Washington, D.C. He also serves as the pro bono chairman of the United States Telecommunications Training Institute, a nonprofit international training initiative that he founded in 1982 while serving as the U.S. ambassador to the ITU Plenipotentiary Conference in Nairobi, Kenya.

Gardner is a graduate of the College at Georgetown University and of the Georgetown University Law School. He is currently an adjunct professor at Georgetown University, where he has taught courses on the modern American presidency and communications public policy. Gardner has served on four presidential commissions under Presidents Nixon, Ford, Reagan, and Bush senior.

9/05   D   6/12